Griddle Cookbook For Beginners

Delight your crowd's taste buds with 450+ delicious recipes! Up your game in the art of grilling, with expert tips, tricks and instruction by Barbecue Pit-masters.

Chris McClure

© Copyright 2022 - All rights reserved

The content contained within this book may not be reproduced, duplicated, or transmitted without direct written permission from the author or the publisher. Under no circumstances will any blame or legal responsibility be held against the publisher, or author, for any damages, reparation, or monetary loss due to the information contained within this book. Either directly or indirectly.

Legal Notice:

This book is copyright protected.

This book is only for personal use. You cannot amend, distribute, sell, use, quote, or paraphrase any part, or the content within this book, without the consent of the author or publisher.

Disclaimer Notice:

Please note the information contained within this document is for educational and

entertainment purposes only. All effort has been executed to present accurate, up-to-date, and reliable, complete information. No warranties of any kind are declared or implied.

Readers acknowledge that the author is not engaging in the rendering of legal, financial, medical, or professional advice. The content within this book has been derived from various sources. Please consult a licensed professional before attempting any techniques outlined in this book.

By reading this document, the reader agrees that under no circumstances is the author responsible for any losses, direct or indirect, which are incurred as a result of the use of the information contained within this document, including, but not limited to, — errors, omissions, or inaccuracies.

Contents

- Introduction 1
- Chapter 1: My Griddle Story 1
- Why Should You Buy an outdoor Griddle? 1
- Features, Specifications and Assembling the Device: 1
- How to use a griddle? 2
  - Before the First Use: 2
  - Set up An Outdoor Griddle 2
  - Grease it Up 2
  - Season It: 3
  - Preheat First 3
  - Start cooking: 3
- Basics of Backyard Cooking 3
- What makes you a Pitmaster? 4
- Griddle Vs Other Smokers 4
  - Propane/Gas smokers 4
  - Offset Smokers 4
  - Pellet Smokers 4
  - Electric Smokers 4
  - Kamado Grills 4
  - Kettle Grills 4
- BBQ-Styles Every Pitmaster must KNOW! 5
  - 1. Kansas City Style BBQ 5
  - 2. Memphis Style BBQ 5
  - 3. Carolina Style BBQ 5
  - 4. Texas Style BBQ 5
- Developing BBQ Styles 5
  - Alabama Style BBQ 5
  - St. Louis Style Barbecue 6
  - Santa Maria Style Barbecue 6
  - Kentucky Style Barbecue 6
  - Vegan BBQ 6
- GRIDDLE VS GRILL 6
- What Type Of Food Do You Cook On A Griddle? 6
- Cleaning and Maintenance 7
- How To Avoid Rust and How to season A griddle? 7
  - What exactly is seasoning? 7
  - How do I season my Griddle? 7
- Griddle Safety Tips 8
- BREAKFAST RECIPES 9
  - Scrambled Eggs with Tomato 10
  - Blueberry Pancakes 10
  - Broccoli Omelet 10
  - Bacon Omelet 11
  - Breakfast bacon Burrito 11
  - Cauliflower Cake 11
  - Tomatoes Omelet 12
  - olives Omelet 12
  - Cheese Sandwiches 12
  - Vanilla Pancakes 12
  - Cheese Omelet with Kale 13
  - Scrambled Spinach Eggs 13
  - French Crepes 13
  - Cauliflower Hash Browns 13
  - Cheese Denver Omelet with Ham 14
  - Cinnamon Toast Sticks 14
  - Pepper Steak with Eggs 14
  - Potatoes Hash Browns with Pepper 14
  - Cauliflower Broccoli Hash Browns 15
  - Cinnamon Almond Pumpkin Pancake 15
  - Bacon, Eggs, and Cheese Sandwich 15
  - Vanilla Oatmeal Pancake 15
  - Mexican Cheese Bean Scramble 16
  - Spinach pancakes 16
  - Zucchini Pancakes 16
  - Cocoa Pancakes 17
  - Avocado Pancakes 17
  - Chocolate Chips Pancakes 17
  - Raspberry Pancakes 18
  - Raisins Pancake 18
  - Egg Dill Scramble 18
  - Egg Mushroom Scramble 19
  - Smoked Salmon Scramble 19
  - Tofu Arugula Scramble 19
  - Tofu Veggie Scramble 19
  - Veggie Scramble 20
  - Apple Omelet 20
  - Asparagus Omelet 20
  - Cheddar Spinach Omelet 20
  - Mushroom Omelet 21
  - Cheese Turkey Omelet 21
  - Smoked Salmon Omelet 21
- SNACK RECIPES 22
  - Figs Stuffed With Goat Cheese 23
  - Bacon-Wrapped Mushrooms 23
  - Goat Cheese-Stuffed Peppadews 23
  - Bacon-Wrapped Asparagus Skewers 23
  - Italian Meatballs With Pecorino 23
  - Sausages stuffed peppers 24
  - Barbecue Meatballs 24
  - Sriracha Hot Wings 25
  - Pig Candy 25
  - Smashed Potatoes 25
  - Hasselback Potatoes 26
  - Hasselback Sweet Potatoes 26
  - Zucchini with Garlic Chili Oil 26
  - Zucchini Rolls With Goat Cheese 26
  - Negimaki 27
  - Homemade Chorizo 27
  - Grilled Potato Wedges 27
  - Bacon-Wrapped Chicken Thighs 28
  - Bison Sliders 28

Hot Dog Burnt Ends 28

Stuffed Mushrooms 28

Manouri Cheese with Caramelized Plums 29

sweet potatoes with Mozzarella 29

HALLOUMI CHEESE WITH MUSHROOMS 29

Bacon-Wrapped Stuffed Jalapenos 30

Avocado fries 30

Bruschetta 30

Avocado Cups 30

Fig & Pork Tenderloln 31

Zucchini Fries 31

Nectarine Cheese Crostini 31

Shrimp Sweet Potato Kabobs 32

Zucchini with Peanut Chicken 32

Maryland Corn Pops 32

Balsamic-Goat Cheese Grilled Plums 32

Loaded Potato Rounds 33

bacon AVOCADO 33

Mushroom Bacon Bites 33

Grilled Potato Skins 33

POULTRY RECIPES 35

Minneola Tangelo Chicken Skewers 36

Greek Chicken Kebabs 36

BBQ Chicken 36

Chicken, Bacon, Ranch Skewers 37

Italian Chicken Veggie Skewers 37

Seared Chicken Breast 37

Sweet Soy Chili Lime Chicken 38

Seared Spicy Citrus Chicken Thigh 38

Honey Paprika Chicken Thighs 38

Garlic Chicken with Salsa Verde 39

Stuffed Chicken Breast 39

Pepper Chicken Stuffed with Cheese 39

Garlic Beer Chicken Thighs 40

Chipotle Adobe Chicken with Oregano 40

Garlic Chicken Tacos 40

Turkey Tacos 41

Chicken Fajitas with Tortillas 41

Hawaiian Chicken Kabob 42

Garlic Chicken Skewers 42

Honey Sriracha Chicken 42

Buffalo Garlic Chicken Wings 43

Chicken Wings with Peach Glaze 43

Pepper Yellow Curry Chicken Wings 43

Korean Pepper Chicken Wings 44

Kale Caesar Salad with Garlic Chicken Breast 44

Teriyaki Chicken with Rice Bowls 44

Chicken Fried Rice with Veggies 45

Buffalo Chicken with Blue cheese 45

Zucchini Basll Crusted Chicken 45

Garlic Chicken and Broccoli 46

Peanut Soy Curried Chicken Kebabs 46

Chicken Fajitas with Corn Tortillas 46

Zucchini Turkey Patties 47

Chicken Drumsticks with Sauce 47

Spicy BBQ Chicken 47

Bacon Chipotle Chicken with Butter 47

Oregano Chicken Bites 48

Honey Jalapeno Chicken 48

Chicken Zucchini Stir Fry 48

Chicken Fritters with Dill 48

Garlic Chicken Wings 49

Pepper Chicken Fajita 49

Coconut Chicken with Butter Sauce 49

Pepper Cheddar Chicken 50

Turkey Patties with Oregano 50

Balsamic Chicken with Rosemary 50

Greek Pepper Chicken 51

Honey-mustard Chicken with Walnut 51

Sambal Chicken with Ginger-sesame 51

Chicken with Fruit Salsa 51

Turkey Burger Patties 52

Lemon Honey Chicken Tenders 52

Spinach Garlic Turkey Patties 52

Taco Turkey Burger Patties 53

Parmesan Chicken Bake 53

BEEF RECIPES 54

BBQ Brisket Burnt Ends 55

London Broil with Herb Butter 55

Caprese Steak 55

Cheesesteak Stuffed Peppers 56

Beef Broccoli Kebabs 56

glazed beef skewers with slaw 57

Satay steak skewers 57

Filet Mignon 57

Beef Tenderloin 58

Lemon Butter Steak 58

Salisbury Steak 58

Balsamic Steak Salad With Peaches 59

Steak Frite Bites 59

Sizzling Steak Fajitas 60

Butter Steak Bites 60

Boyfriend Steak 60

Chimichurri Grilled Steak 60

Steak Fajita Skewers 61

Grilled Skirt Steak with guacamole 61

Jamaican Jerk Steak Tacos 61

Steak Taco on a Stick 62

Grilled Flank Steak with Potato 62

Rib-Eye Steak with Grilled Corn Salad 63

Basil Ground Beef 63

Ground Beef with Cabbage 63

Kale Beef 63

Ground Beef with Veggies 64

Ground Beef with Mushrooms 64

Spiced Beef Meatballs 64

Sesame-Ginger Beef 64

Grilled Steak Skewers with Chimichurri 65

Steak with Onions and Polenta 65

Beef Burger Patties 65

Buffalo Filet Mignon 65

Coffee Crusted Steak 66

Zucchini Beef Skewers 66

Simple Juicy NY Strip Steak 66

Flank Steak Gyros 67

Soy Beef with Vegetables 67

Pineapple Beef Patties 67

Smoked Paprika Brisket 68

Steak au Poivre 68

Reverse Sear Steak 68

Smothered Cube Steak 68

Seared Round Steak 69

PORK RECIPES 70

Pork Chops and Herb Apple Compote 71

Pepper Honey Vinegar Pork Chops 71

Country Pork Ribs 71

Garlic Cayenne Pork Chops 72

Pepper Garlic Soy Pork Chops 72

Montreal Pork Chops 72

Honey Pork Chops with Soy 72

Sesame Boston Butt Pork 73

Garlic Flank Steak with Oregano 73

Cuban Pork Chops 74

Garlic Pepper Pork Chops 74

Dijon Pork Mushrooms Skewers 74

Paprika Cinnamon Pork Tenderloin 74

Pork Chops with Orange Marinade 75

Thyme garlic Pork Patties 75

Garlic Mustard Pork Chops 75

Lemon Pork Tenderloin 76

Grilled cevapi skewers with pickles 76

pork and pineapple skewers 76

Maple caramel pork belly skewers 76

Hot Dog Skewers 77

Miso glazed pork fillet 77

Pork Fillet Saltimbocca 77

Piri Piri Pork Medallions 78

Pork fillet with green vegetable salad 78

Pork Fillet With Fragrant Pilau Rice 78

Cajun Pork Fillet With Sweet Potatoes 79

Pork Fillet With Creamy Wine Sauce 79

Pork With Chilli Sauce 79

Pork Fillet With Chorizo 79

saltimbocca alla Romana 80

Sticky soy and ginger pork 80

Pork stuffed with apricots 80

Chilli-glazed sticky ribs 81

Chinese five-spice spare ribs 81

Mexican pork tenderloin 81

Honey mustard roasted pork fillet 82

LAMB RECIPES 83

greek lamb chops 84

Lamb Chops Sizzled with Garlic 84

Garlic Butter Lamb Chops 84

ROSEMARY LAMB CHOPS 84

Spicy Lamb Chops 85

Lamb kofta flatbreads 85

Tahini BBQ lamb chops 85

Spicy rack of lamb 86

Stuffed leg of lamb 86

Gunpowder lamb 86

Saganaki lamb skewers 86

Crusted lamb rack 87

Herby lamb kebabs 87

Lamb chops with ratatouille 87

Lamb boti kabab 88

Quick lamb kebabs 88

Moroccan lamb chops 88

Spiced lamb lollipops 89

lamb cutlets with coriander potatoes 89

Spicy barbecued leg of lamb 89

Lamb Chop with Veggies 90

Rosemary Lamb Bites 90

Ground Lamb with Peas 90

Lamb Koftas 90

Sizzling lamb with cucumber dip 91

Moroccan-style lamb burgers 91

FISH AND SEAFOOD RECIPES 92

Yummy Grouper 93

Whitefish with Mayonnaise 93

Garlic Fish with Cilantro 93

Chills Amberjack 94

Lemony Cumin Rainbow Trout 94

Shrimp with Pineapple Sauce 94

Snapper Ceviche 95

Honey Tuna Steaks 95

Sweet Potato Snapper Ceviche 95

Clam and Shrimp Bouillabaisse 96

Paprika Shrimp with Honey Lime 96

Orange Lobster Corn Salad 97

Salmon Fillets with Broccolini 97

Spiced Snapper with Salsa 97

Lime Corn Tilapia with cilantro 98

Spinach Halibut with Olives 98

Parsley Garlic Swordfish Skewers 98

Garlic Lime Lobster Tails 99

Chili Oil Crab Legs 99

Mustard Crab Panko Cakes 99

Garlic Pepper Shrimp with Parsley 99

Shrimp Skewers with Pineapple 100

Cajun Shrimp Sausage Skewers 100

Mediterranean Salmon Skewers 100

Cajun Shrimp Kebabs 101

Halibut Parcel 101

Halibut with Veggies 101

Simple Tuna 102

Thyme Tuna 102

Lemony Tuna 102

Spicy Tuna 102

Tuna with Chimichuri 102

Simple Mackerel 103

Herbed Sea Bass 103

Lemony Trout 103

Spiced Shrimp 103

Lemony scallops 104

Garlicky Shrimp 104

Soy Sauce Shrimp 104

Shrimp in Orange Sauce 104

VEGETARIAN RECIPES 106

Burgers with Mushrooms and Arugula 107

Asparagus with Butter 107

Pepper Butternut Squash 107

Cabbage with Thyme and Lemon 108

Broccoli Rice with Herbs 108

Eggplant with Mole 108

Garlic Eggplant with Mint Yogurt 109

Garlicky Lemon Mushrooms 109

Garlic Bell Peppers 109

Rosemary Red Potatoes 110

Garlicy Yukon Gold Potato Hobo Packs 110

Basil Wine Zucchini and Eggplant Salad 110

Tomato and Zucchini Ratatouille 111

Garlic Ginger Tofu with Cilantro 111

Salty Plantains 111

Zucchini and Cauliflower Skewers 112

Tater Tot Skewers 112

Grilled Ranch Potatoes 112

Zucchini mushroom Kabobs 113

Tortellini Skewers 113

Grilled Brussels Sprouts 113

Bang Bang Cauliflower Kebabs 113

Veggie Griddle Cakes 114

Corn on the Cob 114

Cauliflower Wedges With Herb Tarator 114

Carrots With Avocado and Mint 115

Eggplant With Tahini-Yogurt Sauce 115

Caribbean Jerk Vegetables 115

Bacon Green Beans with Pecans 116

Leek Potato Salad 116

Green Beans, Fennel, and Farro 116

Charred Peppers with Queso Blanco 116

Rainbow Veggie Kabobs 117

Seared Peppers 117

Vegetable Skewers 117

Eggplant with Chickpea Croutons 117

Sweet Potatoes With Lemon-Herb Sauce 118

Eggplant Stir-fry 118

DESSERT RECIPES 119

Pineapple with Maple Walnut Ice Cream 120

Sweet Peaches 120

Pineapple Sundaes 120

CINNAMON SUGAR PEACHES 120

RUM-SOAKED PINEAPPLE 120

MONKEY GRILLED CHEESE 121

Grilled Apples 121

Peach Melba 121

Chocolate and Banana Pizza 121

Food Cake with Strawberries 122

Caramelized Pineapple 122

Apricots with Brioche 122

Banana Splits 122

Chocolate Marshmallow Banana 123

Donut Ice Cream Sandwich 123

S'mores Roll-Up 123

Cinnamon Apples 123

Raspberry Cream Cheese Paninis 123

blueberry Cream Cheese Sandwiches 124

Raisins Cookies 124

Orange Marmalade Sandwich 124

Chocolate Chips Cookies 124

Cranberry Cookies 125

gingersnap cookies 125

Double Chocolate Cookies 125

Dulce Cookies sandwich 126

oreo Cookies sandwich 126

vanilla Cookies 127

S'mores Panini 127

Dulce De Leche Panini 127

Chocolate And Brie Panini 127

Brie Cheese Sandwich 128

Peanut Butter Banana Panini 128

Apple Pie Panini 128

Nutella Dessert Panini 128

Measurement Charts 130

Volume equivalent (dry) 130

Volume equivalent (liquid) 130

Weight Equivalents 130

Temperature Equivalents 130

CONCLUSION: 131

INDEX 132

INTRODUCTION

Cooking outdoors, searing hot dogs, and the delicious steak is a festive activity that we all live for. We simply cannot afford to lose money and time experimenting with griddles and cooking stations. We want one quality appliance that could produce great results and require minimum effort. A 36 inches outdoor griddle and the cooking station is that one-stop-shop that lets you cook a grand meal for the whole gang in a single session. This propane run griddle station has a sturdy base, a smooth surface and four burners which offers you a great cooking experience. And if you already have this beauty resting in your backyard, then here comes a great collection of recipes for you to put this griddle to some work. All the 350+ recipes in this cookbook will be enough for you to cook all sorts of juicy steaks, succulent pork chops, roasted poultry, and delicious seafood, along with seared veggies and side meals. So, let's gets started!

CHAPTER 1: MY GRIDDLE STORY

Before we jump straight to the outdoor griddle details, let me first tell you how I ended with this cooking station in the first place. Ever since I planned to enjoy my Saturday afternoon cooking in my backyard, I wanted a cooking station that could be easy to handle and clean. The outdoor griddle cooking station was a recommendation of one of my friends, who himself is a great cook. I was told that this cooking station is best at cooking large batches of meals or several food items at a time. The four-burner heating system, the easy controls and the portability of this cooking station were some other features that inspired me to bring this griddle home.

The best way to introduce 36" griddle is that it is a cooking station that has four propane fueled burners with a flat top gas griddle with a built-in garbage holder, cutting board, and side shelf. It is prepared out of high-quality stainless steel. Thick, hot rolled steel is used to store and distribute heat energy, making food preparation easy for everybody, regardless of skill level. If you're organizing a big family BBQ, the outdoor gas griddle is a must-have.

WHY SHOULD YOU BUY AN OUTDOOR GRIDDLE?

An outdoor gas griddle is lightweight and easy to transport. Every portion of this barbecue may be packed and taken with you wherever you go. You can take it wherever you wish. From sunrise to sundown, prepare whatever cuisine you desire.

On the outdoor gas griddle, you may prepare a variety of meals. Pancakes, quesadillas, tacos, and toast are all options for breakfast, and they can all be cooked on this Griddle. You may also prepare hot dogs, hamburgers, steaks, chicken, and even desserts if it's noon. Make it more special for supper by perfectly preparing fish like tuna and shrimp. You can prepare your meals and much more.

FEATURES, SPECIFICATIONS AND ASSEMBLING THE DEVICE:

Do you know what the essential features of an outdoor gas griddle are? It comes with a flat top surface which allows even cooking and heating all the time. From toast to steaks, it can cook anything while giving things a crunchy exterior, a tender core, and a strong flavour! Do you want to learn more about the fundamentals and advantages of using an outdoor gas griddle for cooking?? Well, following are some of the inspiring benefits of this cooking station that will help you make your mind about it:

Flat Griddle Surface

All of the action takes place here. This is where you cook your meals. Using the necessary ingredients, you can place the food on top of this surface. Your food will be cooked in a matter of minutes. A slab of cold-rolled steel makes up a griddle surface. This indicates that the food cooking does not get any creases, tears, rips, holes, and other marks just even heating. There are no chilly areas because the cooking is done evenly throughout the entire surface.

The Grease Collector

All of the juice from the meat is locked in with the food due to the flat cooking surface. The grease collector gathers all of the extra dripping greases. If you despise doing the dishes after dinner, there's good news! Cleaning this grease collector is a breeze. All you should do now is use soap water to carefully clean the oil. That's all there is to it.

The Burners

All you have to do is swiftly pull the trigger to spark the fire and begin cooking. Light the propane run burners by pressing the ignition button. There are heating zones in a gas griddle since it has more than one burner. At the same time, there are low, medium, and high temperature settings that you can select by turning the temperature dials.

Different Temperature Settings

On its large griddle surface, you can also cook food on different temperature settings. For instance, you can set the two burners on medium heat settings using their respective dials and the other two on high heat setting. In this way you get to cook on different temperature settings at a time.

The Heat controls

The outdoor griddle's heat control is not difficult to use. When using a charcoal griddle, you may feel as if you have no control over the fire, prompting you to consider how much food you are cooking in order to avoid overcooking. The temperature of the burners is regulated by the knobs on the front of the outdoor griddle state. They enable you to precisely select the desired heat level.

HOW TO USE A GRIDDLE?

The griddle top is constructed of stainless steel that has been polished. It's a lot bigger, which makes it ideal for lunch. The application of oil to the top of the pan and spreading it out, wiping away the excess heat, and creating a non-stick surface. The factory-applied a thin layer of rust and oil to the outdoor Gas Griddle. You can clean the surface it with soap and water -before using it for the first time to remove any grease and flush it. Before using the pan for the first time, brush the top edge (both the top and bottom) with oil.

Before the First Use:

If you increase the temperature from low to high, the brown-on-black colour will begin to form at the top of the pan. But don't worry; this is precisely what you want to do. Use some oil to keep the food from clinging to the metal surface if you want a perfect barbeque texture and flavour.

Herbs can also aid in achieving a beautiful finish on the food's outside surface. These techniques can also help prevent rust from accumulating on the pan's surface.

Set up An Outdoor Griddle

To begin cooking your new Griddle, you'll need the appropriate tools. Make sure you get two spatulas; having two spatulas will help you prevent contaminating various foods. Spatulas for grilling come in a variety of shapes and sizes. Many spatulas have gaps on them that allow oil to travel through. You should also bring a nice griddle scraper. The most critical equipment you'll need for your new Griddle is a scraper. It makes cleaning the griddle surface a breeze.

Before cooking, wipe the food particles clean, and thereafter, remove the food residues. I like to have a designated wipe using the scrub's sharp end. Spatula tools allow you to cut and dice veggies while cooking on a griddle. I also use a metal spatula to prepare a variety of foods, including steaks and sausages.

Grease it Up

Last but not least, grab a few pressed oil bottles. Your oil can be stored in bottles. When you're cooking on a griddle, they're little and easy to pick up. I always have a bottle of vegetable or canola oil on hand, as well as a bottle of olive oil. You can have a bottle of beneficial sesame oil if you want to prepare a lot of Asian-inspired recipes. Spray the Griddle with oil if it appears to be dry. We enjoy using 4 burners griddling if you have the 36 inches griddle.

Season It:
Before you start griddling your food on a griddle pan, make sure it's seasoned. Pre-seasoning entails coating the pan with a small layer of oil and slowly heating it. This aids in the creation of a non-stick surface that prevents your food from burning or sticking to the Griddle. Seasoning is also vital in the long run since it prevents rust on your Griddle.

Preheat First
When the cooking station is ready for use, just turn on the burns by rotating the knob given for each burner and rotate them to set the desired temperature. The autoignition will light up the propane fueled burners then leave the griddle for 5 minutes to preheat well then you can start cooking.

Start cooking:
Once the cooking surface is hot enough, all you have to do to begin cooking on a griddle. Food doesn't take long to cook on a griddle, and you only need to flip dishes once or twice to ensure complete cooking!

BASICS OF BACKYARD COOKING

Barbecue is a tradition in almost every country and area. Pitmasters in North America BBQ meals by roasting or smoking them for many hours over wood or charcoal at low temperatures, turning full roasts and difficult chops into soft, delicious morsels of meat. The cooking procedure, equipment, and food are all referred to as BBQ since they are so intertwined. You can cook ribs to perfection, start a fire on the grill, and enjoy a meal of grilled chicken. Barbeque is a verb, noun, and adjective, according to grammarians. It's a way of life for American pit masters. Backyard cooking is a centuries-old culinary culture in the States and here is what you should consider while trying it at home:

Have the necessary equipment
To become a great barbeque expert, you don't have to sear your own flesh. If you utilize the correct tools, cooking outside is much better, safer, and more enjoyable. Heavy-duty oven gloves and fish slices are among them. Don't forget about the tongs. Nothing is more sad than dumping delicious, almost-cooked sausages on the grill or the ground by mistake! If you're on the road, you may utilize a finest fire pit to make your cooking procedure much easier.

Set up the BBQ station:
Where you set up your cooking station in your backyard is a matter of great significance here. Depending on which type of griddle and smoker you are using, you will need properly ventilation. It can neither be a completely closed set up, nor a place where is too much wind blowing, probably somewhere in the backyard where there is wind. Along with the smoker, grill and griddle, arrange all the other needed things on a table nearby so that you could cook without any distractions.

Heat up the Cooking station right
The burner knobs on a gas griddle are given with the aim of providing a better control over the heat of the griddle surface. The knobs are marked with temperature values, you can set it up and then wait for 5 minutes for the griddle station to heat up right according to the set temperature.

Time it properly
Heating properly does not imply putting food in a griddle that is turned. Many professionals suggest that the griddle top must be preheated for 5 minutes at least before you start cooking on it. If you will start cooking on the griddle without preheating it, you food might not get a good texture on the outside. Give the griddle its due time to preheat and cook the food properly, don't rush it!

Pay attention to your sides
Without a delicious side dish or two, no meal is complete. They help to balance your food. Roasted corn on the cob or grilled potato salad are great. Navajo flatbreads and couscous are also available. These go well with your grill and help you get the most out of your marinade.

Don't Check The Temperature Repeatedly.
In two simple words, the correct approach for cooking with a griddle may be summed up: "low and slow." In

other words, have patience! It's best not to constantly check the temperature of the food. Check the temperature at least after every 15 minutes if you cooking red meat or tough cuts.

Allow the meat to rest.
Allow your meat to sit for 10-15 minutes after taking it from the grill. This helps to keep the meat moist and prevents it from drying out.

WHAT MAKES YOU A PITMASTER?
Someone who knows their way around a smoker or grill is known as a pitmaster. A pitmaster is someone a barbeque maestro; ribs, steaks, seafood, poultry—anything that can be grilled or smoked by a pitmaster. In reality, before the emergence of contemporary barbecue grills and smokers, traditionally barbecue cooking was done in holes dug in the ground- PIT, similar to how "pork" is prepared in the traditional fashion, so the term pitmaster emerged from the tradition of using pits for barbecuing. Today, it is used for anyone who is pro at grilling and smoking. And with right techniques, a great grill and cooking station and great recipes, you can to become the pitmaster of your house!

GRIDDLE VS OTHER SMOKERS
When you will be in the market getting a new cooking station, you will definitely come across several other options as well. It is therefore important to know what other varieties are there and how they are different from an outdoor gas griddle.

Propane/Gas smokers
Gas smokers are heated with natural gas or propane, which is surprising. The terms 'gas' and 'propane' are interchangeable when it comes to fueling these smokers. Liquefied petroleum gas-LPG is another name for propane (LPG). Unless you have a direct gas connection to your home, you'll almost definitely be using a refillable gas bottle. Thankfully, they're inexpensive and readily available at most petrol stations and sporting goods stores.

Offset Smokers
The origins of offset smokers may be seen in their barrel-like design, which was inspired by disused oil barrels. Most pit masters' bucket lists include owning one of these monstrosities, which are large, unwieldy, and have enough space to fill an entire city block with properly smoked food. Because the firebox is offset to the side and below the main cooking chamber, the offset smoker gets its name. Smoke and heat are pulled over the food in the cooking chamber and out of a chimney when wood or charcoal is burned in the firebox.

Pellet Smokers
Pellet smokers combine the functions of an oven and a smoker in a high-tech compact. They combine the smokey flavour of genuine combustion with the convenience of an electronic smoker. One of the finest features of a pellet smoker is that it can function as an oven, grill, and smoker all at the same time, making it a one-stop cooking solution.

Electric Smokers
Electric smokers are ideal for "set it and forget it" smoking. You won't have to worry about burning charcoal or wood chips, carrying a propane cylinder around, or cleaning up after you've used one. Choosing the temperature, maybe via a Bluetooth app with some higher-end versions, setting a time, and then locating a beer while the job is done for you are all part of using an electric smoker.

Kamado Grills
When we say Kamado grills are old school, we're referring to the fact that they've been around for approximately 3000 years. Most people aren't familiar with the term Kamado, but they are familiar with the Big Green Egg! While the Big Green Egg smoker is the most well-known Kamado grill brand, it is far from the only one available. There are several great brands to select from, and they all produce fantastic smokes.

Kettle Grills
While a kettle grill isn't strictly a smoker, it is one of the most popular types of live-fire cooking equipment and can easily be used to smoke modest amounts of food. These are one of our favourite types of grill smoker combos since they are inexpensive and easily accessible. If you have one of these in your garage, it might be a simple method to start smoking food.

BBQ-STYLES EVERY PITMASTER MUST KNOW!

There are four major BBQ areas in the United States: Kansas City, Carolina, Memphis, and Texas. The most well-known regional versions of smoked meat are represented by these four barbecue techniques. Techniques, rubs, and sauces from each style are widely imitated across the United States.

1. Kansas City Style BBQ

A smorgasbord of slow-smoked meats are sprinkled in a sweet spice and smothered in a thick, syrupy sauce in Kansas City style BBQ. The base component of Kansas City rub is brown sugar (traditional recipes call for a two-to-one ratio of brown sugar to paprika). Pitmasters maintain the heat low to avoid charring and blackening their meats due to the caramelizing sugar.

While beef, hog, and fowl are all fair game, Kansas City style BBQ is known for its charred ends. Instead of the tiny pieces of bacon provided with flapjacks, try substantial Kansas City bacon. This form of bacon is made by pressing and smoking pork shoulders.

2. Memphis Style BBQ

Memphis, Tennessee produced one of the four prominent kinds of regional BBQ in the United States, which is beloved by smoked meat enthusiasts. Pork is the cornerstone of Memphis style BBQ, and pork ribs are its crown jewel. While you'll find beef and chicken on menus, pork is the foundation of Memphis style BBQ. Ribs are prepared in two ways in Memphis style BBQ: wet and dry.

Slow-smoked pork shoulders are pulled and served with a thin, acidic sauce on the side in a Memphis-style dish. Pulled pork sandwiches are a mainstay of the Memphis BBQ cuisine, and they sell well on their own. Traditional Memphis-style BBQ joints smother their pulled pork sandwiches in creamy coleslaw.

True Memphis BBQ restaurants serve Memphis barbecue spaghetti, which sets them apart from their imitators. Since the 1970s, spaghetti noodles mixed in a half marinara, half barbecue sauce with pulled pork, simmered peppers, and onions has been a Memphis area favourite.

3. Carolina Style BBQ

Carolina style barbecue is based on slow-roasted entire hogs and is one of America's oldest meat-cooking methods. The creative process of grilling a full hog over the span of 12 to 24 hours is known as whole hog BBQ. The stomach, neck, and shoulders are the three main meat sources in a hog. The flesh in the stomach is soft, while the shoulders and neck are rough. Pitmasters must take great care not to scorch the delicate stomach meat while softening the tough sections. Carolina-style whole hog cooking need a moistening mop sauce, whereas Carolinians dress their completed supplies in a variety of regional sauces.

In Western North Carolina, pig shoulders are smoked instead of whole hogs, earning them the title of 'Lexington style BBQ.' North Carolinians debate whether Eastern whole hog BBQ or Lexington style pork shoulder is the official BBQ of their state, from neighborhood squabbles to state legislative action.

4. Texas Style BBQ

The holy trinity of Texas BBQ is ribs, East Texas Hot Links, and melt-in-your-mouth brisket. With a state that stretches over 200,000 miles, it's no surprise that there are many regional customs within the larger Texas barbecue heritage. Central Texas pit masters smoke their brisket over oak, slice it, and serve it plain. It's how mesquite-smoked barbecue is done in South Texas. Eastern Texans prefer spicy, vinegar-based sausages and chopped beef sandwiches that soak through buttered buns and sandwich wrappers (serve with pickles and sliced onions to do as the Eastern Texans do).

DEVELOPING BBQ STYLES

While the four primary kinds of American BBQ are Kansas City, Memphis, Carolina, and Texas, there are innumerable micro barbecue locales around the country. Outside of the basic four, we'll go over a number of the most popular BBQ styles.

Alabama Style BBQ

Alabama style BBQ is defined by its trademark white barbecue sauce, according to smoked meat connoisseurs. Mayonnaise-based Alabama white sauce with apple cider vinegar, brown mustard, and horseradish. It's eaten with grilled poultry and is the secret ingredient in Alabama BBQ restaurants' delectable coleslaw and potato salad.

St. Louis Style Barbecue

Spareribs are famous in the St. Louis region, and when people talk about St. Louis style barbecue, they usually mean this cut of beef. St. Louis ribs are found above the breastbone and below the segment of back ribs on the stomach side of the rib cage. Squaring off the tips is how they're cut. Baby back ribs are fatter and more soft than St. Louis style ribs, but they have a larger bone-to-meat ratio. Unlike typical BBQ techniques, St. Louis style ribs are grilled rather than slow-smoked over indirect fire.

Santa Maria Style Barbecue

Santa Maria style BBQ, which originated on California's Central Coast, focuses on wood-fire grilled tri-tip seasoned with salt, pepper, and garlic powder. An open cast-iron grill filled with coast live oak embers is used for Santa Maria style BBQ. California BBQ lacks the smoky flavour of Southern BBQ because coastal oak (locally known as red oak) emits less smoke than other woods and the grill is open. Santa Maria style tri-tip is served with salsa cruda and Pinquito beans in California.

Kentucky Style Barbecue

Kentucky pit masters mastered the technique of slow smoking mutton and created a unique Worcestershire-based sauce to match the meat's rich, gamey taste. Burgoo, a stew made with sheep and other roasted meats, is another Kentucky barbecue classic.

Vegan BBQ

Though meaty treats are the major attractions for most of us but vegan BBQ is also on the rise these days. You can cook high protein meat-substitutes like tempeh, seitan, or tofu on your griddle as well and enjoy with nicely seared vegetables, and bread.

GRIDDLE VS GRILL

The distinction is clear. Griddles feature flat and smooth surfaces. If griddles have a solid plate like cooking surface, then grills have elevated ridges or bars with gaps in between that allow food on the surface to cook directly over the heat. Griddles and grills can use gas, charcoal, or electricity as a heat source. Griddles effectively distribute heat from the entire metal surface to the food, allowing for even cooking and browning. The food is never in contact with the heat source or flames.

In comparison to griddle cooking, grilling employs higher temperatures. The heat is transferred directly from the fire to the grill grate's metal. The heat is absorbed and intensified by the metal, which causes it to be brown or burn at the point of contact. Grills are therefore used mostly to get nicely charred food.

You cannot cook all sort of food items directly on the grill because of the grill grate's surface, you will need to add them to some other pan to cook on a grill but that is not the case with the griddle. Consider pancakes for instead. On a griddle surface you can pour directly on it and cook golden, fluffy and flat pancakes.

WHAT TYPE OF FOOD DO YOU COOK ON A GRIDDLE?

Griddles can be used to prepare a wide variety of delectable dishes. If you wanted to, you could create breakfast, lunch, and dinner on a griddle.

Poultry, Meat and seafood: You can cook almost any meat cut, poultry or seafood on the griddle surface. Griddles are perfect at doing so, because they give the meat flesh a juicy texture and nice flavor.

Most veggies, such as bell peppers or grilled onions, are ideal for griddling. You can sear any vegetable on the griddle top and serve them as you like.

Pancakes: For breakfast, griddle is great at making pancakes. After you've made your pancake batter, heat up the pancake griddle. If you're afraid of the batter spilling all over the place, you can use a specially designed pancake mould.

Eggs: Cooking eggs on a hot griddle is a dream come true. Simply crack your eggs into the pan and keep an eye on them while they fry in the oil. On griddles, you can make an omelet as well, but scrambled eggs don't work as well.

Hash browns: For breakfast, why not cook a batch of hash browns to go with your fried eggs?

Sausages: While we're on the subject, any other type of breakfast works wonderfully on a griddle! Choose between sausages, tomatoes, and mushrooms.

Grilled Cheeses: If you only need a quick lunch or a light snack, you can make the perfect grilled cheese with griddles. Put some cheese slices between the bread slice and melt it on the griddle.

Burgers: So, griddles are the perfect burger cookers! When you bite into a juicy burger, you'll understand why we adore cooking burgers on griddles.

CLEANING AND MAINTENANCE

It is always suggested that you clean the griddle before and after each use. Because griddles are highly delicate, they must be handled with extreme caution. As a result, you must clean the griddle before cooking, especially if it haven't been used in a long time and you are then using it, because grease accumulates on the griddle top. It is critical to clean the griddle after each usage to prevent grease from accumulating later. The griddle should be cleaned every three weeks, according to the manufacturer's instructions.

It will keep grease and dust from accumulating on it. We recommend that you do this every time you cook on the griddle to ensure that it is properly seasoned.

Because you will most likely not be using the griddle again after it has been used, it is a good idea to do some seasoning. It will maintain the naturally smooth, lustrous surface that is also permanently non-sticky.

When it comes to seasoning your griddle, there is no fixed time. Your griddle should be completely cleaned. For this, you'll need a copper brush and some soap. Simply mix soap and hot water, then pour the water over the griddle carefully while removing any debris and oil residue.

Only use the brush in a gentle manner. We must proceed slowly since we do not want to remove all of the fried food from the griddle.

Remove and clean all the hazardous oils from the griddle surface before you start cooking.

HOW TO AVOID RUST AND HOW TO SEASON A GRIDDLE?

When you open your new Griddle, you'll find that we've included a pre-seasoned oil to keep it from rusting during shipping. Please burn this off first to clean the griddle before continuing with the seasoning steps below.

What exactly is seasoning?

Steel or cast iron cookware is prepared for use by seasoning. This procedure is carried out for two reasons- To prevent rust, coat the cookware and create a natural, permanent non-stick cooking surface.

When using an outdoor griddle, seasoning is a simple but crucial first step. Steel and cast iron, unlike synthetically coated griddles, may be seasoned, re-seasoned, and their cooking surface repaired. When you season your griddle, you are preventing rust and imparting a natural, permanent non-stick surface to the cookware. Remember that a griddle or pan must be seasoned over time and with frequent usage before it develops the lustrous, black surface of your grandmother's cast iron cookware. A well-seasoned griddle is black and glossy.

After the griddle has been seasoned, a basic cleaning with a scouring pad is nearly always possible, but steel wool or anything else will ruin the seasoning. Despite popular belief, a little light soap, such as lye soap, will not remove the seasoning. Detergents that claim to be able to cut grease will do so.

Steel griddle cookware should be stored in a cool, dry location. It's possible that your griddle will rust if you don't dry it after washing it and keep it out of the rain and floods. If rust appears, use steel wool or sandpaper to remove it and re-season. For added protection, look for items like griddle bags and conditioners.

How do I season my Griddle?

The cooking surface of your griddle is coated in shortening before being packed and shipped, and then a light plastic wrap is placed over it. Remove the plastic wrap from the griddle and wash it with hot, soapy water. This is the only time you should use soap at this point. Rinse and dry the utensil thoroughly. It's common for a towel to become discolored.

Using a soft cloth or paper towel, apply a thin, even layer of melted shortening (Crisco, Wesson, etc.) on the griddle. Use on both the top and bottom of your body.

Use boiling water and a plastic scrub bun or brush to clean the griddle after it has been used. If you don't plan on repeating the seasoning procedure, don't use soap. Dishwashers are not recommended.

Always wash while the dish is still hot after usage.

After fully drying the griddle, spray it with vegetable oil (Pam, for example), wipe it with a paper towel, and store it.

Scrub with steel wool, SOS pad, or another scouring tool to remove heavy food or grease build-up, then re-season.

If you follow these simple steps, your Griddle will survive for generations.

Is there a single stage to seasoning?

Seasoning is a continuous procedure. Your griddle will become more seasoned the more you use it. There will very certainly be occasions when you forget and turn on the griddle stove, causing it to become overly hot. You'll notice this because certain portions of the cooking surface may appear dull and dry. If this happens, simply oil the griddle and reheat it.

Do I season the bottom of my griddle as well as the top?

It's entirely up to you. Season the entire griddle, top and bottom, as directed in our seasoning guidelines. If you use your griddle frequently, you'll notice that the bottom season itself over the heat.

GRIDDLE SAFETY TIPS

When you are using an outdoor cooking station which fueled by propane gas, here is how you must take precaution for your own safety and for the safety of people around you:

Check the connection nut for tightness before opening the LP cylinder valve.

Turn off all burn knobs and the LP cylinder valve while the griddle is not in use.

Never move a hot griddle while it is in use.

To avoid burns and splatters, use long-handled barbecue utensils and oven mitts.

The weight limit on the side shelf is 10 pounds.

After each usage, the grease tray must be placed into the griddle and emptied. Remove the greased pan only after the grill has totally cooled.

Clean your griddle frequently, ideally after each picnic. If you use a bristle brush to clean any of the grill's cooking surfaces, be sure no loose bristles remain before grilling.

Turn off the propane supply immediately if you observe grease or other hot material spilling from the grill onto the hose, valve, or regulator. Determine the source of the problem, then fix it before cleaning and inspecting the valve, hose, and regulator. Conduct a leak tests

Keep debris out of the ventilation holes in the cylinder enclosure (grill cart).

During operation, the regulator may generate a humming or whistling noise. This will have no effect on the grill's safety or functionality.

If the regulator frosts, immediately turn off the griddle and the LP cylinder valve. This signifies that the cylinder has a fault and should not be used on any product. Return to the original provider!

BREAKFAST RECIPES

SCRAMBLED EGGS WITH TOMATO
Prep Time: 10 mins. | Cook Time: 10 mins. | Serve: 2

- ✓ 4 eggs
- ✓ 2 tbsp. cilantro, chopped
- ✓ ⅓ cup heavy cream
- ✓ 1 tomato, diced
- ✓ 3 tbsp. butter
- ✓ 1 Serrano chili pepper, chopped
- ✓ 2 tbsp. scallions, sliced
- ✓ ¼ tsp. black pepper
- ✓ ½ tsp. salt

1. Preheat your outdoor Griddle by turning all its burner's knob to medium-heat setting.
2. Grease the griddle top with butter.
3. Add chili pepper and tomato then cook for 2 minutes.
4. Beat cilantro, eggs, black pepper, cream, and salt in a suitable mixing dish.
5. Pour over the veggies, cook and scramble for 8 minutes.
6. Serve warm.

Per Serving:

Calories: 132 | Fat: 1g | Carbohydrates: 21g | Fiber: 1.3g | Sugar: 3.3g | Protein: 10.8g | Sodium: 62mg

BLUEBERRY PANCAKES
Prep Time: 10 mins. | Cook Time: 10 mins. | Serve: 4

- ✓ 1 cup flour
- ✓ ¾ cup milk
- ✓ 2 tbsp. white vinegar
- ✓ 2 tbsp. sugar
- ✓ 1 tsp. baking powder
- ✓ ½ tsp. baking soda
- ✓ ½ tsp. salt
- ✓ 1 egg
- ✓ 2 tbsp. butter, melted
- ✓ 1cup fresh blueberries
- ✓ Butter for cooking

1. Mix well the milk and vinegar in a suitable mixing dish. Allow 2 minutes to pass.
2. Beat together the flour, sugar, baking powder, baking soda, and salt in a suitable mixing bowl.
3. Mix well the milk, egg, blueberries, and melted butter in a suitable mixing bowl.
4. Preheat your outdoor Griddle by turning all its burner's knob to medium-heat setting.
5. Grease the griddle top with butter.
6. Pour a ladle of the prepared pancake batter on the hot griddle top
7. Cook for 5 minutes per side until golden brown.
8. Garnish with maple syrup and serve.

Per Serving:

Calories: 114 | Fat: 6.1g | Carbohydrates: 10g | Fiber: 3.5g | Sugar: 0.9g | Protein: 7.4g | Sodium:54mg

BROCCOLI OMELET
Prep Time: 10 mins. | Cook Time: 10 mins. | Serve: 4

- ✓ 4 eggs
- ✓ 1 cup broccoli, chopped and cooked
- ✓ 1 tbsp. olive oil
- ✓ ¼ tsp. black pepper
- ✓ ½ tsp. salt

1. In a suitable mixing bowl, beat the eggs, broccoli, pepper, and salt.
2. Preheat your outdoor Griddle by turning all its burner's knob to medium-heat setting.

3. Grease the griddle top with cooking spray.
4. Add the broccoli and egg mixture onto the hot griddle top
5. Cook for 5 minutes per side.
6. Serve and enjoy.

Per Serving:
Calories: 163 | Fat: 1.3g | Carbohydrates: 10g | Fiber: 4.3g | Sugar: 2.7g | Protein: 13g | Sodium: 65mg

BACON OMELET

Prep Time: 10 mins. | Cook Time: 20 mins. |Serve: 3
- 6 eggs, beaten
- 6 strips bacon
- ¼ lb. gruyere, shredded
- 1 tsp. black pepper
- 1 tsp. salt
- 1 tbsp. chives, chopped
- Vegetable oil

1. Preheat your outdoor Griddle by turning all its burner's knob to medium-heat setting.
2. Grease the griddle top with cooking spray.
3. Season the beaten eggs with salt and put aside for 10 minutes.
4. Place the bacon strips on the hot griddle top and cook for 5 minutes per side then transfer to any plate lined with parchment paper.
5. Chop the cooked bacon into small pieces once it has been drained.
6. Pour the beaten eggs into two parts on the hot griddle top.
7. Cook for 2 minutes then add cheese and bacon on top.
8. Fold the omelet in half and flip to cook for 5 minutes per side.
9. Serve warm with peppers and chives.

Per Serving:
Calories: 155 | Fat: 1.3g | Carbohydrates: 10g | Fiber: 4.3g | Sugar: 2.7g | Protein: 2.3g | Sodium: 65mg

BREAKFAST BACON BURRITO

Prep Time: 10 mins. | Cook Time: 10 mins. |Serve: 4
- 4 eggs
- 4 strips bacon
- 1 large russet potato, peeled and diced
- 1 red bell pepper
- ½ yellow onion
- 1 ripe avocado, sliced
- 2 tbsp. hot sauce
- 2 large flour tortillas
- Vegetable oil

1. Preheat your outdoor Griddle by turning all its burner's knob to medium-heat setting.
2. Grease the griddle top with cooking spray.
3. Add bacon to one side, and veggies to other side of the griddle.
4. Cook the bacon slices until crispy then transfer to a plate.
5. Sauté veggies until golden brown.
6. Pour beaten eggs on top, stir and cook for 5 minutes.
7. Divide egg, veggies and bacon over the tortillas.
8. Add rest of the fillings on top then serve warm

Per Serving:
Calories: 137 | Fat: 13g | Carbohydrates: 6g | Fiber: 4.3g | Sugar: 0.3g | Protein: 14g | Sodium: 94mg

CAULIFLOWER CAKE

Prep Time: 10 mins. | Cook Time: 18 mins. |Serve: 2
- 2 eggs
- 1 large head cauliflower, cut into florets
- 1 tbsp. butter
- ½ tsp. turmeric
- 1 tbsp. Nutrition yeast
- ⅔ cup almond flour
- ¼ tsp. black pepper
- ½ tsp. salt

1. In a big saucepan, place cauliflower florets.
2. Cover the cauliflower florets with enough water to cover them.
3. Allow 8-10 minutes for the water to boil.
4. Preheat your outdoor Griddle by turning all its burner's knob to medium-heat setting.
5. Grease the griddle top with butter.
6. Drain cauliflower and add to a food processor then blend.
7. Place cauliflower rice in a suitable mixing bowl.
8. Toss in the remaining ingredients, excluding the butter, and whisk to incorporate.
9. Form small patties from the cauliflower mixture and cook for 3-4 minutes per side on the hot griddle top.
10. Serve and enjoy.

Per Serving:
Calories: 140 | Fat: 7.5g | Carbohydrates: 25g | Fiber:

3g | Sugar: 0.6g | Protein: 14.5g | Sodium: 160mg

TOMATOES OMELET

Prep Time: 10 mins. | Cook Time: 12 mins. |Serve: 2

- ✓ 3 eggs
- ✓ 2 tbsp. sun-dried tomatoes, chopped
- ✓ 2 tbsp. mozzarella cheese, shredded
- ✓ 1 tbsp. fresh basil, chopped
- ✓ 2 tbsp. ricotta cheese, shredded

1. Beat the sun-dried tomatoes, eggs, and basil in a suitable mixing dish.
2. Preheat your outdoor Griddle by turning all its burner's knob to medium-heat setting.
3. Grease the griddle top with cooking spray.
4. Pour the egg mixture onto the hot griddle top.
5. Cook for 5 minutes per side.
6. Mix well the mozzarella and ricotta cheeses in a suitable mixing bowl.
7. Top the omelet with the mozzarella mixture and cook for 1-2 minutes.
8. Serve and enjoy.

Per Serving:
Calories: 130 | Fat: 10g | Carbohydrates: 10g | Fiber: 7.5g | Sugar: 0.1g | Protein: 5.5g | Sodium: 175mg

OLIVES OMELET

Prep Time: 10 mins. | Cook Time: 5 mins. |Serve: 2

- ✓ 4 large eggs
- ✓ 2 tbsp. olive oil
- ✓ 1 tsp. herb de Provence
- ✓ 2 oz. cheese
- ✓ 8 olives, pitted
- ✓ ½ tsp. salt

1. In a suitable mixing bowl, beat the eggs, salt, olives, herb de Provence, and olive oil.
2. Preheat your outdoor Griddle by turning all its burner's knob to medium-heat setting.
3. Grease the griddle top with cooking spray.
4. Pour the egg mixture onto the hot griddle top
5. Cook for 3 minutes, or until the omelet is light golden brown.
6. Flip the cooked omelet and cook for another 2 minutes.
7. Serve and enjoy.

Per Serving:
Calories: 40 | Fat: 0.3g | Carbohydrates: 11g | Fiber: 0.8g | Sugar: 1.5g | Protein: 12.5g | Sodium: 43mg

CHEESE SANDWICHES

Prep Time: 10 mins. | Cook Time: 10 mins. |Serve: 1

- ✓ 2 bread slices
- ✓ 2 tsp. butter
- ✓ 2 cheese slices

1. Preheat your outdoor Griddle by turning all its burner's knob to medium-heat setting.
2. Grease the griddle top with cooking spray.
3. Pour the egg mixture onto the hot griddle top
4. Arrange cheese slices on top of one bread slice, then top with another slice of bread.
5. Butter both bread slices and place them on a plate.
6. Cook the sandwich on the hot griddle top until golden brown and the cheese has melted.
7. Serve and enjoy.

Per Serving:
Calories: 76 | Fat: 6.8g | Carbohydrates: 7g | Fiber: 5.5g | Sugar: 0g | Protein: 3.5g | Sodium: 90mg

VANILLA PANCAKES

Prep Time: 10 mins. | Cook Time: 10 mins. |Serve: 2

- ✓ 4 eggs
- ✓ 2 tbsp. swerve
- ✓ 1 tbsp. coconut oil
- ✓ ½ cup butter, melted
- ✓ 2 cups almond flour
- ✓ 1 tsp. baking powder
- ✓ ½ tsp. vanilla
- ✓ ¼ cup of water
- ✓ ½ tsp. of salt

1. In a blender, add all of the recipe ingredients and blend until smooth.
2. Preheat your outdoor Griddle by turning all its burner's knob to medium-heat setting.
3. Grease the griddle top with cooking spray.
4. Pour ⅓ cup of pancake batter onto the hot griddle top.
5. Cook for 5 minutes per side.
6. Serve and enjoy.

Per Serving:
Calories: 107 | Fat: 7.5g | Carbohydrates: 10.1g | Fiber: 6.4g | Sugar: 1.8g | Protein: 4.1g | Sodium: 115mg

CHEESE OMELET WITH KALE

Prep Time: 10 mins. | Cook Time: 8 mins. |Serve: 2

- ✓ 4 eggs
- ✓ 4 cups kale, chopped
- ✓ 1 tbsp. fresh sage, chopped
- ✓ ⅓ cup parmesan cheese, grated
- ✓ ½ tsp. black pepper
- ✓ ½ tsp. salt

1. Place kale on the hot griddle top and cook for a few minutes, or until it has wilted.
2. Beat eggs in a suitable mixing bowl, then add parmesan cheese, sage, pepper, and salt.
3. Preheat your outdoor Griddle by turning all its burner's knob to medium-heat setting.
4. Grease the griddle top with cooking spray.
5. Pour the egg mixture onto the hot griddle top then cook for 4 minutes per side.
6. Serve and enjoy.

Per Serving:
Calories: 157 | Fat: 13g | Carbohydrates: 8g | Fiber: 5.1g | Sugar: 1.5g | Protein: 6.8g | Sodium: 160mg

SCRAMBLED SPINACH EGGS

Prep Time: 10 mins. | Cook Time: 10 mins. |Serve: 2

- ✓ 3 eggs, beaten
- ✓ 4 mushrooms, chopped
- ✓ ½ cup spinach, chopped
- ✓ ¼ cup bell peppers, chopped
- ✓ ½ tsp. black pepper
- ✓ ½ tsp. salt

1. Preheat your outdoor Griddle by turning all its burner's knob to medium-heat setting.
2. Grease the griddle top with cooking spray.
3. Place chopped vegetables on the hot griddle top and cook until they are softened.
4. Stir in the eggs, pepper, and salt until the eggs are scrambled and set.
5. Serve and enjoy.

Per Serving:
Calories: 127 | Fat: 9.5g | Carbohydrates: 11g | Fiber: 6.3g | Sugar: 1.5g | Protein: 15g | Sodium: 190mg

FRENCH CREPES

Prep Time: 10 mins. | Cook Time: 4 mins. |Serve: 2

- ✓ 1 ¼ cups flour
- ✓ ¾ cup whole milk
- ✓ ½ cup water
- ✓ 2 eggs
- ✓ 3 tbsp. butter, melted
- ✓ 1 tsp. vanilla
- ✓ 2 tbsp. sugar

1. Beat all of the recipe ingredients in a suitable mixing bowl.
2. Check to see if the prepared batter is smooth. Let stand for 1 hour.
3. Preheat your outdoor Griddle by turning all its burner's knob to medium-heat setting.
4. Grease the griddle top with butter.
5. Pour a ladle of the prepared batter onto the hot griddle top, spread it well and cook for 1-2 minutes per side.
6. For a sweet crepe, top with Nutella and strawberries.
7. Serve.

Per Serving:
Calories: 195 | Fat: 15g | Carbohydrates: 14g | Fiber: 5.4g | Sugar: 0.8g | Protein: 5.4g | Sodium:45mg

CAULIFLOWER HASH BROWNS

Prep Time: 10 mins. | Cook Time: 10 mins. |Serve: 2

- ✓ 3 eggs
- ✓ 3 oz. (85 g) onion, chopped
- ✓ 1 lb. cauliflower, grated
- ✓ ½ cup parmesan cheese, grated
- ✓ ½ cup almond flour
- ✓ 1½ tsp. lemon pepper
- ✓ ½ tsp. baking powder
- ✓ 1 tsp. salt

1. In a suitable mixing bowl, add all of the recipe ingredients and stir until well blended.
2. Preheat your outdoor Griddle by turning all its burner's knob to medium-heat setting.
3. Grease the griddle top with cooking spray.
4. Form patties out of the mixture and cook on the hot griddle top until browned on both the two sides.
5. Serve and enjoy.

Per Serving:
Calories: 177 | Fat: 14g | Carbohydrates: 7g | Fiber: 0.4g | Sugar: 0g | Protein: 8.4g | Sodium: 0mg

CHEESE DENVER OMELET WITH HAM
Prep Time: 10 mins. | Cook Time: 10 mins. | Serve: 3

- 6 large eggs
- ¼ cup country ham, diced
- ¼ cup yellow onion, chopped
- ¼ cup green bell pepper, chopped
- ⅔ cup cheddar cheese, shredded
- ¼ tsp. cayenne pepper
- ½ tsp. salt and black pepper
- 2 tbsp. butter

1. In a suitable skillet, melt the butter and sauté the ham, onion, and pepper until the veggies are just cooked.
2. In a suitable mixing bowl, beat the eggs with a pinch of salt and cayenne pepper.
3. Preheat your outdoor Griddle by turning all its burner's knob to medium-heat setting.
4. Grease the griddle top with cooking spray.
5. Divide the veggie mixture on top of griddle into 4 parts.
6. Pour ¼ of the egg mixture on each section of the veggies on the hot griddle top.
7. Cook each omelet for 3-5 minutes per side.
8. Serve warm.

Per Serving:
Calories: 262 | Fat: 17.5g | Carbohydrates: 25g | Fiber: 5.4g | Sugar: 0.1g | Protein: 14.5g | Sodium:195mg

CINNAMON TOAST STICKS
Prep Time: 10 mins. | Cook Time: 35 mins. | Serve: 2

- 2 eggs
- 4 bread slices, cut each bread slice into 3 pieces vertically
- ⅔ cup milk
- ¼ tsp. ground cinnamon
- 1 tsp. vanilla

1. Preheat your outdoor Griddle by turning all its burner's knob to medium-heat setting.
2. Grease the griddle top with cooking spray.
3. Beat the eggs, cinnamon, vanilla, and milk in a suitable mixing dish.
4. Coat each slice of bread with the egg mixture thoroughly.
5. Place the coated bread pieces on the hot griddle top and cook until both the two sides are golden brown.
6. Serve and enjoy.

Per Serving:
Calories: 195 | Fat: 13.5g | Carbohydrates: 23g | Fiber: 4.4g | Sugar: 0.6g | Protein: 10.8g | Sodium:35mg

PEPPER STEAK WITH EGGS
Prep Time: 10 mins. | Cook Time: mins. | Serve: 2

- 1 lb. Sirloin, cut into 4½ - inch thick pieces
- 8 large eggs
- 3 tbsp. vegetable oil
- ½ tsp. salt and black pepper

1. Preheat your outdoor Griddle by turning all its burner's knob to medium-high heat setting.
2. Grease the griddle top with cooking spray.
3. Season both the two sides of the steaks with salt and black pepper.
4. Cook the steaks for 3 minutes per side on medium-high heat on the hot griddle top.
5. Crack the eggs on one side of the griddle and cook until set.
6. Serve the steak with eggs.

Per Serving:
Calories: 230 | Fat: 15g | Carbohydrates: 11g | Fiber: 3.4g | Sugar: 0.1g | Protein: 11.8g | Sodium:50mg

POTATOES HASH BROWNS WITH PEPPER
Prep Time: 10 mins. | Cook Time: 15 mins. | Serve: 3

- 3 russet potatoes, peeled
- 1 tbsp. onion powder
- 1 tbsp. salt
- 1 tsp. black pepper
- 3 tbsp. vegetable oil

1. Grate the potatoes with a grater then mix with onion powder, salt, and black pepper in a bowl.
2. Preheat your outdoor Griddle by turning all its burner's knob to medium-heat setting.
3. Grease the griddle top with cooking oil.
4. Divide the potato mixture on the hot griddle top into hash browns.
5. Cook for 3-5 minutes per side until golden brown.
6. Serve warm

Per Serving:

Calories: 197 | Fat: 12.5g | Carbohydrates: 23g | Fiber: 2.8g | Sugar: 1g | Protein: 6.3g | Sodium: 189mg

CAULIFLOWER BROCCOLI HASH BROWNS
Prep Time: 10 mins. | Cook Time: 10 mins. | Serve: 2

- 1 egg
- 4 oz. cheddar cheese, shredded
- 3 cups broccoli rice
- ¼ tsp. garlic powder
- ¼ tsp. onion powder
- 3 cups cauliflower rice
- ½ tsp. black pepper
- ½ tsp. salt

1. Microwave broccoli rice and cauliflower rice for 5 minutes in a microwave-safe bowl.
2. Squeeze the broccoli and cauliflower rice to remove any extra moisture.
3. Preheat your outdoor Griddle by turning all its burner's knob to medium-heat setting.
4. Grease the griddle top with cooking spray.
5. Place the veggie rice in a suitable mixing bowl.
6. Mix well the egg, garlic powder, onion powder, cheese, pepper, and salt in a suitable mixing bowl.
7. Form patties from the mixture and fry until browned on both the two sides on the hot griddle top.
8. Serve and enjoy.

Per Serving:
Calories: 104 | Fat: 6.5g | Carbohydrates: 10g | Fiber: 3g | Sugar: 6g | Protein: 2.1g | Sodium: 90mg

CINNAMON ALMOND PUMPKIN PANCAKE
Prep Time: 10 mins. | Cook Time: 10 mins. | Serve: 2

- 4 eggs
- ½ tsp. cinnamon
- ½ cup pumpkin puree
- 1 cup almond flour
- 2 tsp. liquid stevia
- 1 tsp. baking powder

1. In a suitable mixing bowl, whisk almond flour, stevia, baking powder, cinnamon, pumpkin puree, and eggs.
2. Preheat your outdoor Griddle by turning all its burner's knob to medium-heat setting.
3. Grease the griddle top with cooking spray.
4. Pour a ladle of the prepared batter onto the hot griddle top and cook for 5 minutes per side.
5. Serve and enjoy.

Per Serving:
Calories: 190 | Fat: 11.3g | Carbohydrates: 18g | Fiber: 4.1g | Sugar: 2g | Protein: 0.4g | Sodium: 150mg

BACON, EGGS, AND CHEESE SANDWICH
Prep Time: 10 mins. | Cook Time: 15 mins. | Serve: 2

- 4 large eggs
- 8 strips of bacon
- 4 slices cheddar or American cheese
- 8 slices sourdough bread
- 2 tbsp. butter
- 2 tbsp. vegetable oil

1. Preheat your outdoor Griddle by turning all its burner's knob to medium-heat setting.
2. Grease the griddle top with cooking spray.
3. Add bacon to the hot griddle top and cook until brown then transfer to a plate.
4. Crack egg, scramble and cook for 5 minutes then transfer to a bowl.
5. Butter top side of each slice of bread and set it on the hot griddle top with butter-side down.
6. Place a cheese slice on four slices of bread.
7. Stack the eggs on the bread when the cheese has just begun to melt and the eggs are done.
8. Top the sandwiches with the bacon and the second slice of bread.
9. Serve right away.

Per Serving:
Calories: 90 | Fat: 1.8g | Carbohydrates: 16g | Fiber: 2.5g | Sugar: 0g | Protein: 3.5g | Sodium: 7mg

VANILLA OATMEAL PANCAKE
Prep Time: 10 mins. | Cook Time: 10 mins. | Serve: 6

- 6 egg whites
- 1 cup steel-cut oats
- ¼ tsp. vanilla
- 1 cup Greek yogurt
- ½ tsp. baking powder
- 1 tsp. liquid stevia
- ¼ tsp. cinnamon

1. Preheat your outdoor Griddle by turning all its burner's knob to medium-heat setting.

2. Grease the griddle top with cooking spray.
3. Add oats to your food blender and process until a fine powder forms.
4. In a blender, mix well the other ingredients and blend until smooth.
5. Pour ¼ cup batter over the griddle's hot surface.
6. Cook pancakes for 5 minutes per side until golden brown.
7. Serve and enjoy.

Per Serving:
Calories: 162 | Fat: 0.8g | Carbohydrates: 10.1g | Fiber: 1.3g | Sugar: 0.3g | Protein: 3g | Sodium: 22mg

MEXICAN CHEESE BEAN SCRAMBLE
Prep Time: 10 mins. | Cook Time: 10 mins. | Serve: 4

- 8 eggs, beaten
- 1 lb. Chorizo
- ½ yellow onion
- 1 cup cooked black beans
- ½ cup green chilies
- ½ cup jack cheese
- ¼ cup green onion, chopped
- ½ tsp. black pepper
- 2 tbsp. vegetable oi

1. Preheat your outdoor Griddle by turning all its burner's knob to medium-heat setting.
2. Grease the griddle top with cooking spray.
3. Brush the chorizo on one side and place the onions on the other side of the griddle with vegetable oil.
4. Mix well the onion, beans, chorizo, and chilies.
5. Add the cheese, eggs, and green onion to the pan and cook until the eggs are set.
6. Remove the scrambled egg from the griddle and season with black pepper.
7. Serve scrambled eggs with beans mixture.
8. Cover the jar and refrigerate overnight before serving.

Per Serving:
Calories: 95 | Fat: 3.3g | Carbohydrates: 14.5g | Fiber: 2.5g | Sugar: 0.5g | Protein: 3g | Sodium: 90mg

SPINACH PANCAKES
Prep Time: 10 mins. | Cook Time: 10 mins. | Serve: 6

- 1 cup flour
- ¾ cup milk
- 2 tbsp. white vinegar
- 2 tbsp. sugar
- 1 tsp. baking powder
- ½ tsp. baking soda
- ½ tsp. salt
- 1 egg
- 2 tbsp. butter, melted
- 1 cup spinach leaves
- 1 banana
- Butter for cooking

1. Blanch spinach leave in boiling water for 2 minutes then drain and add to a food processor.
2. Add banana and blend until smooth.
3. Mix well the milk and vinegar in a suitable mixing dish. Allow 2 minutes to pass.
4. Beat together the flour, sugar, baking powder, baking soda, and salt in a suitable mixing bowl.
5. Stir in the milk, egg, and melted butter the mix until smooth.
6. Fold in spinach-banana mixture and mix evenly.
7. Preheat your outdoor Griddle by turning all its burner's knob to medium-heat setting.
8. Grease the griddle top with butter.
9. Pour a ladle of the prepared pancake batter on the hot griddle top
10. Cook for 5 minutes per side until golden brown.
11. Garnish with maple syrup and serve.

Per Serving:
Calories: 154 | Fat: 6.1g | Carbohydrates: 25g | Fiber: 3.5g | Sugar: 0.9g | Protein: 7.4g | Sodium: 54mg

ZUCCHINI PANCAKES
Prep Time: 10 mins. | Cook Time: 10 mins. | Serve: 8

- 1 cup flour
- ¾ cup milk
- 2 tbsp. white vinegar
- 2 tbsp. sugar
- 1 tsp. baking powder
- ½ tsp. baking soda
- ½ tsp. salt
- 1 egg
- 2 tbsp. butter, melted
- 1 cup zucchini, grated
- Butter for cooking

1. Mix well the milk and vinegar in a suitable mixing dish. Allow 2 minutes to pass.
2. Beat together the flour, sugar, baking powder, baking soda, and salt in a suitable mixing bowl.

3. Stir in the milk, egg, and melted butter the mix until smooth.
4. Fold in zucchini and mix evenly.
5. Preheat your outdoor Griddle by turning all its burner's knob to medium-heat setting.
6. Grease the griddle top with butter.
7. Pour a ladle of the prepared pancake batter on the hot griddle top
8. Cook for 5 minutes per side until golden brown.
9. Garnish with maple syrup and serve.

Per Serving:
Calories: 174 | Fat: 6.1g | Carbohydrates: 24g | Fiber: 3.5g | Sugar: 0.9g | Protein: 7.4g | Sodium:54mg

COCOA PANCAKES

Prep Time: 10 mins. | Cook Time: 10 mins. |Serve: 6

- 1 cup flour
- ¾ cup milk
- 2 tbsp. white vinegar
- 2 tbsp. sugar
- 1 tsp. baking powder
- ½ tsp. baking soda
- ½ tsp. salt
- 1 egg
- 2 tbsp. butter, melted
- ¼ cup cocoa powder
- Butter for cooking

1. Mix well the milk and vinegar in a suitable mixing dish. Allow 2 minutes to pass.
2. Beat together the flour, sugar, baking powder, baking soda, and salt in a suitable mixing bowl.
3. Stir in the milk, cocoa powder, egg, and melted butter the mix until smooth.
4. Preheat your outdoor Griddle by turning all its burner's knob to medium-heat setting.
5. Grease the griddle top with butter.
6. Pour a ladle of the prepared pancake batter on the hot griddle top
7. Cook for 5 minutes per side until golden brown.
8. Garnish with maple syrup and serve.

Per Serving:
Calories: 153 | Fat: 6.1g | Carbohydrates: 7g | Fiber: 3.5g | Sugar: 0.9g | Protein: 7.4g | Sodium:54mg

AVOCADO PANCAKES

Prep Time: 10 mins. | Cook Time: 10 mins. |Serve: 4

- 1 cup flour
- ¾ cup milk
- 2 tbsp. white vinegar
- 2 tbsp. sugar
- 1 tsp. baking powder
- ½ tsp. baking soda
- ½ tsp. salt
- 1 egg
- 2 tbsp. butter, melted
- ½ cup avocado, mashed
- Butter for cooking

1. Mix well the milk and vinegar in a suitable mixing dish. Allow 2 minutes to pass.
2. Beat together the flour, sugar, baking powder, baking soda, and salt in a suitable mixing bowl.
3. Stir in the milk, egg, and melted butter the mix until smooth.
4. Fold in avocado mash and mix evenly.
5. Preheat your outdoor Griddle by turning all its burner's knob to medium-heat setting.
6. Grease the griddle top with butter.
7. Pour a ladle of the prepared pancake batter on the hot griddle top
8. Cook for 5 minutes per side until golden brown.
9. Garnish with maple syrup and serve.

Per Serving:
Calories: 155 | Fat: 6.1g | Carbohydrates: 18g | Fiber: 3.5g | Sugar: 0.9g | Protein: 7.4g | Sodium:54mg

CHOCOLATE CHIPS PANCAKES

Prep Time: 10 mins. | Cook Time: 10 mins. |Serve: 6

- 1 cup flour
- ¾ cup milk
- 2 tbsp. white vinegar
- 2 tbsp. sugar
- 1 tsp. baking powder
- ½ tsp. baking soda
- ½ tsp. salt
- 1 egg
- 2 tbsp. butter, melted
- ½ cup chocolate chips
- Butter for cooking

1. Mix well the milk and vinegar in a suitable mixing dish. Allow 2 minutes to pass.
2. Beat together the flour, sugar, baking powder, baking soda, and salt in a suitable mixing bowl.

3. Stir in the milk, egg, and melted butter the mix until smooth.
4. Fold in chocolate chips and mix evenly.
5. Preheat your outdoor Griddle by turning all its burner's knob to medium-heat setting.
6. Grease the griddle top with butter.
7. Pour a ladle of the prepared pancake batter on the hot griddle top
8. Cook for 5 minutes per side until golden brown.
9. Garnish with maple syrup and serve.

Per Serving:
Calories: 171 | Fat: 3.1g | Carbohydrates: 17g | Fiber: 3.5g | Sugar: 0.9g | Protein: 7.4g | Sodium:54mg

RASPBERRY PANCAKES

Prep Time: 10 mins. | Cook Time: 10 mins. |Serve: 4

- 1 cup flour
- ¾ cup milk
- 2 tbsp. white vinegar
- 2 tbsp. sugar
- 1 tsp. baking powder
- ½ tsp. baking soda
- ½ tsp. salt
- 1 egg
- 2 tbsp. butter, melted
- 1 cup fresh raspberries
- Butter for cooking

1. Mix well the milk and vinegar in a suitable mixing dish. Allow 2 minutes to pass.
2. Beat together the flour, sugar, baking powder, baking soda, and salt in a suitable mixing bowl.
3. Stir in the milk, egg, and melted butter the mix until smooth.
4. Fold in raspberries and mix evenly.
5. Preheat your outdoor Griddle by turning all its burner's knob to medium-heat setting.
6. Grease the griddle top with butter.
7. Pour a ladle of the prepared pancake batter on the hot griddle top
8. Cook for 5 minutes per side until golden brown.
9. Garnish with maple syrup and serve.

Per Serving:
Calories: 134 | Fat: 6.1g | Carbohydrates: 12g | Fiber: 3.5g | Sugar: 0.9g | Protein: 7.4g | Sodium:54mg

RAISINS PANCAKE

Prep Time: 10 mins. | Cook Time: 10 mins. |Serve: 4

- 1 cup flour
- ¾ cup milk
- 2 tbsp. white vinegar
- 2 tbsp. sugar
- 1 tsp. baking powder
- ½ tsp. baking soda
- ½ tsp. salt
- 1 egg
- 2 tbsp. butter, melted
- ½ cup raisins
- Butter for cooking

1. Mix well the milk and vinegar in a suitable mixing dish. Allow 2 minutes to pass.
2. Beat together the flour, sugar, baking powder, baking soda, and salt in a suitable mixing bowl.
3. Stir in the milk, egg, and melted butter the mix until smooth.
4. Fold in raisins and mix evenly.
5. Preheat your outdoor Griddle by turning all its burner's knob to medium-heat setting.
6. Grease the griddle top with butter.
7. Pour a ladle of the prepared pancake batter on the hot griddle top
8. Cook for 5 minutes per side until golden brown.
9. Garnish with maple syrup and serve.

Per Serving:
Calories: 114 | Fat: 6.1g | Carbohydrates: 15g | Fiber: 3.5g | Sugar: 0.9g | Protein: 7.4g | Sodium:54mg

EGG DILL SCRAMBLE

Prep Time: 5 mins. | Cook Time: 8 mins. |Serve: 1

- 1 tsp. olive oil
- 2 eggs, beaten
- 2 tsp. dried dill weed
- Salt and black pepper, to taste

1. Preheat your outdoor Griddle by turning all its burner's knob to medium-heat setting.
2. Grease the griddle top with olive oil.
3. Beat eggs, black pepper, dill, and salt in a suitable mixing dish.
4. Pour over the griddle top, cook and scramble for 8 minutes.
5. Serve warm.

Per Serving:
Calories: 172 | Fat: 13.5g | Carbohydrates: 18g | Fiber: 0.3g | Sugar: 0.7g | Protein: 11.5g | Sodium: 200mg

EGG MUSHROOM SCRAMBLE

Prep Time: 10 mins. | Cook Time: 10 mins. | Serve: 1

- 1 large egg
- 1 large egg white
- Salt and black pepper, to taste
- 1 tsp. olive oil
- ½ cup fresh mushrooms, sliced thinly
- 1 tbsp. low-fat cheddar cheese, shredded

1. Preheat your outdoor Griddle by turning all its burner's knob to medium-heat setting.
2. Grease the griddle top with olive oil.
3. Add mushroom then cook for 2 minutes.
4. Beat egg, egg white, black pepper, cheese, , and salt in a suitable mixing dish.
5. Pour over the mushroom, cook and scramble for 8 minutes.
6. Serve warm.

Per Serving:
Calories: 155 | Fat: 7.5g | Carbohydrates: 21g | Fiber: 0.4g | Sugar: 3.3g | Protein: 15.4g | Sodium: 165mg

SMOKED SALMON SCRAMBLE

Prep Time: 5 mins. | Cook Time: 8 mins. | Serve: 1

- ½ tbsp. olive oil
- 1 cup fresh kale, tough ribs removed and chopped
- Black pepper, to taste
- ¼ cup smoked salmon, crumbled
- 2 eggs, beaten

1. Preheat your outdoor Griddle by turning all its burner's knob to medium-heat setting.
2. Grease the griddle top with olive oil.
3. Beat eggs, black pepper, salmon, kale, and salt in a suitable mixing dish.
4. Pour over the griddle top, cook and scramble for 8 minutes.
5. Serve warm.

Per Serving:
Calories: 240 | Fat: 15g | Carbohydrates: 23g | Fiber: 1g | Sugar: 0.7g | Protein: 16.8g | Sodium: 365mg

TOFU ARUGULA SCRAMBLE

Prep Time: 10 mins. | Cook Time: 8 mins. | Serve: 1

- ½ tbsp. olive oil
- 1 small garlic clove, minced
- 3 oz. medium-firm tofu, pressed, drained and crumbled
- ¼-1/3 cup water
- 1¼ cups fresh arugula
- 2 tbsp. tomato, chopped
- ¼ tsp. ground turmeric
- ½ tsp. fresh lemon juice

1. Preheat your outdoor Griddle by turning all its burner's knob to medium-heat setting.
2. Grease the griddle top with olive oil.
3. Beat eggs, black pepper, arugula, garlic, water, tomato, turmeric, lemon juice, and salt in a suitable mixing dish.
4. Pour over the griddle top, cook and scramble for 8 minutes.
5. Serve warm.

Per Serving:
Calories: 137 | Fat: 10.8g | Carbohydrates: 24g | Fiber: 1.4g | Sugar: 1.7g | Protein: 8.1g | Sodium: 21mg

TOFU VEGGIE SCRAMBLE

Prep Time: 10 mins. | Cook Time: 10 mins. | Serve: 1

- ½ tbsp. olive oil
- ½ of small onion, chopped
- ½ of small red bell pepper, chopped
- ¼ cup cherry tomatoes, chopped
- ¾ cup firm tofu, crumbled and chopped
- Pinch of cayenne pepper
- Pinch of ground turmeric
- Salt, to taste

1. Preheat your outdoor Griddle by turning all its burner's knob to medium-heat setting.
2. Grease the griddle top with butter.
3. Add red pepper and tomato then cook for 2 minutes.
4. Stir in tofu, salt, turmeric, cayenne pepper, and onion.
5. Cook the tofu scramble for 8 minutes.
6. Serve warm.

Per Serving:

Calories: 224 | Fat: 15g | Carbohydrates: 10g | Fiber: 2.4g | Sugar: 4g | Protein: 16.4g | Sodium: 265mg

VEGGIE SCRAMBLE

Prep Time: 10 mins. | Cook Time: 10 mins. |Serve: 1

- 2 tbsp. chickpea flour
- ½ tbsp. nutritional yeast
- Pinch of paprika
- Pinch of ground turmeric
- Pinch of tsp. ground cumin
- Black pepper, to taste
- 2 tbsp. water
- 2 tbsp. cooked chickpeas
- ½ tbsp. fresh parsley, chopped
- ½ of garlic clove, minced
- ½ tbsp. olive oil
- 2 tbsp. bell pepper, seeded and chopped
- 2 tbsp. tomato, chopped

1. Preheat your outdoor Griddle by turning all its burner's knob to medium-heat setting.
2. Grease the griddle top with olive oil.
3. Mash chickpeas in a bowl and stir in flour, water and rest of the ingredients.
4. Mix well until smooth and pour a dollop of this batter on the griddle top.
5. Cook the chickpea omelet for 5 minutes per side.
6. Serve warm.

Per Serving:
Calories: 144 | Fat: 7.5g | Carbohydrates: 13g | Fiber: 4.3g | Sugar: 2.5g | Protein: 5.8g | Sodium: 16mg

APPLE OMELET

Prep Time: 10 mins. | Cook Time: 10 mins. |Serve: 1

- 2 tsp. olive oil, divided
- ½ of small green apple, cored and sliced
- ¼ tsp. ground cinnamon
- 1/8 tsp. ground nutmeg
- 2 eggs
- 1/8 tsp. organic vanilla extract
- Pinch of salt

1. Preheat your outdoor Griddle by turning all its burner's knob to medium-heat setting.
2. Grease the griddle top with butter.
3. Beat eggs, green apple, cinnamon, nutmeg, vanilla and salt in a suitable mixing dish.
4. Pour over the griddle, cook for 5 minutes per side.
5. Serve warm.

Per Serving:
Calories: 242 | Fat: 17.5g | Carbohydrates: 18g | Fiber: 1.3g | Sugar: 5g | Protein: 11.3g | Sodium: 165mg

ASPARAGUS OMELET

Prep Time: 10 mins. | Cook Time: 15 mins. |Serve: 1

- 2 large eggs
- Salt and black pepper, to taste
- ½ tbsp. olive oil
- scallion, chopped
- 4 asparagus spears, chopped
- 1 tbsp. tomato, chopped

1. Preheat your outdoor Griddle by turning all its burner's knob to medium-heat setting.
2. Grease the griddle top with olive oil.
3. Add asparagus and tomato then cook for 5 minutes.
4. Beat eggs, black pepper, scallion, black pepper and salt in a suitable mixing dish.
5. Pour over the asparagus, cook 5 minutes per side.
6. Serve warm.

Per Serving:
Calories: 212 | Fat: 17g | Carbohydrates: 8g | Fiber: 0.5g | Sugar: 1.7g | Protein: 13.1g | Sodium:144mg

CHEDDAR SPINACH OMELET

Prep Time: 10 mins. | Cook Time: 10 mins. |Serve: 1

- 2 large eggs
- ¼ cup cooked spinach, squeezed
- 2 scallions, chopped
- tbsp. fresh parsley, chopped
- 2 tbsp. low-fat cheddar cheese, shredded
- Salt and black pepper, to taste
- tsp. olive oil

1. Preheat your outdoor Griddle by turning all its burner's knob to medium-heat setting.
2. Grease the griddle top with olive oil.
3. Beat eggs, black pepper, spinach, cheese, scallions, and salt in a suitable mixing dish.
4. Pour over the griddle top, cook 5 minutes per side.
5. Serve warm.

Per Serving:
Calories: 254 | Fat: 17.5g | Carbohydrates: 3.5g | Fiber: 1.1g | Sugar: 1.6g | Protein: 16g | Sodium: 200mg

MUSHROOM OMELET

Prep Time: 10 mins. | Cook Time: 15 mins. |Serve: 1

- ✓ 2 small eggs
- ✓ Salt and black pepper, to taste
- ✓ ¼ cup unsweetened almond milk
- ✓ ¼ of onion, chopped
- ✓ ¼ cup fresh mushrooms, cut into slices
- ✓ ½ tbsp. chives, minced

1. Preheat your outdoor Griddle by turning all its burner's knob to medium-heat setting.
2. Grease the griddle top with cooking spray.
3. Add mushrooms and chives then cook for 5 minutes.
4. Beat eggs, milk, onion, black pepper, and salt in a suitable mixing dish.
5. Pour over the mushrooms, cook 5 minutes per side.
6. Serve warm.

Per Serving:
Calories: 132 | Fat: 7.5g | Carbohydrates: 23g | Fiber: 1.1g | Sugar: 2.1g | Protein: 10.5g | Sodium:151mg

CHEESE TURKEY OMELET

Prep Time: 10 mins. | Cook Time: 15 mins. |Serve: 1

- ✓ ¼ lb. lean ground turkey
- ✓ 2 eggs
- ✓ 2 tbsp. low-fat cheddar cheese, shredded
- ✓ 2 tbsp. unsweetened almond milk
- ✓ Pinch of red pepper flakes, crushed
- ✓ Salt and black pepper, to taste

1. Preheat your outdoor Griddle by turning all its burner's knob to medium-heat setting.
2. Grease the griddle top with butter.
3. Add ground turkey then cook for 5 minutes.
4. Beat eggs, milk, red pepper, black pepper, salt and cheese in a suitable bowl.
5. Pour over the turkey, cook 5 minutes per side.
6. Serve warm.

Per Serving:
Calories: 317 | Fat: 17.5g | Carbohydrates: 13g |Fiber: 0.3g | Sugar: 0.8g | Protein: 36g | Sodium: 365mg

SMOKED SALMON OMELET

Prep Time: 5 mins. | Cook Time: 10 mins. |Serve: 1

- ✓ 2 large eggs
- ✓ Black pepper, to taste
- ✓ 1 tbsp. olive oil
- ✓ 1½ oz. smoked salmon, chopped
- ✓ tbsp. low-fat cheddar cheese, shredded

1. Preheat your outdoor Griddle by turning all its burner's knob to medium-heat setting.
2. Grease the griddle top with olive oil.
4. Beat eggs, cheese, salmon and black pepper in a bowl.
5. Pour over the griddle top, cook 5 minutes per side.
6. Serve warm.

Per Serving:
Calories: 335 | Fat: 27.3g | Carbohydrates: 11g |Fiber: 0g | Sugar: 0.8g | Protein: 22.4g | Sodium: 423mg

SNACK RECIPES

FIGS STUFFED WITH GOAT CHEESE
Prep Time: 10 mins. | Cook Time: 10 mins. | Serve: 10

- 20 ripe figs
- 4 oz soft goat cheese
- 2 tbsp. olive oil
- 2 tbsp. balsamic vinegar
- 1 tbsp. chopped fresh rosemary

1. Preheat your outdoor Griddle by turning all its burner's knobs to low-heat setting.
2. Grease the griddle top with cooking spray.
3. Make a cross cut on top of the figs.
4. Mix goat cheese, balsamic vinegar and rosemary in a bowl.
5. Stuff the figs with the goat cheese mixture.
6. Place the figs on the hot griddle top and cook for 10 minutes.
7. Serve warm.

Per Serving:
Calories: 284 | Fat: 19g | Carbohydrates: 8g | Fiber: 0.8g | Sugar: 1.5g | Protein: 23.8g | Sodium: 465mg

BACON-WRAPPED MUSHROOMS
Prep Time: 10 mins. | Cook Time: 10 mins. | Serve: 4

- 1 lb. bacon, cut in half
- 1 lb. of cremini mushrooms, scrubbed
- Olive oil
- Kosher salt, to taste
- black pepper

1. Wrap the mushrooms with bacon half and seal with a toothpick.
2. Preheat your outdoor Griddle by turning all its burner's knob to medium-heat setting.
3. Grease the griddle top with cooking oil.
4. Season the wrapped mushrooms and place them on the hot griddle top.
5. Cook for almost 5 minutes per side.
6. Serve warm.

Per Serving:
Calories: 130 | Fat: 18.1g | Carbohydrates: 13g | Fiber: 0.1g | Sugar: 0.8g | Protein: 8.3g | Sodium: 265mg

GOAT CHEESE-STUFFED PEPPADEWS
Prep Time: 10 mins. | Cook Time: 10 mins. | Serve: 4

- 5 oz. spreadable goat cheese
- 2 tbsp. chopped chives, divided
- 1 tbsp. parsley leaves, chopped
- 1 14-oz. jar Peppadews, drained
- 1 tbsp. olive oil

1. Preheat your outdoor Griddle by turning all its burner's knobs to low-heat setting.
2. Grease the griddle top with cooking spray.
3. Make a cut on top of the peppadews.
4. Mix goat cheese, balsamic vinegar and rosemary in a bowl.
5. Stuff the peppadews with the goat cheese mixture.
6. Place the peppadews on the hot griddle top and cook for 5 minutes per side.
7. Serve warm.

Per Serving:
Calories: 30 | Fat: 18.1g | Carbohydrates: 13g | Fiber: 0.1g | Sugar: 0.8g | Protein: 28.3g | Sodium: 265mg

BACON-WRAPPED ASPARAGUS SKEWERS
Prep Time: 10 mins. | Cook Time: 10 mins. | Serve: 2

- 1 tbsp. sweet paprika
- 2 tsp. ground coriander
- 1 tsp. ground cumin
- 1 (16-oz.) package bacon, cut into 4 pieces
- 1 lb. asparagus, cut into 3 pieces
- Vegetable oil

1. Wrap the asparagus spears with bacon and rub them with all the spices.
2. Preheat your outdoor Griddle by turning all its burner's knob to medium-heat setting.
3. Grease the griddle top with cooking spray.
4. Place the asparagus spears on the hot griddle top.
5. Cook for almost 5 minutes per side.
6. Serve warm.

Per Serving:
Calories: 127 | Fat: 12.5g | Carbohydrates: 3.5g | Fiber: 0.4g | Sugar: 0.7g | Protein: 27.3g | Sodium: 365mg

ITALIAN MEATBALLS WITH PECORINO
Prep Time: 15 mins. | Cook Time: 10 mins. | Serve: 6

- 1 lb. ground chuck
- ½ lb. ground pork

- 3/4 cup fresh breadcrumbs
- 2 large eggs, beaten
- 1/3 cup Parmesan, grated
- 1/3 cup grated Pecorino Romano
- 2 garlic cloves, minced
- 2 tbsp. fresh parsley, chopped
- ¼ tsp. red pepper flakes
- Kosher salt, to taste
- black pepper, to taste
- Olive oil
- Marinara sauce, for dipping

1. Blend ground chuck, pork and rest pf the ingredients in a food processor for 2 minutes.
2. Make 1-2 inches sized meatballs out of this mixture.
3. Preheat your outdoor Griddle by turning all its burner's knob to medium-heat setting.
4. Grease the griddle top with cooking spray.
5. Place the meatballs on the hot griddle top.
6. Cook for almost 5 minutes per side.
7. Dip the meatballs in the marinara sauce.
8. Serve warm.

Per Serving:
Calories: 164 | Fat: 8.5g | Carbohydrates: 15.1g | Fiber: 3.3g | Sugar: 3.1g | Protein: 5.4g | Sodium: 175mg

SAUSAGES STUFFED PEPPERS
Prep Time: 10 mins. | Cook Time: 10 mins. |Serve: 4

- 4 oz. cream cheese
- ½ cup shredded sharp cheddar cheese
- 1 tbsp. chopped cilantro
- 6 large jalapeños, halved and seeded
- 2 lbs. loose breakfast sausage
- 1 tbsp. favorite barbecue rub

1. Mix cheddar cheese, cream cheese, cilantro, and sausage in a bowl.
2. Stuff the jalapenos with cream cheese mixture.
3. Preheat your outdoor Griddle by turning all its burner's knob to medium-low heat setting.
4. Grease the griddle top with cooking spray.
5. Season the peppers with barbecue rub and place them on the hot griddle top.
6. Cook for almost 10 minutes.
7. Serve warm.

Per Serving:

Calories: 185 | Fat: 11.8g | Carbohydrates: 23g |Fiber: 1.3g | Sugar: 2.6g | Protein: 15.3g | Sodium:195mg

BARBECUE MEATBALLS
Prep Time: 10 mins. | Cook Time: 10 mins. |Serve: 4

- For the Rub
- 2 tsp. paprika
- 2 tsp. Kosher salt, to taste
- 1 tsp. dark brown sugar
- ½ tsp. garlic powder
- ½ tsp. chili powder
- ½ tsp. ground cumin
- ½ tsp. black pepper
- ¼ tsp. mustard powder
- 1/8 tsp. cayenne pepper
- 1 tbsp. vegetable oil
- 1 small onion, minced
- 2 gloves garlic, minced
- 1 ½ tsp. chili powder
- 3/4lb ground beef chuck
- 3/4lb ground pork
- 1 egg, beaten
- 1 cup of your favorite barbecue sauce

1. Blend pork ground, and rest of the ingredients in a food processor except the barbecue sauce in a food processor.
2. Make 1-2 inches meatballs out of the mixture.
3. Preheat your outdoor Griddle by turning all its burner's knob to medium-heat setting.
4. Grease the griddle top with cooking spray.
5. Place the meatballs on the hot griddle top.
6. Cook for almost 5 minutes per side.
7. Dip the meatballs in the sauce.
8. Serve warm.

Per Serving:
Calories: 185 | Fat: 11.8g | Carbohydrates: 23g |Fiber:

1.3g | Sugar: 2.6g | Protein: 15.3g | Sodium:195mg

SRIRACHA HOT WINGS
Prep Time: 10 mins. | Cook Time: 30 mins. |Serve: 8

- ✓ 4 lbs. chicken wings, cut into drumettes and flats
- ✓ 1 tbsp. baking powder
- ✓ 1 tsp. kosher salt, to taste
- ✓ For the Sauce
- ✓ 4 tbsp. butter
- ✓ ½ cup Sriracha
- ✓ 2 tbsp. honey
- ✓ 1 ½ tbsp. soy sauce
- ✓ 1 tbsp. chopped cilantro
- ✓ 1 tbsp. squeezed lime juice
- ✓ 1 tsp. rice vinegar

1. Prepare the sauce for the wings by mixing all its ingredients in a saucepan.
2. Cook this sauce to a simmer then keep it aside.
3. Season the chicken wings with rest of the ingredients.
4. Preheat your outdoor Griddle by turning all its burner's knob to medium-heat setting.
5. Grease the griddle top with cooking spray.
6. Place the chicken wings on the hot griddle top.
7. Cook for almost 10 minutes per side.
8. Brush the wings with the prepared sauce.
9. Cook the wings for 5 minutes per side.
10. Serve warm.

Per Serving:

Calories: 200 | Fat: 14.8g | Carbohydrates: 3.5g | Fiber: 1g | Sugar: 1.6g | Protein: 11.8g | Sodium: 201mg

PIG CANDY
Prep Time: 10 mins. | Cook Time: 12 mins. |Serve: 4

- ✓ ½ cup dark brown sugar
- ✓ 1/8 tsp. cayenne pepper
- ✓ 1 lb. thick cut bacon
- ✓ ¼ cup maple syrup

1. Mix maple syrup, cayenne pepper and brown sugar in a bowl.
2. Brush the bacon slices with the maple mixture.
3. Preheat your outdoor Griddle by turning all its burner's knob to medium-heat setting.
4. Grease the griddle top with cooking spray.
5. Place the bacon slices on the hot griddle top.
6. Cook for almost 6 minutes per side while brushing them with the maple syrup.
7. Serve warm.

Per Serving:
Calories: 214 | Fat: 15g | Carbohydrates: 21g | Fiber: 1.5g | Sugar: 1.9g | Protein: 14.5g | Sodium:232mg

SMASHED POTATOES
Prep Time: 10 mins. | Cook Time: 10 mins. |Serve: 8

- ✓ 16 small potatoes, mix variety of red, white, and/or purple skinned
- ✓ 2 tbsp. olive oil
- ✓ 2 tbsp. chopped fresh rosemary leaves, divided
- ✓ Kosher salt, to taste
- ✓ black pepper

1. Boil potatoes in pot filled with boiling water until soft.
2. Drain and allow them to cool and smash the potatoes with your palm.
3. Rub the potato with oil, rosemary, black pepper and salt.
4. Preheat your outdoor Griddle by turning all its burner's knob to medium-heat setting.
5. Grease the griddle top with cooking spray.
6. Place the potatoes on the hot griddle top.
7. Cook for almost 5 minutes per side.
8. Serve warm.

Per Serving:
Calories: 150 | Fat: 9.4g | Carbohydrates: 18g | Fiber: 0.5g | Sugar: 1g | Protein: 15.1g | Sodium: 185mg

HASSELBACK POTATOES

Prep Time: 10 mins. | Cook Time: 40 mins. |Serves: 4

- ✓ 4 medium russet potatoes, scrubbed
- ✓ 4 large garlic cloves, sliced
- ✓ 4 oz Parmesan cheese, 2oz sliced, 2oz grated
- ✓ 2 tbsp. olive oil
- ✓ Kosher salt, to taste
- ✓ black pepper

1. Rub the potatoes with oil, black pepper and salt.
2. Make cut on top of the potato with ½ inch gaps in between.
3. Drizzle oil, parmesan cheese, salt and black pepper in the cuts.
4. Wrap the potatoes with aluminum foil and place them on the griddle top.
5. Preheat your outdoor Griddle by turning all its burner's knob to medium-heat setting.
6. Grease the griddle top with cooking spray.
7. Cook for almost 40 minutes while rotating after every 5 minutes.
8. Serve warm.

Per Serving:
Calories: 176 | Fat: 10g | Carbohydrates: 38g | Fiber: 1.4g | Sugar: 3.3g | Protein: 14.8g | Sodium:181mg

HASSELBACK SWEET POTATOES

Prep Time: 10 mins. | Cook Time: 40 mins. | Serve: 4

- ✓ 6 medium garlic cloves, minced
- ✓ 2 tsp. chopped fresh rosemary
- ✓ 1 tbsp., plus 1 tsp. olive oil, divided
- ✓ 4 medium sweet potatoes, scrubbed
- ✓ Kosher salt, to taste
- ✓ black pepper, to taste

1. Rub the sweet potatoes with oil, black pepper and salt.
2. Make cut on top of the potato with ½ inch gaps in between.
3. Drizzle oil, rosemary, garlic, salt and black pepper in the cuts.
4. Wrap the sweet potatoes with aluminum foil and place them on the griddle top.
5. Preheat your outdoor Griddle by turning all its burner's knob to medium-heat setting.
6. Grease the griddle top with cooking spray.
7. Cook for almost 40 minutes while rotating after every 5 minutes.
8. Serve warm.

Per Serving:
Calories: 132 | Fat: 8g | Carbohydrates: 25.1g | Fiber: 1.1g | Sugar: 1.9g | Protein: 1.5g | Sodium: 280mg

ZUCCHINI WITH GARLIC CHILI OIL

Prep Time: 10 mins. | Cook Time: 10 mins. |Serves: 2

- ✓ 4 medium zucchini, washed and split in half
- ✓ ¼ cup olive oil
- ✓ 1 tbsp. kosher salt, to taste
- ✓ 1 tbsp. black pepper
- ✓ 1 cup Parmesan, grated cheese
- ✓ ½ cup garlic chili oil

1. Preheat your outdoor Griddle by turning all its burner's knob to medium-heat setting.
2. Grease the griddle top with cooking spray.
3. Place the zucchini slices on the hot griddle top.
4. Cook for almost 5 minutes per side.
5. Drizzle parmesan and rest of the ingredients on top.
6. Serve warm.

Per Serving:
Calories: 106 | Fat: 7.1g | Carbohydrates: 24g | Fiber: 1g | Sugar: 1.1g | Protein: 9.3g | Sodium: 190mg

ZUCCHINI ROLLS WITH GOAT CHEESE

Prep Time: 10 mins. | Cook Time: 10 mins. |Serve: 4

- ✓ 1 small bunch fresh chives
- ✓ 4-5 medium zucchinis (2 lbs.), sliced
- ✓ 3 tbsp. olive oil
- ✓ Kosher salt, to taste
- ✓ black pepper, to taste
- ✓ 4 oz. fresh goat cheese, at room temperature

- ✓ 1 small bunch fresh mint leaves, chopped
- ✓ 2 tbsp. balsamic vinegar
- ✓ 1 handful baby arugula
- ✓ 2 Fresno peppers, cut into 1/8" matchsticks

1. Rub the black pepper and salt over the zucchini slices.
2. Preheat your outdoor Griddle by turning all its burner's knob to medium-heat setting.
3. Grease the griddle top with cooking spray.
4. Place the zucchini slices on the griddle top and cook for 5 minutes per side.
5. Mix goat cheese and rest of the ingredients in a bowl.
6. Divide the goat cheese mixture at the center of each zucchini slice on top.
7. Roll the zucchini slices and serve.

Per Serving:

Calories: 165 | Fat: 13g | Carbohydrates: 15g | Fiber: 2.3g | Sugar: 3.8g | Protein: 8.1g | Sodium:175mg

NEGIMAKI

Prep Time: 10 mins. | Cook Time: 10 mins. |Serve: 2

- ✓ 2 quarts water
- ✓ 1 tbsp. kosher salt, to taste, divided
- ✓ 12 small scallions, trimmed to 6-inches in length
- ✓ 1 lb. flank steak, 6 to 7 inches square
- ✓ ¼ cup sake
- ✓ ¼ cup mirin
- ✓ 3 tbsp. soy sauce
- ✓ 1 tbsp. sugar
- ✓ 1 tbsp. vegetable oil

1. Boil water with salt, sake, scallions, sugar, and soy sauce in a saucepan.
2. Remove from the heat and allow the water to cool.
3. Soak the steak in the water, cover and refrigerate overnight.
4. Preheat your outdoor Griddle by turning all its burner's knob to medium-heat setting.
5. Grease the griddle top with cooking oil.
6. Place the steak on the griddle top and cook for 5 minutes per side.
7. Serve warm.

Per Serving:
Calories: 155 | Fat: 7.5g | Carbohydrates: 21g | Fiber: 0.4g | Sugar: 3.3g | Protein: 15.4g | Sodium: 165mg

HOMEMADE CHORIZO

Prep Time: 10 mins. | Cook Time: 10 mins. |Serve: 4

- ✓ 2 ½ lbs. pork shoulder, minced
- ✓ For the dry seasoning
- ✓ ¼ cup ferment
- ✓ 1 tbsp. paprika
- ✓ 1 tbsp. mild chili powder
- ✓ 2 tsp. corn syrup
- ✓ 2 tsp. kosher salt, to taste
- ✓ 1 tsp. cayenne pepper
- ✓ ¾ tsp. garlic powder
- ✓ ½ tsp. pink curing salt

1. Mix all the dry seasoning ingredients in a bowl.
2. Stir in pork mince then mix well.
3. Stuff the pork mince in a hot casings to make sausage links and refrigerate overnight.
4. Preheat your outdoor Griddle by turning all its burner's knob to medium-heat setting.
5. Grease the griddle top with cooking spray.
6. Place the sausages on the hot griddle top.
7. Cook for almost 5 minutes per side.
8. Serve warm.

Per Serving:
Calories: 152 | Fat: 13g | Carbohydrates: 28g | Fiber: 1g | Sugar: 2.3g | Protein: 7.1g | Sodium: 205mg

GRILLED POTATO WEDGES

Prep Time: 5 mins. | Cook Time: 20 mins. |Serve: 4

- ✓ 4-6 russet potatoes medium-sized
- ✓ ½ cup cooking oil
- ✓ 2 tbsp. paprika
- ✓ ¼ cup salt
- ✓ 1 tbsp. black pepper
- ✓ ⅔ cup potato flakes

1. Mix potato wedges with paprika, salt, potato flakes and black pepper in a bowl.
2. Preheat your outdoor Griddle by turning all its burner's knob to medium-heat setting.
3. Grease the griddle top with cooking oil.
4. Place potato wedges on the hot griddle top.
5. Cook for almost 20 minutes and flip every 5 minutes.
6. Serve warm.

Per Serving:

Calories: 137 | Fat: 7.8g | Carbohydrates: 35g | Fiber: 1g | Sugar: 2.1g | Protein: 11.4g | Sodium: 160mg

BACON-WRAPPED CHICKEN THIGHS

Prep Time: 10 mins. | Cook Time: 50 mins. | Serve: 6

- 12 chicken thighs
- 12 strips bacon
- BBQ rub
- 2 tbsp. paprika
- 2 tbsp. chili powder
- 1 tbsp. thyme
- 2 tbsp. garlic powder
- 2 tbsp. cumin
- 1 tbsp. salt
- 2 tbsp. black pepper

1. Wrap the chicken thighs with bacon slices and rub them with the spices.
2. Preheat your outdoor Griddle by turning all its burner's knob to medium-heat setting.
3. Grease the griddle top with cooking oil.
4. Place the wrapped chicken thighs on the hot griddle top.
5. Cook for almost 50 minutes while turning the thighs every 10 minutes.
6. Serve warm.

Per Serving:

Calories: 207 | Fat: 13.5g | Carbohydrates: 25g | Fiber: 4.8g | Sugar: 0.7g | Protein: 6.8g | Sodium: 201mg

BISON SLIDERS

Prep Time: 10 mins. | Cook Time: 10 mins. | Serve: 4

- 1 lb. ground buffalo meat
- 3 garlic cloves minced
- 2 tbsp. Worcestershire sauce
- 1 tsp. table/kosher salt, to taste
- 1 tsp. black pepper
- cheese sliced

1. Mix buffalo meat with garlic, Worcestershire sauce, black pepper and salt in a bowl.
2. Make 8 small patties out of this mixture.
3. Preheat your outdoor Griddle by turning all its burner's knob to medium-heat setting.
4. Grease the griddle top with cooking spray.
5. Place the patties on the hot griddle top.
6. Cook for almost 5 minutes per side.
7. Top the patties with cheese and place each patty in a bun.
8. Serve warm.

Per Serving:

Calories: 137 | Fat: 9.5g | Carbohydrates: 23g | Fiber: 0.5g | Sugar: 0.6g | Protein: 5.4g | Sodium: 217mg

HOT DOG BURNT ENDS

Prep Time: 10 mins. | Cook Time: 12 mins. | Serve: 4

- 1 pack hot dogs
- ½ cup BBQ sauce
- 2 tbsp. butter
- ¼ cup brown sugar
- Seasoning
- 2 tbsp. mustard
- 2 tbsp. dry rub

1. Mix bbq sauce, butter, brown sugar, mustard and dry rub in a bowl.
2. Coat the hot dogs with this mixture.
3. Preheat your outdoor Griddle by turning all its burner's knob to medium-heat setting.
4. Grease the griddle top with cooking spray.
5. Place them on the hot griddle top.
6. Cook for almost 6 minutes per side.
7. Serve warm.

Per Serving:

Calories: 124 | Fat: 0.4g | Carbohydrates: 21g | Fiber: 0.4g | Sugar: 0.6g | Protein: 1.3g | Sodium: 165mg

STUFFED MUSHROOMS

Prep Time: 10 mins. | Cook Time: 22 minute | Serve: 8

- 8 portobello mushrooms
- cheddar cheese grated or shredded
- Filling

- 4 slices bacon
- ½ lb. cream cheese
- 1 large red onion sliced
- 1 jalapeño pepper sliced

1. Preheat your outdoor Griddle by turning all its burner's knob to medium-heat setting.
2. Grease the griddle top with cooking spray.
3. Place bacon on the hot griddle top.
4. Cook for almost 6 minutes per side.
5. Chop the bacon and mix well cream cheese, red onion and jalapeno in a bowl.
6. Divide the mixture into the mushrooms.
7. Place the mushrooms on the hot griddle top.
8. Drizzle cheese on top and cook for 10 minutes.
9. Serve warm.

Per Serving:
Calories: 126| Fat: 0.5g | Carbohydrates: 5g | Fiber:1g | Sugar: 0.7g | Protein: 1.5g | Sodium: 166mg

MANOURI CHEESE WITH CARAMELIZED PLUMS
Prep Time: 5 mins. | Cook Time: 15 mins. |Serve: 6

- 2 tbsp. honey
- 6 medium plums, halved and pitted
- 2 tbsp. sherry vinegar
- 2 tbsp. lemon juice
- 2 tbsp. olive oil
- Salt and black pepper
- ½ lb. manouri cheese, cut into rounds
- ½ tsp. dried Greek oregano
- 6 cups packed arugula
- 2 tbsp. basil, sliced

1. Brush honey, vinegar, lemon juice and oil over the plums.
2. Preheat your outdoor Griddle by turning all its burner's knob to medium-heat setting.
3. Grease the griddle top with cooking spray.
4. place them on the hot griddle top and cook for 5 minutes from the cut side.
5. Sauté arugula on the griddle for 5 minutes.
6. Divide the cheese and rest of the ingredients on the plums.
7. Serve.

Per Serving:
Calories: 165 | Fat: 6g | Carbohydrates: 7g | Fiber:3.1g | Sugar: 0.7g | Protein: 19.3g | Sodium: 265mg

SWEET POTATOES WITH MOZZARELLA
Prep Time: 10 mins. | Cook Time: 16 mins. |Serve: 3

- 3 sweet potatoes (1 lb.), cut into ¼-inch slices
- 2 tbsp. olive oil
- Salt
- Fresh-black pepper, to taste
- ¼ tsp. wine vinegar
- 1 garlic clove, minced
- 1 tbsp. chopped flat-leaf parsley
- ½ lb. salted fresh mozzarella, cut into thick slices

1. Season sweet potato slices with salt, black pepper, vinegar, garlic, and parsley.
2. Preheat your outdoor Griddle by turning all its burner's knob to medium-heat setting.
3. Grease the griddle top with cooking spray.
4. Place sweet potatoes slices on the hot griddle top.
5. Cook for almost 6 minutes per side.
6. Top the sweet potato with mozzarella and cook for 2 minutes.
7. Serve warm.

Per Serving:
Calories: 192 | Fat: 1.8g | Carbohydrates: 13g | Fiber: 2.3g | Sugar: 1.9g | Protein: 7.3g | Sodium: 230mg

HALLOUMI CHEESE WITH MUSHROOMS
Prep Time: 10 mins. | Cook Time: 12 mins. |Serve: 4

- 8 oz. brown mushrooms, diced
- 1 small sweet onion, diced
- 8 oz. Halloumi cheese, diced
- MARINADE
- 3 tbsp. lemon juice
- 2 tsp. red wine vinegar
- 2 tbsp. olive oil
- 1 tsp. Greek Seasoning
- ½ tsp. Spike Seasoning

1. Mix mushroom, cheese and onion cubes with marinade ingredients in a bowl.
2. Cover and marinate for 20 minutes.
3. Preheat your outdoor Griddle by turning all its burner's knob to medium-heat setting.
4. Grease the griddle top with cooking spray.
5. Thread the mushrooms, cheese and onion on the skewers alternately.
6. Place mushroom skewers on the hot griddle top.
7. Cook for almost 6 minutes per side.

8. Serve warm.
Per Serving:

Calories: 160 | Fat: 7g | Carbohydrates: 18g | Fiber: 2.4g | Sugar: 4g | Protein: 7.3g | Sodium: 205mg

BACON-WRAPPED STUFFED JALAPENOS
Prep Time: 10 mins. | Cook Time: 30 mins. | Serve: 12

- ✓ 24 medium jalapeno peppers, cut in half, seeded
- ✓ 1 lb. uncooked chorizo or bulk spicy pork sausage
- ✓ 2 cups shredded cheddar cheese
- ✓ 12 bacon strips, cut in half

1. Preheat your outdoor Griddle by turning all its burner's knob to medium-heat setting.
2. Grease the griddle top with cooking spray.
3. Place sausage on the hot griddle top.
4. Crumble and cook for almost 10 minutes until brown.
5. Mix the sausage with cheese in a bowl.
6. Divide the cheese mixture in the peppers and wrap each with a bacon pieces.
7. Place the wrapped peppers on the griddle.
8. Cook for 20 minutes while flipping after every 5 minutes.
9. Serve warm.

Per Serving:
Calories: 124 | Fat: 3.8g | Carbohydrates: 12.1g | Fiber: 2.3g | Sugar: 1.8g | Protein: 10.5g | Sodium: 149mg

AVOCADO FRIES
Prep Time: 10 mins. | Cook Time: 10 mins. | Serve: 4

- ✓ 1 tsp. grated lemon zest
- ✓ 1 tbsp. lemon juice
- ✓ 1/8 tsp. salt
- ✓ 1/8 tsp. pepper
- ✓ 4 avocado, cut into sticks
- ✓ 1 egg, beaten
- ✓ 1 cup breadcrumbs

1. Season the avocado sticks with lemon zest, black pepper, salt and lemon juice.
2. Dip each into beaten egg and then coat with the breadcrumbs.
3. Preheat your outdoor Griddle by turning all its burner's knob to medium-heat setting.
4. Grease the griddle top with cooking spray.
5. Place avocado fries on the hot griddle top.
6. Cook for 5 minutes per side until crispy and golden brown.
7. Serve warm.

Per Serving:
Calories: 117 | Fat: 6g | Carbohydrates: 11.1g | Fiber: 1.4g | Sugar: 0.2g | Protein: 6.1g | Sodium:209mg

BRUSCHETTA
Prep Time: 10 mins. | Cook Time: 6 mins. | Serve: 4

- ✓ ½ cup balsamic vinegar
- ✓ 1-½ cups chopped and seeded plum tomatoes
- ✓ 2 tbsp. chopped shallot
- ✓ 1 tbsp. minced fresh basil
- ✓ 2 tsp. plus 3 tbsp. olive oil, divided
- ✓ 1 garlic clove, minced
- ✓ 16 slices French bread baguette (½ inch thick)
- ✓ Sea salt and Parmesan, grated cheese

1. Preheat your outdoor Griddle by turning all its burner's knob to medium-heat setting.
2. Grease the griddle top with cooking spray.
3. Brush the baguette slices with oil.
4. Place the slices on the hot griddle top.
5. Cook for 3 minutes per side.
6. Mix rest of the ingredients in bowl.
7. Divide the mixture on top of the baguette slices.
8. Serve.

Per Serving:
Calories: 135 | Fat: 6.3g | Carbohydrates: 14g | Fiber: 3g | Sugar: 3.1g | Protein: 5.5g | Sodium: 165mg

AVOCADO CUPS
Prep Time: 10 mins. | Cook Time: 5 mins. | Serve: 3

- ✓ 1 medium red onion, cut into ½-inch slices
- ✓ 2 plum tomatoes, halved and seeded
- ✓ 1 jalapeno pepper, halved and seeded
- ✓ 2 tbsp. canola oil, divided
- ✓ 3 medium ripe avocados, halved and pitted
- ✓ ¼ cup fresh cilantro leaves, chopped
- ✓ 2 tbsp. lime juice
- ✓ 2 tsp. ground cumin
- ✓ 3/4 tsp. salt

1. Preheat your outdoor Griddle by turning all its

burner's knob to medium-heat setting.
2. Grease the griddle top with cooking spray.
3. Place avocado on the hot griddle top with the cut sides downwards.
4. Cook for 5 minutes and scoop out some flesh from the center
5. Mix rest of the ingredients with scooped avocado and divide into the avocado cups.
6. Serve.

Per Serving:
Calories: 136 | Fat: 7.1g | Carbohydrates: 12.1g | Fiber: 6.1g | Sugar: 3.2g | Protein: 7.4g | Sodium: 205mg

FIG & PORK TENDERLOIN
Prep Time: 10 mins. | Cook Time: 20 mins. |Serve: 4

- ✓ 1-½ lbs. pork tenderloin, cubed
- ✓ 1 tbsp. smoked paprika
- ✓ 1 tsp. salt
- ✓ 1 tsp. pepper
- ✓ 1 tsp. onion powder
- ✓ ½ tsp. garlic powder
- ✓ ½ tsp. white pepper
- ✓ ¼ tsp. cayenne pepper
- ✓ ¼ cup balsamic vinegar
- ✓ 3 tbsp. honey
- ✓ 1 tbsp. Dijon mustard
- ✓ 2 tsp. olive oil
- ✓ Skewers
- ✓ 12 dried figs, halved
- ✓ 12 cherry tomatoes
- ✓ ½ cup crumbled blue cheese
- ✓ 4 fresh basil leaves, sliced

1. Mix pork cubes with all the spices, honey, vinegar, mustard and oil in a bowl.
2. Thread the pork, tomatoes, and figs on the skewers alternately.
3. Preheat your outdoor Griddle by turning all its burner's knob to medium-heat setting.
4. Grease the griddle top with cooking spray.
5. Place skewers on the hot griddle top.
6. Cook for 10 minutes per side.
7. Serve warm.

Per Serving:
Calories: 187 | Fat: 9.5g | Carbohydrates: 3.4g |Fiber: 1.4g | Sugar: 0.9g | Protein: 4.5g | Sodium:265mg

ZUCCHINI FRIES
Prep Time: 10 mins. | Cook Time: 10 mins. |Serve: 4

- ✓ 1 tsp. grated lemon zest
- ✓ 1 tbsp. lemon juice
- ✓ 1/8 tsp. salt
- ✓ 1/8 tsp. pepper
- ✓ 4 medium zucchini, cut into sticks
- ✓ 1 egg, beaten
- ✓ 1 cup breadcrumbs

1. Season the zucchini sticks with lemon zest, black pepper, salt and lemon juice.
2. Dip each into beaten egg and then coat with the breadcrumbs.
3. Preheat your outdoor Griddle by turning all its burner's knob to medium-heat setting.
4. Grease the griddle top with cooking spray.
5. Place zucchini fries on the hot griddle top.
6. Cook for 5 minutes per side until crispy and golden brown.
7. Serve warm.

Per Serving:
Calories: 67 | Fat: 2.5g | Carbohydrates: 9g | Fiber: 5.3g | Sugar: 1g | Protein: 2.1g | Sodium: 55mg

NECTARINE CHEESE CROSTINI
Prep Time: 5 mins. | Cook Time: 16 mins. |Serve: 4

- ✓ ½ cup balsamic vinegar
- ✓ 1 tbsp. olive oil
- ✓ 12 slices French bread baguette (¼ inch thick)
- ✓ 2 medium nectarines, halved
- ✓ ¼ cup fresh goat cheese, softened
- ✓ ¼ cup loosely packed basil leaves, sliced

1. Preheat your outdoor Griddle by turning all its burner's knob to medium-heat setting.
2. Grease the griddle top with cooking spray.
3. Brush the baguette slices with oil.
4. Place the slices on the hot griddle top.
5. Cook for 5 minutes per side.
6. Sear the nectarines on the griddle for 2-3 minutes.
7. Divide the nectarine slices on top of the baguette.
8. Add rest of the ingredients on top.
9. Serve.

Per Serving:

Calories: 200 | Fat: 11.5g | Carbohydrates: 4g | Fiber: 1g | Sugar: 1.9g | Protein: 14.3g | Sodium: 155mg

SHRIMP SWEET POTATO KABOBS
Prep Time: 5 mins. | Cook Time: 10 mins. | Serve: 4

- ✓ 2 medium sweet potatoes (1-¼ lbs.)
- ✓ 2 tbsp. plus ¼ cup olive oil, divided
- ✓ 1-½ tsp. minced fresh rosemary
- ✓ 1 tsp. chili powder, divided
- ✓ 3 tbsp. lemon juice
- ✓ 12 uncooked jumbo shrimp (3/4 lb.), peeled and deveined
- ✓ ¼ tsp. salt
- ✓ ¼ tsp. pepper

1. Peel and dice the sweet potatoes into cubes.
2. Cook the sweet potatoes in boiling water until soft then drain.
3. Mix shrimp with sweet potato cubes and rest of the ingredients in a bowl.
4. Thread sweet potatoes and shrimp on the skewers alternately.
5. Preheat your outdoor Griddle by turning all its burner's knob to medium-heat setting.
6. Grease the griddle top with cooking spray.
7. Place the skewers on the hot griddle top.
8. Cook for 10 minutes while flipping every 5 minutes.
9. Serve warm.

Per Serving:
Calories: 120 | Fat: 6.5g | Carbohydrates: 15g | Fiber: 0g | Sugar: 0.5g | Protein: 14.3g | Sodium: 164mg

ZUCCHINI WITH PEANUT CHICKEN
Prep Time: 5 mins. | Cook Time: 10 mins. | Serve: 2

- ✓ 2 medium zucchini, cut diagonally into ½-in. slices
- ✓ 1/8 tsp. salt
- ✓ 1/8 tsp. pepper
- ✓ topping:
- ✓ ¼ cup water
- ✓ 3 tbsp. brown sugar
- ✓ 2 tbsp. reduced-sodium soy sauce
- ✓ 1 tbsp. creamy peanut butter
- ✓ 1 tsp. lime juice
- ✓ ¼ tsp. ground ginger
- ✓ ¼ tsp. cayenne pepper
- ✓ 1 cup shredded cooked chicken
- ✓ 2 tbsp. chopped red onion
- ✓ Julienned carrot and chopped fresh cilantro

1. Season the zucchini with black pepper and salt.
2. Preheat your outdoor Griddle by turning all its burner's knob to medium-heat setting.
3. Grease the griddle top with cooking spray.
4. Place zucchini slices on the hot griddle top.
5. Sear them for 5 minutes per side.
6. Meanwhile, mix the topping ingredients in a bowl.
7. Divide the topping mixture over the zucchini slices.
8. Serve.

Per Serving:
Calories: 160 | Fat: 10.5g | Carbohydrates: 25g | Fiber: 1.5g | Sugar: 2g | Protein: 9.5g | Sodium: 149mg

MARYLAND CORN POPS
Prep Time: 10 mins. | Cook Time: 20 mins. | Serve: 8

- ✓ 8 medium ears sweet corn, cut into quarters
- ✓ 2 tbsp. canola oil
- ✓ 1-½ cups mayonnaise
- ✓ 1-½ tsp. garlic powder
- ✓ ¼ tsp. pepper
- ✓ 2 cups crumbled feta cheese
- ✓ 2 tbsp. seafood seasoning
- ✓ ¼ cup minced fresh cilantro
- ✓ Lime wedges, optional

1. Preheat your outdoor Griddle by turning all its burner's knob to medium-heat setting.
2. Grease the griddle top with cooking spray.
3. Place corn cobs on the hot griddle top.
4. Cook for 20 minutes while flipping every 5 minutes.
5. Mix mayonnaise, cilantro, garlic powder, black pepper, and seafood seasoning in a bowl.
6. Dip the corn on cobs into the mayo mixture then coat with the feta cheese
7. Serve warm.

Per Serving:
Calories: 264 | Fat: 0.3g | Carbohydrates: 14g | Fiber: 2.5g | Sugar: 2.9g | Protein: 1.3g | Sodium: 39mg

BALSAMIC-GOAT CHEESE GRILLED PLUMS
Prep Time: 5 mins. | Cook Time: 5 mins. | Serve: 4

- ✓ 1 cup balsamic vinegar

- ✓ 2 tsp. grated lemon zest
- ✓ 4 medium firm plums, halved and pitted
- ✓ ½ cup crumbled goat cheese

1. Preheat your outdoor Griddle by turning all its burner's knob to medium-heat setting.
2. Grease the griddle top with cooking spray.
3. Place plums on the hot griddle top and cook for 5 minutes.
4. Mix goat cheese with lemon zest and vinegar.
5. Divide this mixture into the plum.
6. Serve.

Per Serving:
Calories: 230 | Fat: 12.5g | Carbohydrates: 25g | Fiber: 0.1g | Sugar: 0.4g | Protein: 21.4g | Sodium: 260mg

LOADED POTATO ROUNDS

Prep Time: 10 mins. | Cook Time: 14 mins. | Serves: 4

- ✓ 4 large potatoes, baked and cooled
- ✓ ¼ cup butter, melted
- ✓ ¼ tsp. salt
- ✓ ¼ tsp. pepper
- ✓ 1 cup sour cream
- ✓ 1-½ cups shredded cheddar cheese
- ✓ 8 bacon strips, cooked and crumbled
- ✓ 3 tbsp. minced chives

1. Preheat your outdoor Griddle by turning all its burner's knob to medium-heat setting.
2. Grease the griddle top with cooking spray.
3. Place potatoes round on the hot griddle top.
4. Cook them for 7 minutes per side.
5. Mix cheese and rest of the ingredients in a bowl.
6. Divide this mixture over the potato rounds.
7. Serve.

Per Serving:
Calories: 124 | Fat: 7.5g | Carbohydrates: 13g | Fiber: 2.4g | Sugar: 1.4g | Protein: 4.1g | Sodium: 93mg

BACON AVOCADO

Prep Time: 15 mins. | Cook Time: 15 mins. | Serves: 4

- ✓ 4 avocado, cut into wedges
- ✓ 12 bacon strips, halved

1. Wrap the avocado wedges with bacon pieces.
2. Preheat your outdoor Griddle by turning all its burner's knob to medium-heat setting.
3. Grease the griddle top with cooking spray.
4. Place the wrapped avocado on the hot griddle top.
5. Cook for 15 minutes while flipping every 5 minutes.
6. Serve warm.

Per Serving:
Calories: 76 | Fat: 3.8g | Carbohydrates: 14g | Fiber: 2.8g | Sugar: 0.4g | Protein: 2.8g | Sodium: 169mg

MUSHROOM BACON BITES

Prep Time: 10 mins. | Cook Time: 17 mins. | Serves: 12

- ✓ 24 medium fresh mushrooms
- ✓ 12 bacon strips, halved
- ✓ 1 cup barbecue sauce

1. Wrap the mushrooms with bacon slices.
2. Brush the bites with barbecue sauce.
3. Preheat your outdoor Griddle by turning all its burner's knob to medium-heat setting.
4. Grease the griddle top with cooking spray.
5. Place mushroom bites on the hot griddle top.
6. Cook for 15 minutes while flipping every 5 minutes.
7. Serve warm.

Per Serving:
Calories: 105 | Fat: 8.5g | Carbohydrates: 28g | Fiber: 0.8g | Sugar: 0.4g | Protein: 2.4g | Sodium: 121mg

GRILLED POTATO SKINS

Prep Time: 10 mins. | Cook Time: 15 mins. | Serves: 2

- ✓ 2 large baking potatoes
- ✓ 2 tbsp. butter, melted
- ✓ 2 tsp. minced fresh rosemary
- ✓ ½ tsp. salt
- ✓ ½ tsp. pepper
- ✓ 1 cup shredded cheddar cheese
- ✓ 3 bacon strips, cooked and crumbled
- ✓ 2 green onions, chopped
- ✓ Sour cream

1. Place the potatoes in a pot filled with boiling water.
2. Cook just until the potatoes are tender.
3. Allow the potatoes to cool and scoop the flesh out from the center.

4. Mix the flesh with bacon and rest of the ingredients in a bowl.
5. Divide the mixture into the potato skins.
6. Preheat your outdoor Griddle by turning all its burner's knob to medium-heat setting.
7. Grease the griddle top with cooking spray.
8. Place the potato skins on the hot griddle top.
9. Cover the potatoes with a lid and cook for 10 minutes
10. Serve warm.

Per Serving:
Calories: 174 | Fat: 13g | Carbohydrates: 13g | Fiber: 4.3g | Sugar: 1.1g | Protein: 9.3g | Sodium: 210mg

POULTRY RECIPES

MINNEOLA TANGELO CHICKEN SKEWERS
Prep Time: 10 mins. | Cook Time: 10 mins. | Serve: 2

- 1 lb. boneless chicken breasts, diced
- 1 red bell pepper, diced
- 1 Sunkist Minneola tangelo, cut into wedges
- ½ large red onion, diced
- 1 ½ cup Sunkist Minneola tangelo juice
- 5 tbsp. cider vinegar
- 3 tbsp. honey
- 3 tbsp. Dijon mustard
- 3 tbsp. Worcestershire sauce
- 3 garlic cloves, peeled and smashed
- Kosher salt, to taste
- black pepper, to taste

1. Season chicken with vinegar, honey, Worcestershire sauce, garlic, black pepper, salt and tangelo juice in a bowl.
2. Thread the chicken, tangelo, onion and red bell pepper on the skewers alternately.
3. Preheat your outdoor Griddle by turning all its burner's knob to medium-heat setting.
4. Grease the griddle top with cooking spray.
5. Place the skewers on the hot griddle top.
6. Cook for almost 5 minutes per side.
7. Serve warm.

Per Serving:
Calories: 184 | Fat: 5.4g | Carbohydrates: 24g | Fiber: 0.4g | Sugar: 1.1g | Protein: 26.1g | Sodium: 245mg

GREEK CHICKEN KEBABS
Prep Time: 10 mins. | Cook Time: 12 mins. | Serve: 2

- 1 cup olive oil
- 3 tbsp. red wine vinegar
- 1 tbsp. dried oregano
- kosher salt, to taste
- black pepper, to taste
- 1 lb. boneless chicken breasts, diced
- 2 large zucchini, sliced
- 1 cup chopped red onion
- 4 pita bread
- ½ cup crumbled feta
- ¼ cup torn fresh dill

1. Mix chicken with vinegar, oregano, black pepper, salt, zucchini dill and red onion in a bowl.
2. Thread the chicken, onion and zucchini on the skewers alternately.
3. Preheat your outdoor Griddle by turning all its burner's knob to medium-heat setting.
4. Grease the griddle top with cooking spray.
5. Place the skewers on the hot griddle top.
6. Cook for almost 6 minutes per side.
7. Serve warm.

Per Serving:
Calories: 146 | Fat: 3g | Carbohydrates: 28g | Fiber: 0.8g | Sugar: 1.6g | Protein: 26.3g | Sodium: 280mg

BBQ CHICKEN
Prep Time: 10 mins. | Cook Time: 40 mins. | Serves: 6

- 3 lbs. whole chicken, cut into pieces
- Salt, to taste
- 1-tsp. Olive oil
- ½ cup barbecue sauce

1. Preheat your outdoor Griddle by turning all its burner's knob to medium-heat setting.
2. Grease the griddle top with cooking spray.
3. Season the chicken well with salt and olive oil.
4. On the hot griddle top, sear the chicken skin side down for 5-minutes per side.
5. Reduce the heat to medium-low, cover with foil, and cook for 30 minutes.
6. Flip the chicken and baste it with the barbecue sauce.
7. Baste with extra barbecue sauce then serve warm.

Per Serving:

Calories: 162 | Fat: 13g | Carbohydrates: 5g | Fiber: 2.5g | Sugar: 1.1g | Protein: 8.8g | Sodium: 169mg

CHICKEN, BACON, RANCH SKEWERS
Prep Time: 10 mins. | Cook Time: 10 mins. | Serve: 1

- 1 cup ranch dressing
- Juice of ½ lemon
- Pinch of cayenne pepper
- kosher salt, to taste
- black pepper, to taste
- 1 lb. chicken breasts, cut into 1" chunks
- 16 slices bacon, cut in half
- 1 cup cherry tomatoes
- Chopped chives, to garnish

1. Season chicken cubes with black pepper, salt, cayenne pepper, lemon juice and ranch dressing in a bowl.
2. Wrap the chicken cubes with bacon pieces.
3. Thread the wrapped chicken and tomatoes on the skewers alternately.
4. Preheat your outdoor Griddle by turning all its burner's knob to medium-heat setting.
5. Grease the griddle top with cooking spray.
6. Place the skewers on the hot griddle top.
7. Cook for almost 5 minutes per side.
8. Garnish with chives.
9. Serve warm.

Per Serving:
Calories: 215 | Fat: 9.8g | Carbohydrates: 25g | Fiber: 0.8g | Sugar: 1.3g | Protein: 26.3g | Sodium:305mg

ITALIAN CHICKEN VEGGIE SKEWERS
Prep Time: 10 mins. | Cook Time: 10 mins. | Serve: 4

- 1 tbsp. olive oil
- ½ tsp. garlic powder
- 1 tsp. Italian seasoning
- Kosher salt, to taste
- black pepper, to taste
- ½ yellow bell pepper
- ½ red bell pepper, diced
- ½ green bell pepper, diced
- 2 boneless chicken breasts, diced
- Bamboo skewers

1. Season the chicken and veggies with Italian seasoning and rest of the ingredients.
2. Preheat your outdoor Griddle by turning all its burner's knob to medium-heat setting.
3. Grease the griddle top with cooking spray.
4. Thread the chicken and rest of the veggies on the skewers alternately.
5. Place the skewers on the hot griddle top.
6. Cook for almost 5 minutes per side.
7. Serve warm.

Per Serving:
Calories: 285 | Fat: 15.5g | Carbohydrates: 15g | Fiber: 4.1g | Sugar: 0.5g | Protein: 27.1g | Sodium:237mg

SEARED CHICKEN BREAST
Prep Time: 10 mins. | Cook Time: 16 mins. | Serves: 4

- 2-lb. Boneless chicken breasts
- ¾ cup balsamic vinegar
- 1-tbsp. olive oil
- ½-tbsp. honey
- 1-tsp. oregano
- 1-tsp. basil
- 1-tsp. garlic powder
- To garnish:
- Sea salt
- ½-tsp. Black pepper, fresh ground
- 1 cup Slices fresh mozzarella cheese
- 4 slices avocado
- 4 slices beefsteak tomato
- Balsamic glaze, for drizzling

1. In a suitable mixing bowl, whisk honey, balsamic vinegar, oregano, olive oil, basil, and garlic powder.
2. Toss in the chicken and cover, and marinate in the refrigerator for almost 30 minutes.
3. Preheat your outdoor Griddle by turning all its burner's knob to medium-heat setting.
4. Grease the griddle top with cooking spray.
5. Sear the chicken for 7 minutes per side on the hot griddle top.
6. Top each chicken breast with avocado, mozzarella, and tomato, then cover with foil and cook for 2 minutes.

7. Drizzle with balsamic glaze and drizzle sea salt and black pepper.
8. Serve warm.

Per Serving:

Calories: 162 | Fat: 13g | Carbohydrates: 5g | Fiber: 2.5g | Sugar: 1.1g | Protein: 8.8g | Sodium: 169mg

SWEET SOY CHILI LIME CHICKEN
Prep Time: 15 mins. | Cook Time: 14 mins. |Serves: 8

- ½ cup sweet chili sauce
- ¼ cup soy sauce
- 1-tsp. mirin
- ½-tsp. orange juice
- 1-tsp. orange marmalade
- 1-tbsp. lime juice
- 1 tbsp. brown sugar
- 1 garlic clove, minced
- 4-lb. Boneless chicken breasts
- Sesame seeds, to garnish

1. In a suitable mixing bowl, combine soy sauce, brown sugar, sweet chili sauce, orange marmalade, mirin, lime and orange juice, and minced garlic.
2. Reserve ¼ cup of this orange sauce.
3. Add the chicken to the remaining sauce, mix well to coat and set aside for 30 minutes to marinate.
4. Preheat your outdoor Griddle by turning all its burner's knob to medium-heat setting.
5. Grease the griddle top with cooking spray.
6. Place the chicken on the hot griddle top and cook for 7 minutes per side.
7. Garnish with sesame seeds and serve.

Per Serving:
Calories: 156 | Fat: 8.5g | Carbohydrates: 25g | Fiber: 0.8g | Sugar: 2g | Protein: 15.8g | Sodium: 138mg

SEARED SPICY CITRUS CHICKEN THIGH
Prep Time: 10 mins. | Cook Time: 16 mins. |Serves: 4

- 2-lb. boneless chicken thighs
- For the marinade:
- ¼ cup fresh lime juice
- 2-tsp. lime zest
- ¼ cup honey
- 2 tbsp. olive oil
- ½-tbsp. balsamic vinegar
- ½-tsp. sea salt
- ½-tsp. black pepper
- ½ Garlic cloves, minced
- ¼-tsp. onion powder

1. In a suitable mixing bowl, whisk all marinade ingredients; keep 2 tbsp. of the marinade for basting.
2. Mix the chicken with marinade in a sealable plastic bag, shake and refrigerate overnight.
3. Preheat your outdoor Griddle by turning all its burner's knob to medium-heat setting.
4. Grease the griddle top with cooking oil.
5. Cook the marinated chicken for 8 minutes per side while basting on the hot griddle top.
6. Serve and enjoy

Per Serving:

Calories: 145 | Fat: 6.5g | Carbohydrates: 11g | Fiber: 0.3g | Sugar: 0.7g | Protein: 19.3g | Sodium:160mg

HONEY PAPRIKA CHICKEN THIGHS
Prep Time: 15 mins. | Cook Time: 14 mins. |Serves: 4

- 2-lb. boneless chicken thighs
- 1-tsp. olive oil
- ½-tsp. sea salt
- ¼-tsp. black pepper
- ½-tsp. paprika
- ¾-tsp. onion powder
- For the Marinade:
- 1-tbsp. honey
- 1-tbsp. balsamic vinegar
- 2-tbsp. tomato paste
- ½-tsp. garlic, minced

1. In a sealable plastic bag, mix the chicken, salt, olive oil, paprika, black pepper, and onion powder.
2. Seal and set aside the chicken to coat it in spices and oil.
3. Mix the tomato paste, balsamic vinegar, garlic, and honey in a suitable mixing bowl.
4. Split the marinade in two. Combine one half with the chicken in the bag and keep the other half in the refrigerator in a covered container.
5. Close the bag and shake the chicken in it to coat it. Refrigerate for 30 to 4 hours.
6. Preheat your outdoor Griddle by turning all its burner's knob to medium-heat setting.
7. Grease the griddle top with cooking spray.

8. Cook the marinated chicken for 7 minutes per side on the hot griddle top, or until juices flow clear and a meat thermometer reads 165°F.
9. Brush the remaining marinade on top of the chicken thighs during the last minute of cooking.
10. Serve right away

Per Serving:

Calories: 152 | Fat: 8.1g | Carbohydrates: 3.3g | Fiber: 1g | Sugar: 1.4g | Protein: 16.3g | Sodium: 127mg

GARLIC CHICKEN WITH SALSA VERDE
Prep Time: 10 mins. | Cook Time: 14 mins. |Serves: 6

- 3-lb. Boneless chicken breasts
- 1-tbsp. olive oil
- 1-tsp. sea salt
- 1-tsp. chili powder
- 1-tsp. ground cumin
- 1-tsp. garlic powder
- For the salsa Verde marinade:
- ½-tsp. garlic, minced
- 1 small onion, chopped
- 6 Tomatillos, husked, rinsed and chopped
- 1 medium jalapeño pepper, cut in half, seeded
- ¼ cup fresh cilantro, chopped
- ½-tsp. sugar or sugar substitute

1. In a food processor, mix well all of the ingredients for the salsa Verde marinade and pulse until smooth.
2. In a suitable mixing bowl, mix well the sea salt, chili powder, cumin, and garlic powder. Place chicken breasts in a glass baking dish and season with olive oil and seasoning mix.
3. Cover each chicken breast with a tbsp. of salsa Verde marinade, reserving the rest for serving.
4. Refrigerate for 4 hours after covering the dish with plastic wrap.
5. Preheat your outdoor Griddle by turning all its burner's knob to medium-heat setting.
6. Grease the griddle top with cooking spray.
7. Cook 7 minutes per side on the hot griddle top
8. Serve with more salsa Verde on the side and enjoy.

Per Serving:

Calories: 145 | Fat: 7.8g | Carbohydrates: 13g | Fiber: 0.3g | Sugar: 0.6g | Protein: 16.5g | Sodium:265mg

STUFFED CHICKEN BREAST
Prep Time: 10 mins. | Cook Time: 20 mins. |Serves: 4

- 2-½-lb. Boneless chicken breasts
- 2-tbsp. olive oil
- 2-tbsp. taco seasoning
- ½ red, yellow, and green pepper, very sliced
- ½ Small red onion, very sliced
- ½ cup shredded Mexican cheese
- Guacamole, for serving
- Sour cream, for serving
- Salsa, for serving

1. Make small horizontal incisions across the chicken breasts.
2. Coat the chicken in olive oil and taco seasoning evenly.
3. Preheat your outdoor Griddle by turning all its burner's knob to medium-heat setting.
4. Grease the griddle top with cooking spray.
5. Fill each cut with a mixture of bell peppers and red onions, then set the breasts on the hot griddle top.
6. Allow 15 minutes for the chicken to cook.
7. Top the chicken with cheese, cover with foil and cook for 5 minutes.
8. Remove from the griddle and serve with sour cream, guacamole, and salsa on the side.
9. Serve with.

Per Serving:
Calories: 132 | Fat: 8.4g | Carbohydrates: 18g | Fiber: 0.3g | Sugar: 0.6g | Protein: 12.4g | Sodium:220mg

PEPPER CHICKEN STUFFED WITH CHEESE
Prep Time: 15 mins. | Cook Time: 16 mins. |Serves: 4

- ¾-lb. Boneless chicken breasts
- 8 mini sweet peppers, sliced thin and seeded
- 2 slices pepper jack cheese, cut in half
- 2 slices Colby jack cheese, cut in half
- 1-tbsp. Creole seasoning, like Emeril's
- 1-tsp. black pepper
- 1-tsp. garlic powder
- 1-tsp. onion powder
- 1-tsp. olive oil, separated
- Toothpicks

1. In a suitable mixing bowl, combine garlic powder, pepper, creole seasoning, and onion powder.
2. Cut a slit down the side of each chicken breast,

taking care not to cut all the way through.
3. Drizzle 1 tsp. olive oil over each breast.
4. Evenly coat each chicken breast with the spice mix.
5. Stuff each chicken piece with 1 half pepper jack cheese slice, 1 half Colby cheese slice, and a handful of pepper pieces into each chicken breast.
6. Use 4 or 5 toothpicks to close the chicken.
7. Preheat your outdoor Griddle by turning all its burner's knob to medium-heat setting.
8. Grease the griddle top with cooking spray.
9. Cook the chicken rolls for 8 minutes per side.
10. Serve.

Per Serving:
Calories: 146 | Fat: 11.5g | Carbohydrates: 25g | Fiber: 3g | Sugar: 0.7g | Protein: 4.1g | Sodium: 154mg

GARLIC BEER CHICKEN THIGHS
Prep Time: 10 mins. | Cook Time: 14 mins. | Serves: 2

- 1-lb. boneless chicken thighs
- (12 oz.) can root beer
- 1 teaspoon Olive oil
- For the rub:
- ½-tbsp. garlic powder
- ¾-tbsp. sea salt
- ½-tbsp. white pepper
- 1-tsp. smoked paprika
- ½-tsp. garlic powder
- 1-tsp. dried thyme
- ⅛-tsp. cayenne pepper

1. In a suitable mixing bowl, mix well all of the rub ingredients; set aside half in an airtight container until ready to use.
2. Drizzle olive oil over chicken thighs and coat each with the spice rub.
3. Arrange the chicken in a baking dish that measures 13 by 9 inches.
4. Cover with two root beer cans.
5. Preheat your outdoor Griddle by turning all its burner's knob to medium-heat setting.
6. Grease the griddle top with cooking oil.
7. In a small dish, gently fold the remaining rub and half of the third can of root beer.
8. Cook the chicken for 7 minutes per side, basting with the root beer rub mixture.
9. Serve.

Per Serving:
Calories: 94 | Fat: 3.5g | Carbohydrates: 11g | Fiber: 0.8g | Sugar: 1g | Protein: 4.1g | Sodium: 124mg

CHIPOTLE ADOBE CHICKEN WITH OREGANO
Prep Time: 10 mins. | Cook Time: 14 mins. | Serves: 4

- 2-lb. chicken thighs or breasts (boneless,)
- For the marinade:
- ¼ cup olive oil
- 2 chipotle peppers in adobo sauce, plus 1-tsp. adobo sauce from the can
- 1-tbsp. garlic, minced
- 1 shallot, chopped
- 1 ½ tbsp. cumin
- 1-tbsp. cilantro, super-chopped or dried
- 2-tsp. chili powder
- 1-tsp. dried oregano
- ½-tsp. salt
- 2 Fresh limes, garnish
- 1 Cilantro, garnish

1. Pulse the marinade ingredients into a paste in a food processor or blender.
2. Place the chicken in a sealable plastic bag with the marinade and massage well to coat.
3. Refrigerate for 24 hours prior to cooking.
4. Preheat your outdoor Griddle by turning all its burner's knob to medium-heat setting.
5. Grease the griddle top with cooking spray.
6. Cook for 7 minutes on one side, then flip and cook for another 7 minutes.
7. Reduce the heat to low and simmer until the chicken reaches an internal temperature of 165°F.
8. To serve, top with fresh lime juice and cilantro.

Per Serving:
Calories: 35 | Fat: 2.3g | Carbohydrates: 18g | Fiber: 0.3g | Sugar: 0.5g | Protein: 2.5g | Sodium: 27mg

GARLIC CHICKEN TACOS
Prep Time: 10 mins. | Cook Time: 10 mins. | Serves: 2

- ½-lb. Boneless chicken breasts, sliced thin
- Chicken marinade:
- 1 serrano pepper, minced
- 1-tsp. garlic, minced
- 1 lime, juiced
- 1-tsp. ground cumin
- ⅓ cup olive oil
- Sea salt, to taste
- Black pepper, to taste

- Avocado crema:
- 1 cup sour cream
- 2-tsp. lime juice
- 1-tsp. lime zest
- 1 serrano pepper, diced and seeded
- 1 garlic clove, minced
- 1 large Hass avocado
- Garnish:
- ½ cup queso fresco, crumbled
- 2-tsp. cilantro, chopped
- 1 lime sliced into wedges
- 10 corn tortillas

1. In a sealable plastic bag, mix well all of the chicken marinade ingredients.
2. Toss in the chicken and toss well to coat.
3. Refrigerate for 1 hour to marinate.
4. In a food processor, blend all of the avocado crema ingredients and pulse until smooth.
5. Preheat your outdoor Griddle by turning all its burner's knob to medium-heat setting.
6. Grease the griddle top with cooking spray.
7. Cook the chicken on the hot griddle top for 5 minutes per side
8. Top chicken with a dollop of queso fresco, cilantro, avocado crema, and lime wedges.
9. Serve warm on tortillas.

Per Serving:
Calories: 185 | Fat: 14.4g | Carbohydrates: 18g | Fiber: 5.8g | Sugar: 1g | Protein: 6.5g | Sodium: 82mg

TURKEY TACOS

Prep Time: 10 mins. | Cook Time: 10mins. | Serves: 2

- ½-lb. ground turkey
- marinade:
- 1 serrano pepper, minced
- 1-tsp. garlic, minced
- 1 lime, juiced
- 1-tsp. ground cumin
- ⅓ cup olive oil
- Sea salt, to taste
- Black pepper, to taste
- Avocado crema:
- 1 cup sour cream
- 2-tsp. lime juice
- 1-tsp. lime zest
- 1 serrano pepper, diced and seeded
- 1 garlic clove, minced
- 1 large Hass avocado
- Garnish:
- ½ cup queso fresco, crumbled
- 2-tsp. cilantro, chopped
- 1 lime sliced into wedges
- 10 corn tortillas

1. In a sealable plastic bag, mix well all of the marinade ingredients.
2. Toss in the turkey and toss well to coat.
3. In a food processor, blend all of the avocado crema ingredients and pulse until smooth.
4. Preheat your outdoor Griddle by turning all its burner's knob to medium-heat setting.
5. Grease the griddle top with cooking spray.
6. Cook the turkey mince on the hot griddle top for 10 minutes.
7. Top turkey with a dollop of queso fresco, cilantro, avocado crema, and lime wedges.
8. Serve warm on tortillas.

Per Serving:
Calories: 154 | Fat: 1.5g | Carbohydrates: 19.1g | Fiber: 4.5g | Sugar: 0g | Protein: 4.5g | Sodium: 159mg

CHICKEN FAJITAS WITH TORTILLAS

Prep Time: 10 mins. | Cook Time: 20 mins | Serves: 4

- 2-lb. Boneless chicken breast halves, sliced
- ¼ cup Yellow onion, sliced
- 1 Large green bell pepper, sliced
- 1 large red bell pepper, sliced
- 1-tsp. ground cumin
- 1-tsp. garlic powder
- 1-tsp. onion powder
- 1-tbsp. lime juice
- 1-tbsp. olive oil
- ½-tsp. black pepper
- 1-tsp. salt
- 1-tbsp. vegetable oil
- 10 flour tortillas

1. Toss chicken with garlic, cumin, salt, lime juice, onion, pepper, and olive oil in a zip-lock bag then marinated for 39 minutes.
2. Preheat your outdoor Griddle by turning all its burner's knob to medium-heat setting.
3. Grease the griddle top with cooking spray.
4. Cook until the onion and bell pepper on the griddle top until softened.
5. Add the marinated chicken on the other side of the griddle until cook until browned.

6. Mix with the onion and pepper and cook until the internal temperature of the chicken reaches 165°F.
7. Serve on warm tortillas.

Per Serving:
Calories: 117 | Fat: 5.4g | Carbohydrates: 13.5g | Fiber: 2.3g | Sugar: 0g | Protein: 3.4g | Sodium: 50mg

HAWAIIAN CHICKEN KABOB
Prep Time: 15 mins. | Cook Time: 10 mins. | Serves: 2

- ½-lb. boneless chicken breast, diced
- 2 cups pineapple, diced
- 3 green peppers, diced
- 1 red onion, diced
- 2-tsp. olive oil, to coat veggies
- For the marinade:
- ⅓ cup tomato paste
- ⅓ cup brown sugar, packed
- ⅓ cup soy sauce
- ¼ cup pineapple juice
- 2-tbsp. olive oil
- 1 ½-tsp. mirin
- ½-tsp. garlic cloves, minced
- 1-tsp. ginger, minced
- ½-tsp. sesame oil
- 1 pinch sea salt
- 1 pinch black pepper
- 10 wooden skewers

1. In a suitable mixing bowl, whisk the marinade ingredients until smooth.
2. Half a cup of the marinade should be kept in the refrigerator.
3. Place the chicken in a sealable plastic bag with the remaining marinade, seal and refrigerate for 1 hour.
4. Toss the red onion, bell pepper, and pineapple in a suitable mixing bowl with 2 tbsp. olive oil.
5. Preheat your outdoor Griddle by turning all its burner's knob to medium-heat setting.
6. Grease the griddle top with cooking spray.
7. Thread the skewers with bell pepper, red onion, pineapple, and chicken alternately.
8. Place the skewers on the hot griddle top and cook for 5 minutes per side.
9. Brush the chicken with the marinade once cooked halfway through.
10. Serve

Per Serving:
Calories: 197| Fat: 15.4g | Carbohydrates: 3.4g |Fiber: 3g | Sugar: 3.3g | Protein: 4.1g | Sodium: 148mg

GARLIC CHICKEN SKEWERS
Prep Time: 10 mins. | Cook Time: 10 mins. |Serve: 6

- 10 boneless chicken thighs, diced
- 1 red onion, wedged
- 1 red pepper, stemmed, seeded, diced
- For the marinade:
- ⅓ cup toasted pine nuts
- 1 ½ cups roasted red peppers, sliced
- Hot cherry peppers, seeded, or to taste
- 1 cup packed fresh basil leaves
- 2 garlic cloves, peeled
- ¼ cup Parmesan, grated cheese
- 1-tbsp. paprika
- Olive oil, as needed

1. In a food processor, blend the toasted pine nuts, hot cherry peppers, roasted red peppers, garlic, basil, Parmesan, and paprika until smooth
2. Stir in the olive oil and mix until the pesto gets a thin consistency.
3. Spoon half of the pesto into a big sealable plastic bag and set rest aside for serving.
4. Place the chicken thigh chunks in the pesto bag, shut it, and rub the chicken to coat it.
5. Set aside for 1 hour in the refrigerator for marination.
6. Using metal skewers, thread the pesto chicken cubes, red onion, and red pepper, alternately.
7. Brush the chicken with the pesto that was set aside.
8. Preheat your outdoor Griddle by turning all its burner's knob to medium-heat setting.
9. Grease the griddle top with cooking spray.
10. Cook the pesto skewers for about 5 minutes per side.
11. Serve.

Per Serving:
Calories: 214 | Fat: 17.5g | Carbohydrates: 24g |Fiber: 1.4g | Sugar: 1.6g | Protein: 5.8g | Sodium: 165mg

HONEY SRIRACHA CHICKEN
Prep Time: 10 mins. | Cook Time: 17 mins. | Serve: 6

- 3-lb. boneless chicken thighs
- 3-tbsp. butter, unsalted
- 1-tbsp. fresh ginger, minced

- ✓ 3 Garlic cloves, minced
- ✓ ¼-tsp. smoked paprika
- ✓ ¼-tsp. chili powder
- ✓ ¼-tbsp. honey
- ✓ 1-tbsp. Sriracha
- ✓ 1-tbsp. lime juice

1. In a suitable saucepan over medium-low heat, melt butter; add ginger and garlic.
2. Stir and cook for about 2 minutes.
3. Mix the ground cloves, smoked paprika, honey, Sriracha, and lime juice in a suitable mixing bowl.
4. Stir to mix, then reduce to a low heat and cook for almost 5 minutes.
5. Season both the two sides of the chicken with salt and black pepper.
6. Brush the glaze on both the two sides of the chicken during the last 5 minutes of griddling.
7. Preheat your outdoor Griddle by turning all its burner's knob to medium-heat setting.
8. Grease the griddle top with cooking spray.
9. Cook the chicken for 5 minutes per side on the hot griddle.
10. Serve.

Per Serving:
Calories: 180 | Fat: 14.4g | Carbohydrates: 10g | Fiber: 7.4g | Sugar: 0.4g | Protein: 6,3g | Sodium: 88mg

BUFFALO GARLIC CHICKEN WINGS

Prep Time: 8 mins. | Cook Time: 24 mins. | Serves: 8

- ✓ 1-tbsp. sea salt
- ✓ 1-tsp. black pepper
- ✓ ½-tsp. garlic powder
- ✓ 4-lb. chicken wings
- ✓ 2-tbsp. butter
- ✓ ⅓ cup buffalo sauce, like Moore's
- ✓ 1-tbsp. apple cider vinegar
- ✓ 1-tbsp. honey

1. In a suitable mixing bowl, combine salt, garlic powder and pepper,.
2. Season the wings by tossing them in the spice mixture.
3. Preheat your outdoor Griddle by turning all its burner's knob to medium-heat setting.
4. Grease the griddle top with cooking spray.
5. Place the wings on the hot griddle top and cook for almost 20 minutes, flipping every 5 minutes.
6. In a suitable saucepan over low heat, melt the butter and stir in the vinegar, buffalo sauce, and honey.
7. Toss the wings in a suitable mixing bowl with the prepared sauce.
8. Return the wings to the griddle and cook for 1 to 2 minutes per side on high heat.
9. Serve warm with remaining sauce

Per Serving:
Calories: 200| Fat: 7.5g | Carbohydrates: 14g | Fiber: 3.8g | Sugar: 1.8g | Protein: 7.8g | Sodium:167mg

CHICKEN WINGS WITH PEACH GLAZE

Prep Time: 15 mins. | Cook Time: 28 mins. | Serve: 4

- ✓ 1 (12 oz.) Jar peach preserves
- ✓ 1 cup sweet red chili sauce
- ✓ 1-tsp. lime juice
- ✓ 1 tbsp. fresh cilantro, minced
- ✓ 1 (2-½-lb.) bag chicken wing sections
- ✓ Non-stick cooking spray

1. In a suitable mixing bowl, mix the preserves, lime juice, red chili sauce, and cilantro.
2. Divide this mixture in half and set aside one half for serving.
3. Preheat your outdoor Griddle by turning all its burner's knob to medium-heat setting.
4. Grease the griddle top with cooking spray.
5. Cook wings on the hot griddle top for 25 minutes, flipping every 5 minutes.
6. Toss them with ½ of the glaze and cook for 3 minutes more on high heat.
7. Serve with left over glaze.

Per Serving:

Calories: 232 | Fat: 17.5g | Carbohydrates: 10.4g | Fiber: 3.4g | Sugar: 4g | Protein: 0.8g | Sodium: 82mg

PEPPER YELLOW CURRY CHICKEN WINGS

Prep Time: 15 mins. | Cook Time: 20 mins. | Serve: 4

- ✓ 2-lb. chicken wings
- ✓ Marinade:
- ✓ ½ cup Greek yogurt, plain
- ✓ ½-tbsp. mild yellow curry powder
- ✓ 1-tbsp. olive oil
- ✓ ½-tsp. sea salt

- ½-tsp. black pepper
- 1-tsp. red chili flakes

1. In a suitable mixing bowl, mix marinade ingredients until blended.
2. Toss the wings in the bowl to coat them well.
3. Refrigerate for marination for 30 minutes after covering bowl with plastic wrap.
4. Preheat your outdoor Griddle by turning all its burner's knob to medium-heat setting.
5. Grease the griddle top with cooking spray.
6. Place the wings on the hot griddle top, flipping every 5 minutes, cook for 20 minutes.
7. Serve warm.

Per Serving:

Calories: 177 | Fat: 11.5g | Carbohydrates: 25g | Fiber: 3.4g | Sugar: 2g | Protein: 2.4g | Sodium: 211mg

KOREAN PEPPER CHICKEN WINGS
Prep Time: 10 mins. | Cook Time: 20 mins. | Serve: 4

- 2 lbs. chicken wings
- Marinade:
- ½-tbsp. olive oil
- 1-tsp. sea salt, plus more
- ½-tsp. black pepper
- ½ cup Korean hot pepper paste
- 1 scallion, sliced, to garnish

1. In a suitable mixing bowl, mix well all of the marinade ingredients until blended.
2. Toss the wings in the bowl to coat well.
3. Refrigerate for marination for 30 minutes after covering with plastic wrap.
4. Preheat your outdoor Griddle by turning all its burner's knob to medium-heat setting.
5. Grease the griddle top with cooking spray.
6. Place the wings on the hot griddle top, flipping every 5 minutes, cook for 20 minutes.
7. Serve warm.

Per Serving:
Calories: 142 | Fat: 12.3g | Carbohydrates: 23g | Fiber: 2.3g | Sugar: 1.1g | Protein: 3.4g | Sodium: 106mg

KALE CAESAR SALAD WITH GARLIC CHICKEN BREAST
Prep Time: 10 mins. | Cook Time: 14 mins. | Serve: 2

- 1-lb. Chicken breast
- 1-tsp. garlic powder
- ½-tsp. black pepper
- ½-tsp. sea salt
- 2 kale leaves, chopped
- Shaved parmesan, for serving
- For the dressing:
- 1-tbsp. mayonnaise
- ½-tbsp. Dijon mustard
- ½-tsp. garlic powder
- ½-tsp. Worcestershire sauce
- ¼ lemon, juice of (or ½ a small lime)
- ¼-tsp. anchovy paste
- Pinch sea salt
- Pinch black pepper

1. In a suitable mixing bowl, mix well black pepper, garlic powder, and sea salt.
2. Season and rub the chicken well with the spice mixture.
3. Preheat your outdoor Griddle by turning all its burner's knob to medium-heat setting.
4. Grease the griddle top with cooking oil.
5. Sear the chicken on the hot griddle top for 7 minutes per side.
6. Mix well all of the dressing ingredients in a suitable mixing bowl.
7. Place the kale on a plate and drizzle with the dressing, tossing to mix.
8. Arrange the chicken on top of the salad in a diagonal cut.
9. Serve with shaved parmesan on top.

Per Serving:
Calories: 220 | Fat: 9.8g | Carbohydrates: 28g | Fiber: 1.4g | Sugar: 4g | Protein: 25.4g | Sodium: 60mg

TERIYAKI CHICKEN WITH RICE BOWLS
Prep Time: 10 mins. | Cook Time: 16 mins. | Serve: 4

- 2 Bag brown rice
- For the skewers:
- 2-lb. Boneless skinless chicken breasts, cubed
- 1 red onion, quartered
- 1 red pepper, cut into cube slices
- 1 green pepper, cut into cube slices
- ½ pineapple, cut into cubes
- For the marinade:
- ¼ cup light soy sauce
- ¼ cup sesame oil

- 1-tbsp. ginger, fresh grated
- 1 garlic clove, crushed
- ½ lime, juiced

1. In a suitable mixing bowl, mix well the marinade ingredients.
2. Toss the chicken with the marinade in a resealable plastic bag, seal, and toss to coat well.
3. Preheat your outdoor Griddle by turning all its burner's knob to medium-heat setting.
4. Grease the griddle top with cooking spray.
5. Thread the chicken and cubed vegetables alternately onto 8 metal skewers.
6. Sear the prepared skewers on hot griddle top for 8 minutes per side.
7. Serve warm.

Per Serving:
Calories: 122 | Fat: 5.3g | Carbohydrates: 23g | Fiber: 1.4g | Sugar: 2g | Protein: 14.5g | Sodium: 65mg

CHICKEN FRIED RICE WITH VEGGIES

Prep Time: 10 mins. | Cook Time: 15 mins. | Serve: 4

- 2 boneless chicken breasts, diced
- 4 Cups long grain rice, cooked and allowed to air dry
- ⅓ cup soy sauce
- 1 Yellow onion, chopped
- 3 Garlic cloves, chopped
- ½ Cups petite peas
- 2 carrots sliced into thin rounds
- ½ cup corn kernels
- ¼ cup vegetable oil
- ½-tbsp. butter

1. Preheat your outdoor Griddle by turning all its burner's knob to medium-heat setting.
2. Grease the griddle top with cooking oil.
3. Add the carrot, onion, peas, and corn to the griddle top.
4. Cook for a few minutes, until the edges are browned.
5. Toss in the chicken and cook until it is browned.
6. Mix well the rice, soy sauce, garlic, and butter in a suitable mixing bowl.
7. Stir in rice and cook until vegetables have softened.
8. Serve.

Per Serving:

Calories: 115 | Fat: 5.1g | Carbohydrates: 25g | Fiber: 1.1g | Sugar: 1.2g | Protein: 14.3g | Sodium: 190mg

BUFFALO CHICKEN WITH BLUE CHEESE

Prep Time: 10 mins. | Cook Time: 28 mins. | Serve: 4

- 2 cups shredded cooked chicken
- 1 large sweet onion, sliced
- 8 slices seedless rye
- 8 slices Swiss cheese
- ¼ cup blue cheese dressing
- 1 cup mayonnaise
- 1 cup buffalo hot sauce
- 2-tbsp. Butter
- Blue cheese dressing

1. In a suitable skillet over medium heat, melt the butter.
2. Stir in onion and sauté for almost 20 minutes.
3. Toss the chicken with the buffalo sauce and mayonnaise in a suitable mixing bowl.
4. On a piece of bread, set a slice of cheese, onions, the chicken, and another slice of cheese, followed by another piece of bread.
5. Repeat with the rest of the sandwiches in the same manner.
6. Brush both the sides of the sandwich with butter.
7. Preheat your outdoor Griddle by turning all its burner's knob to medium-heat setting.
8. Grease the griddle top with cooking spray.
9. Cook the sandwiches on the hot griddle top for 4 minutes per side.
10. Serve with blue cheese dressing.

Per Serving:
Calories: 137 | Fat: 5g | Carbohydrates: 178g | Fiber: 2.3g | Sugar: 5.3g | Protein: 13.8g | Sodium: 188mg

ZUCCHINI BASIL CRUSTED CHICKEN

Prep Time: 10 mins. | Cook Time: 15 mins. | Serve: 2

- Salt and black pepper for taste
- 1 lb. boneless chicken meat, cut into bite-sized pieces
- 1 red bell pepper, washed and diced
- 8-oz. mushrooms, cleaned and sliced
- 2 cups zucchini or other summer squash (washed, stemmed, and sliced)
- 3 garlic cloves (minced or pressed)
- 8-oz. fresh basil (chopped)

1. Preheat your outdoor Griddle by turning all its burner's knob to medium-heat setting.
2. Grease the griddle top with cooking spray.
3. Season and rub the chicken to taste with salt and black pepper.
4. Place the chicken on the hot griddle top and brown on both the two sides.
5. Add the other ingredients and cook for another 3 minutes.
6. Serv.

Per Serving:
Calories: 134 | Fat: 6.5g | Carbohydrates: 3.8g | Fiber: 1.3g | Sugar: 1.7g | Protein: 14.3g | Sodium:265mg

GARLIC CHICKEN AND BROCCOLI
Prep Time: 10 mins. | Cook Time: 10 mins. |Serve: 2

- 1-lb. chicken breast, skinless, boneless, and cut into chunks
- 1-tbsp. soy sauce
- 1-tbsp. ginger, minced
- ½-tsp. garlic powder
- 1-tbsp. olive oil
- ½ onion, sliced
- 2 cups broccoli florets
- 2-tsp. hot sauce
- 2-tsp. vinegar
- 1-tsp. sesame oil
- Black pepper, to taste
- Salt, to taste

1. Toss all of the recipe ingredients together in a large mixing dish.
2. Preheat your outdoor Griddle by turning all its burner's knob to medium-heat setting.
3. Grease the griddle top with cooking spray.
4. Place the chicken and broccoli mixture on the hot griddle top.
5. Cook until the broccoli is soft and the chicken is done.
6. Serve and enjoy.

Per Serving:
Calories: 114 | Fat: 5.1g | Carbohydrates: 25g | Fiber: 0.8g | Sugar: 1.6g | Protein: 14.4g | Sodium:160mg

PEANUT SOY CURRIED CHICKEN KEBABS
Prep Time: 10 mins. | Cook Time: 15 mins. |Serve: 2

- 1 ½-lb. chicken breasts, boneless and cut into 1-inch pieces
- ½ cup soy sauce
- 1-tbsp. olive oil
- 1-tbsp. curry powder
- 1-tbsp. brown sugar
- 2-tbsp. peanut butter

1. Place the chicken in a big zip-lock bag and seal it.
2. Mix well olive oil, soy sauce, brown sugar, curry powder, and peanut butter in a suitable mixing dish and pour over chicken.
3. Seal the bag and shake it well then refrigerate overnight.
4. Thread marinated chicken onto the skewers.
5. Preheat your outdoor Griddle by turning all its burner's knob to medium-heat setting.
6. Grease the griddle top with cooking spray.
7. Cook the prepared for 12-15 minutes on the hot griddle top, flipping every 5 minutes.
8. Serve and enjoy.

Per Serving:
Calories: 60 | Fat: 1.1g | Carbohydrates: 15g | Fiber: 0.4g | Sugar: 0.8g | Protein: 10.3g | Sodium: 32mg

CHICKEN FAJITAS WITH CORN TORTILLAS
Prep Time: 10 mins. | Cook Time: 14 mins. |Serve: 4

- 4 boneless chicken breasts, sliced
- 1 small red onion, sliced
- 2 red bell peppers, sliced
- ½ cup spicy ranch salad dressing, divided
- ½-tsp. dried oregano
- 8 corn tortillas
- 2 cups torn butter lettuce
- 4 avocados, peeled and chopped

1. In a suitable mixing dish, mix well the onion, chicken, and pepper.
2. Drizzle 1 tbsp. salad dressing and oregano on top then mix well.
3. Preheat your outdoor Griddle by turning all its burner's knob to medium-heat setting.
4. Grease the griddle top with cooking spray.
5. Add the chicken to the hot griddle top and cook for 14 minutes, until tender.
6. Toss the chicken and veggies with the remaining salad dressing in a bowl.
7. Divide the chicken mixture, lettuce, and avocados

in the tortillas and serve warm.

Per Serving:
Calories: 260 | Fat: 20.8g | Carbohydrates: 10g | Fiber: 6.8g | Sugar: 0.7g | Protein: 12.88g | Sodium: 195mg

ZUCCHINI TURKEY PATTIES

Prep Time: 15 mins. | Cook Time: 10 mins. |Serve: 2

- ✓ 1-lb. ground turkey
- ✓ ¼ cup breadcrumbs
- ✓ 6 oz. zucchini, grated
- ✓ 1-tbsp. onion, grated
- ✓ 1 garlic clove, grated
- ✓ Pepper
- ✓ Salt

1. In a suitable mixing bowl, mix well the ground turkey and the remaining ingredients.
2. Preheat your outdoor Griddle by turning all its burner's knob to medium-heat setting.
3. Grease the griddle top with cooking spray.
4. Shape the mixture into patties and set them on the hot griddle top.
5. Cook the patties for 5 minutes per side until golden brown.
6. Serve and enjoy.

Per Serving:
Calories: 640 | Fat: 33g | Carbohydrates: 13g | Fiber: 0.1g | Sugar: 0.2g | Protein: 55.4g | Sodium:274mg

CHICKEN DRUMSTICKS WITH SAUCE

Prep Time: 15 mins. | Cook Time: 40 mins. | Serves: 3

- ✓ ¼ cup minced garlic
- ✓ ¼ cup tomato paste
- ✓ ¾ cup minced onion
- ✓ ¾ cup sugar
- ✓ 1 cup soy sauce
- ✓ 1 cup water
- ✓ 1 cup white vinegar
- ✓ 6 chicken drumsticks
- ✓ Salt and black pepper to taste

1. In a large bowl, add all the recipe ingredients In a Ziploc bag, mix well all of the recipe ingredients.
2. Marinate for at least 2 hours in the refrigerator.

3. Preheat your outdoor Griddle by turning all its burner's knob to medium-heat setting.
4. Grease the griddle top with cooking spray.
5. Sear the chicken for 40 minutes on the hot griddle top, flip every 10 minutes.
6. In the meantime, boil the leftover marinade in a suitable skillet over medium heat until it thickens.
7. Brush the glaze liberally over the chicken and serve.

Per Serving:
Calories: 477 | Fat: 21.5g | Carbohydrates: 15g |Fiber: 0.5g | Sugar: 0.2g | Protein: 65.8g | Sodium:223mg

SPICY BBQ CHICKEN

Prep Time: 10 mins. | Cook Time: 15 mins. |Serve: 2

- ✓ 4 chicken breasts and boneless.
- ✓ 1-tbsp. Red pepper flakes
- ✓ 1-tbsp. Chili powder
- ✓ 6-tbsp. Brown sugar
- ✓ 6-tbsp. BBQ sauce
- ✓ 1 cup Pineapple juice

1. Place the chicken breasts in a zip-lock bag.
2. Add pineapple juice, BBQ sauce, chili powder, brown sugar, and red pepper flakes.
3. Seal, shake well and place the Ziploc bag in the refrigerator overnight.
4. Preheat your outdoor Griddle by turning all its burner's knob to medium-heat setting.
5. Grease the griddle top with cooking spray.
6. Cook the marinated chicken breasts for 12-15 minutes.
7. Serve.

Per Serving:
Calories: 402 | Fat: 17.5g | Carbohydrates: 25g |Fiber: 1.4g | Sugar: 2g | Protein: 32.8g | Sodium: 365mg

BACON CHIPOTLE CHICKEN WITH BUTTER

Prep Time: 5 mins. | Cook Time: 10 mins. |Serve: 1

- ✓ 2 slices sourdough bread
- ✓ ¼ cup Caesar salad dressing
- ✓ 1 cooked chicken breast, diced
- ✓ ½ cup shredded cheddar cheese
- ✓ 1-tbsp. bacon bits
- ✓ 1-½-tsp. chipotle chili powder, or to taste
- ✓ 2-tbsp. softened butter

1. On one side of two pieces of bread, spread the salad dressing.
2. Then add a layer of chicken, bacon, cheese, and chipotle chili powder on top.
3. Place the last slice of bread on top, dressing side down.
4. Brush both the sides of the sandwich with butter.
5. Preheat your outdoor Griddle by turning all its burner's knob to medium-heat setting.
6. Sear the sandwiches on the hot griddle top for 5 minutes per side.
7. Serve warm.

Per Serving:
Calories: 300 | Fat: 10g | Carbohydrates: 18g | Fiber: 0.4g | Sugar: 0g | Protein: 46.8g | Sodium:265mg

OREGANO CHICKEN BITES

Prep Time: 5 mins. | Cook Time: 10 mins. | Serve: 2

- ✓ 1-lb. chicken breasts, skinless, boneless, and cut into cubes
- ✓ 2-tbsp. fresh lemon juice
- ✓ 1-tbsp. fresh oregano, chopped
- ✓ 2-tbsp. olive oil
- ✓ ⅛-tsp. cayenne pepper

1. Place the chicken breasts in a suitable mixing bowl.
2. Mix well the remaining ingredients and pour over the chicken.
3. Refrigerate the chicken for 1 hour before cooking.
4. Thread the marinated chicken cubes.
5. Preheat your outdoor Griddle by turning all its burner's knob to medium-heat setting.
6. Grease the griddle top with cooking spray.
7. Cook the skewers on the hot griddle top until the chicken is cooked.
8. Serve and enjoy.

Per Serving:
Calories: 295 | Fat: 10.3g | Carbohydrates: 18g | Fiber: 0.4g | Sugar: 0.1g | Protein: 46.8g | Sodium:205mg

HONEY JALAPENO CHICKEN

Prep Time: 10 mins. | Cook Time: 20 mins. | Serve: 1

- ✓ 1-½-lb. chicken thighs and boneless.
- ✓ 1-tsp. garlic, crushed.
- ✓ 1 jalapeno pepper, minced.
- ✓ 3-tbsp. fresh lime juice
- ✓ 3-tbsp. honey

- ✓ 3-tbsp. olive oil
- ✓ 1-tsp. kosher salt, to taste

1. Mix well the chicken and the rest of the ingredients in a zip-lock bag.
2. Refrigerate overnight after sealing the bag.
3. Preheat your outdoor Griddle by turning all its burner's knob to medium-heat setting.
4. Grease the griddle top with cooking spray.
5. Cook the marinated chicken on the hot griddle top for 8-10 minutes per side.
6. Serve.

Per Serving:
Calories: 236 | Fat: 13.5g | Carbohydrates: 14g | Fiber: 0.1g | Sugar: 0.1g | Protein: 25.3g | Sodium:265mg

CHICKEN ZUCCHINI STIR FRY

Prep Time: 10 mins. | Cook Time: 10 mins. | Serve: 2

- ✓ 6 oz. chicken breast, boneless and cut into cubes
- ✓ ¼ onion, sliced
- ✓ ½ bell pepper, chopped
- ✓ ½ zucchini, chopped
- ✓ 1-tbsp. olive oil
- ✓ ¼-tsp. dried thyme
- ✓ ½-tsp. garlic powder
- ✓ 1-tsp. dried oregano

1. Toss all of the recipe ingredients together in a large mixing dish.
2. Preheat your outdoor Griddle by turning all its burner's knob to medium-heat setting.
3. Grease the griddle top with cooking spray.
4. Place the chicken mixture on the hot griddle top and sear for 5 minutes per side.
5. Serve and enjoy.

Per Serving:
Calories: 297 | Fat: 9.5g | Carbohydrates: 23g | Fiber: 0.4g | Sugar: 0.5g | Protein: 47.1g | Sodium:269mg

CHICKEN FRITTERS WITH DILL

Prep Time: 10 mins. | Cook Time: 10 mins. | Serve: 4

- ✓ 1-lb. ground chicken
- ✓ 1-tsp. onion powder
- ✓ 1-tsp. garlic powder
- ✓ ½ cup parmesan cheese, shredded
- ✓ 1-tbsp. dill, chopped

- ½ cup breadcrumbs
- Pepper
- Salt

1. In a suitable mixing bowl, mix well all of the ingredients and stir until well blended.
2. Preheat your outdoor Griddle by turning all its burner's knob to medium-heat setting.
3. Grease the griddle top with cooking spray.
4. Shape the chicken mixture into patties and set them on the hot griddle top, cook for 5 minutes per side.
5. Serve and enjoy.

Per Serving:
Calories: 377 | Fat: 17.5g | Carbohydrates: 24g | Fiber: 0.8g | Sugar: 0g | Protein: 30.4g | Sodium: 275mg

GARLIC CHICKEN WINGS

Prep Time: 5 mins. | Cook Time: 20 mins. | Serve: 6

- 3-lb. chicken wings
- 1-½-tsp. garlic, minced
- 1-tbsp. fresh thyme leaves, chopped
- 1-tbsp. fresh parsley, chopped
- 2-tsp. lemon zest, grated
- 3-tbsp. soy sauce
- 1-tbsp. Dijon mustard
- 3-tbsp. brown sugar
- ½ cup olive oil
- ¾-tsp. black pepper
- 1-tsp. salt

1. Place the chicken wings in a zip-lock bag.
2. Mix well the other ingredients in a medium bowl and pour over the chicken wings.
3. Refrigerate for 8 hours after sealing the Ziplock bag.
4. Preheat your outdoor Griddle by turning all its burner's knob to medium-heat setting.
5. Grease the griddle top with cooking spray.
6. Pour the egg mixture onto the hot griddle top
7. Cook the chicken wings for 10 minutes per side on the hot griddle top.
8. Serve.

Per Serving:
Calories: 172 | Fat: 7.5g | Carbohydrates: 50g | Fiber: 0g | Sugar: 0g | Protein: 25.3g | Sodium: 185mg

PEPPER CHICKEN FAJITA

Prep Time: 10 mins. | Cook Time: 10 mins. | Serve: 2

- 1-lb. chicken breast, boneless and sliced
- 2-tsp. olive oil
- 1 onion, sliced
- 2 bell peppers, sliced
- ⅛-tsp. cayenne
- 1-tsp. cumin
- 2-tsp. chili powder
- Pepper
- Salt

1. In a suitable mixing dish, mix well the chicken, onion, and sliced bell peppers.
2. Toss in the cayenne, oil, chili powder, cumin, pepper, and salt.
3. Preheat your outdoor Griddle by turning all its burner's knob to medium-heat setting.
4. Grease the griddle top with cooking spray.
5. Pour the egg mixture onto the hot griddle top
6. Transfer the chicken mixture to the hot griddle and cook until chicken is done.
7. Serve and enjoy.

Per Serving:
Calories: 147 | Fat: 4.3g | Carbohydrates: 10g | Fiber: 0.5g | Sugar: 0.1g | Protein: 25.1g | Sodium: 205mg

COCONUT CHICKEN WITH BUTTER SAUCE

Prep Time: 10 mins. | Cook Time: 10 mins. | Serve: 2

- 1-lb. boneless chicken thighs, cut into thin strips
- Olive oil, for brushing
- For the marinade:
- ½ cup canned light coconut milk
- ½ lime, juiced
- 1-tbsp. honey
- 2-tsp. soy sauce
- 1 ½-tsp. fish sauce
- ½-tsp. red chili flakes
- 2-tsp. ginger, grated
- 1 clove of garlic, grated
- ½-tsp. curry powder
- ¼-tsp. ground coriander
- For the almond butter sauce:
- ¼ cup almond butter
- ¼ cup water
- 2-tbsp. canned, light coconut milk
- 1-tbsp. honey

- ½ lime, juiced
- 1-tsp. fish sauce
- 1-tsp. grated ginger
- ½-tsp. low sodium soy sauce
- ½-tsp. Sriracha

1. In a medium mixing bowl, beat all of the marinade ingredients.
2. Toss the chicken in the mixing bowl to coat it.
3. Refrigerate for 2 hours or overnight, covered.
4. Preheat your outdoor Griddle by turning all its burner's knob to medium-heat setting.
5. Grease the griddle top with cooking spray.
6. Using metal skewers, thread the chicken strips.
7. Cook the chicken skewers for 4 minutes per side on the prepared griddle
8. In a suitable saucepan, mix well all of the recipe ingredients for the almond butter sauce.
9. Bring this sauce to a boil over medium heat, then reduce to low heat and cook for 2 minutes.
10. Enjoy the warm chicken satay with the almond butter sauce

Per Serving:
Calories: 195 | Fat: 9.3g | Carbohydrates: 14g | Fiber: 0.3g | Sugar: 0.1g | Protein: 27.4g | Sodium:265mg

PEPPER CHEDDAR CHICKEN
Prep Time: 10 mins. | Cook Time: 16 mins. |Serve: 2

- 1-lb. boneless skinless chicken breasts
- 4 oz. taco seasoning
- 1-tsp. cayenne pepper
- Kosher salt, to taste, to taste
- 2 cloves minced garlic
- 1 chopped small red onion
- 2 chopped red bell peppers
- 15-oz. Can black beans (drained)
- 2 cups shredded cheddar
- ½ cup chopped fresh cilantro

1. Season the chicken with cayenne pepper, salt, and taco seasoning.
2. Preheat your outdoor Griddle by turning all its burner's knob to medium-heat setting.
3. Grease the griddle top with cooking spray.
4. Cook it for 6 minutes per side on the hot griddle top.
5. Add the remaining ingredients and cook for another 7 minutes.
6. Garnish and serve

Per Serving:
Calories: 247 | Fat: 12.5g | Carbohydrates: 6g | Fiber: 1.3g | Sugar: 3.3g | Protein: 28g | Sodium:275mg

TURKEY PATTIES WITH OREGANO
Prep Time: 10 mins. | Cook Time: 10 mins. |Serve: 4

- 8 oz. ground turkey
- 2-tsp. fresh oregano, chopped
- 2 garlic cloves, minced
- ½-tsp. red pepper, crushed
- ¼-tsp. salt

1. Preheat your outdoor Griddle by turning all its burner's knob to medium-heat setting.
2. Grease the griddle top with cooking spray.
3. In a suitable mixing bowl, mix well the ground turkey and the additional ingredients.
4. Form the mixture into two patties and set them on the hot griddle top, cooking for 5 minutes per side.
5. Serve and enjoy.

Per Serving:
Calories: 180 | Fat: 7.8g | Carbohydrates: 15g | Fiber: 0.5g | Sugar: 0.2g | Protein: 25.4g | Sodium:65mg

BALSAMIC CHICKEN WITH ROSEMARY
Prep Time: 10 mins. | Cook Time: 12 mins. |Serve: 4

- ½ cup balsamic vinegar
- 2-tbsp. olive oil
- 2 rosemary sprigs, chopped
- 2 lbs. boneless chicken breasts, ½-inch thickness

1. In a suitable baking dish, mix well the balsamic vinegar, olive oil, and rosemary.
2. Add chicken breasts and rub with the sauce.
3. Refrigerate for at least 30 minutes after covering with plastic wrap.
4. Preheat your outdoor Griddle by turning all its burner's knob to medium-heat setting.
5. Grease the griddle top with cooking spray.
6. Place the chicken breasts on the hot griddle top and cook for 6 minutes per side.
7. Serve warm.

Per Serving:
Calories: 180 | Fat: 7.8g | Carbohydrates: 15g | Fiber: 0.5g | Sugar: 0.2g | Protein: 25.4g | Sodium:65mg

GREEK PEPPER CHICKEN
Prep Time: 5 mins. | Cook Time: 16 mins. |Serve: 2

- 2 chicken breasts and boneless
- 2-tbsp. olive oil
- 1-tsp. Italian seasoning
- 1 ½ cup grape tomatoes, cut in half
- ½ cup olives
- ¼-tsp. black pepper
- ¼-tsp. salt

1. Season the chicken with black pepper, salt, and Italian seasoning.
2. Preheat your outdoor Griddle by turning all its burner's knob to medium-heat setting.
3. Grease the griddle top with cooking spray.
4. Season the chicken and place it on the hot griddle top.
5. Cook for almost 6 minutes per side. Place the chicken on a serving plate.
6. Cook for 4 minutes on the hot griddle top with the tomatoes and olives.
7. Toss the chicken with the olive and tomato mixture and serve.

Per Serving:
Calories: 260 | Fat: 6.3g | Carbohydrates: 10g | Fiber: 0g | Sugar: 0g | Protein: 24g | Sodium: 213mg

HONEY-MUSTARD CHICKEN WITH WALNUT
Prep Time: 10 mins. | Cook Time: 6 mins. |Serve: 4

- ½ cup Dijon mustard
- 2-tbsp. honey
- 2-tbsp. olive oil
- 1-tsp. black pepper
- 2 lbs. chicken tenders
- ½ cup walnuts

1. In a medium mixing bowl, mix well the honey, mustard, olive oil, and black pepper.
2. Toss in the chicken to coat it.
3. Pulse the walnuts in a food processor.
4. Toss the chicken tenders in a thin coating of ground walnuts.
5. Preheat your outdoor Griddle by turning all its burner's knob to medium-heat setting.
6. Grease the griddle top with cooking spray.
7. Sear the chicken tenders for 3 minutes per side.
8. Serve.

Per Serving:
Calories: 222 | Fat: 10.5g | Carbohydrates: 0g | Fiber: 0g | Sugar: 0g | Protein: 30.1g | Sodium: 225mg

SAMBAL CHICKEN WITH GINGER-SESAME
Prep Time: 10 mins. | Cook Time: 6 mins. |Serve: 4

- 8 boneless chicken thighs
- For the glaze:
- 3-tbsp. dark brown sugar
- 2 ½-tbsp. soy sauce
- 1-tbsp. fresh garlic, minced
- 2-tsp. sesame seeds
- 1-tsp. fresh ginger, minced
- 1-tsp. sambal Oelek
- ⅓ cup scallions, sliced
- Non-stick cooking spray

1. In a suitable mixing bowl, mix well all the glaze ingredients and set aside half for serving.
2. Toss the chicken in the bowl to evenly coat it.
3. Preheat your outdoor Griddle by turning all its burner's knob to medium-heat setting.
4. Grease the griddle top with cooking spray.
5. Cook this marinated chicken for 6 minutes.
6. Transfer the chicken to plates and garnish with the remaining glaze.
7. Serve warm

Per Serving:
Calories: 212 | Fat: 11.3g | Carbohydrates: 13g | Fiber: 0.5g | Sugar: 0.1g | Protein: 25.4g | Sodium: 195mg

CHICKEN WITH FRUIT SALSA
Prep Time: 10 mins. | Cook Time: 14 mins. |Serve: 4

- 4 boneless chicken breasts
- For the marinade:
- ½ cup fresh lemon juice
- ½ cup soy sauce
- 1-tbsp. fresh ginger, minced
- 1-tbsp. lemon-pepper seasoning
- 2 garlic cloves, minced
- For the salsa:
- 1 ½ cups pineapple, chopped
- ¾ cup kiwi fruit, chopped
- ½ cup mango, chopped
- ½ cup red onion, chopped
- 2-tbsp. fresh cilantro, chopped
- 1 small jalapeño pepper, seeded and chopped

- ✓ 1 ½-tsp. ground cumin
- ✓ ¼-tsp. sea salt
- ✓ ⅛-tsp. black pepper
- ✓ ½-tsp. olive oil

1. In a big sealable plastic bag, mix well the marinade ingredients.
2. Place the chicken in the bag, seal it, and shake it to coat it.
3. Refrigerate for 1 hour to marinate.
4. In a suitable mixing bowl, mix well all of the salsa ingredients.
5. Preheat your outdoor Griddle by turning all its burner's knob to medium-heat setting.
6. Grease the griddle top with cooking spray.
7. Cook the marinated chicken for 7 minutes per side.
8. Serve the salsa-topped chicken with your favorite side dishes

Per Serving:
Calories: 287 | Fat: 17.5g | Carbohydrates: 13g | Fiber: 0.5g | Sugar: 0.1g | Protein: 30.3g | Sodium:215mg

TURKEY BURGER PATTIES

Prep Time: 1 mins. | Cook Time: 10 mins. |Serves: 2

- ✓ 1-lb. ground turkey
- ✓ 1-tbsp. garlic powder
- ✓ 1 ½-tbsp. dried parsley
- ✓ 3 oz. onion, diced
- ✓ Black pepper, to taste
- ✓ Salt, to taste

1. In a suitable mixing bowl, mix well all of the ingredients and stir until well blended.
2. Preheat your outdoor Griddle by turning all its burner's knob to medium-heat setting.
3. Grease the griddle top with cooking spray.
4. Make patties out this mixture and cook for 5 minutes per side on the hot griddle top.
5. Serve and enjoy.

Per Serving:
Calories: 312 | Fat: 17.5g | Carbohydrates: 3.4g | Fiber: 0.4g | Sugar: 1.5g | Protein: 32.1g | Sodium: 205mg

LEMON HONEY CHICKEN TENDERS

Prep Time: 10 mins. | Cook Time: 10 mins. |Serve: 2

- ✓ 1 ½-lb. chicken tenders
- ✓ 1-tsp. dried oregano
- ✓ 1-tsp. dried rosemary
- ✓ 2-tbsp. Herb de province
- ✓ 2-tbsp. lemon juice
- ✓ 2-tbsp. olive oil
- ✓ 4-tbsp. honey
- ✓ 1 shallot, minced
- ✓ ⅓ cup Dijon mustard
- ✓ Black pepper, to taste
- ✓ Salt, to taste

1. In a zip-lock bag, mix well the chicken and the remaining ingredients.
2. Refrigerate overnight after sealing the bag and shaking it well.
3. Preheat your outdoor Griddle by turning all its burner's knob to medium-heat setting.
4. Grease the griddle top with cooking spray.
5. Cook the marinated chicken tenders for 5 minutes per side on the hot griddle top.
6. Serve and enjoy.

Per Serving:
Calories: 196 | Fat: 10.5g | Carbohydrates: 13g | Fiber: 0g | Sugar: 0.2g | Protein: 24.1g | Sodium: 205mg

SPINACH GARLIC TURKEY PATTIES

Prep Time: 10 mins. | Cook Time: 10 mins. |Serve: 6

- ✓ 3-lb. ground turkey
- ✓ 3-tbsp. garlic, minced
- ✓ 1 onion, chopped
- ✓ 5 cups spinach, sautéed
- ✓ 3-tbsp. mustard
- ✓ Pepper
- ✓ Salt

1. Preheat your outdoor Griddle by turning all its burner's knob to medium-heat setting.
2. Grease the griddle top with cooking spray.
3. In a suitable mixing bowl, mix well all of the ingredients and stir until well blended.
4. Make patties out of this mixture and fry them for 5 minutes per side on the hot griddle top.
5. Serve and enjoy.

Per Serving:
Calories: 215 | Fat: 11.4g | Carbohydrates: 28g |Fiber: 1.3g | Sugar: 0.1g | Protein: 25.4g | Sodium:195mg

TACO TURKEY BURGER PATTIES

Prep Time: 10 mins. | Cook Time: 10 mins. |Serve: 2

- 1-lb. ground turkey
- 1-tbsp. taco seasoning
- ½ cup red peppers, chopped
- ½ cup green peppers, chopped
- Black pepper, to taste
- Salt, to taste

1. In a suitable mixing bowl, mix well all of the ingredients and stir until well blended.
2. Preheat your outdoor Griddle by turning all its burner's knob to medium-heat setting.
3. Grease the griddle top with cooking spray.
4. Make patties out of this mixture and fry them for 5 minutes per side on the hot griddle top.
5. Serve and enjoy.

Per Serving:
Calories: 190| Fat: 5.1g | Carbohydrates: 28g | Fiber: 0.3g | Sugar: 1.3g | Protein: 33g | Sodium:55mg

PARMESAN CHICKEN BAKE

Prep Time: 10 mins. | Cook Time: 20 mins. |Serve: 4

- 4 tbsp. fat-free plain Greek yogurt
- 1 tbsp. low-fat Parmesan cheese, grated
- Salt and black pepper, to taste
- 1 (4-oz.) boneless, skinless chicken breast

1. In a bowl, add the yogurt, cheese, garlic powder and black pepper and mix well. Add the chicken breast and coat with theyogurt mixture evenly.
2. Arrange the chicken breast in a foil container.
3. Preheat your outdoor Griddle by turning all its burner's knob to medium-heat setting.
4. Place the chicken container on the griddle and cook for 20 minutes.
5. Serve warm.

Per Serving:
Calories: 155 | Fat: 3.5g | Carbohydrates: 23g | Fiber: 0g | Sugar: 0g | Protein: 26.3g | Sodium: 285mg

BEEF RECIPES

BBQ BRISKET BURNT ENDS
Prep Time: 10 mins. | Cook Time: 4 hrs. |Serve: 8

- 1 tsp. olive oil
- 1 (8 lbs.) brisket
- 2 tsp. kosher salt
- 2 tsp. black pepper
- BBQ rub
- 1 cup BBQ sauce
- ½ cup brown sugar
- 2 tbsp. garlic powder

1. Rub the brisket with black pepper, salt and oil.
2. Cover and refrigerate the brisket for 1 hour.
3. Mix bbq sauce, sugar and garlic powder in a bowl.
4. Preheat your outdoor Griddle by turning all its burner's knob to medium-heat setting.
5. Grease the griddle top with cooking spray.
6. Make criss cross cuts on top of the brisket.
7. Place the brisket on the griddle top and brush it with the bbq sauce mixture.
8. Cook for almost 4 hours and keep flipping it after every 30 minutes.
9. Slice and serve warm.

Per Serving:
Calories: 105 | Fat: 5g | Carbohydrates: 15.1g | Fiber: 2.8g | Sugar: 5.3g | Protein: 1.8g | Sodium:162mg

LONDON BROIL WITH HERB BUTTER
Prep Time: 10 mins. | Cook Time: 16 mins. |Serve: 4

- 1 (2-lb.) London broil top-round steak
- Kosher salt, to taste
- black pepper, to taste
- ¼ cup olive oil
- Juice of ½ lemon
- 2 tbsp. packed brown sugar
- 1 tbsp. Worcestershire sauce
- 4 garlic cloves, minced
- FOR THE HERB BUTTER
- ½ cup (1 stick) butter, softened
- 1 tbsp. parsley leaves, chopped
- 2 tsp. chopped chives
- Zest of ½ lemon
- ½ tsp. kosher salt, to taste
- Pinch crushed red pepper flakes

1. Mix brown sugar, Worcestershire sauce, garlic, lemon juice, salt and black pepper in a bowl.
2. Season the steak with the prepared sauce.
3. Preheat your outdoor Griddle by turning all its burner's knob to medium-heat setting.
4. Grease the griddle top with cooking spray.
5. Place the steak on the hot griddle top.
6. Cook for almost 7-8 minutes per side until tender.
7. Meanwhile, mix the herb butter ingredients in a bowl.
8. Slice the steak and top it with herb butter.
9. Serve warm.

Per Serving:
Calories: 252 | Fat: 12.5g | Carbohydrates: 28g | Fiber: 3.5g | Sugar: 1g | Protein: 29g | Sodium: 287mg

CAPRESE STEAK
Prep Time: 10 mins. | Cook Time: 22 mins. |Serve: 4

- 3/4 cup balsamic vinegar
- 3 garlic cloves, minced
- 2 tbsp. honey
- 2 tbsp. olive oil
- 1 tbsp. dried thyme
- 1 tbsp. dried oregano
- 4 (6-oz.) filet mignon
- 2 beefsteak tomatoes, sliced
- kosher salt, to taste
- 4 slices mozzarella
- Fresh basil leaves, for serving

1. Mix balsamic vinegar, garlic, honey, dried thyme, and dried oregano in a bowl
2. Season the steak with this mixture, cover and refrigerate for 1 hour.
3. Preheat your outdoor Griddle by turning all its burner's knob to medium-heat setting.

4. Grease the griddle top with cooking oil.
5. Place the steak on the hot griddle top.
6. Cook for almost 6 minutes per side.
7. Brush the leftover marinade over tomatoes and place on the griddle to cook for 5 minutes per side.
8. Top the steak with tomatoes and mozzarella.
9. Serve warm.

Per Serving:
Calories: 315 | Fat: 13.8g | Carbohydrates: 28g | Fiber: 1.8g | Sugar: 1g | Protein: 27.3g | Sodium: 215mg

CHEESESTEAK STUFFED PEPPERS
Prep Time: 10 mins. | Cook Time: 20 mins. | Serve: 4

- 4 bell peppers, halved
- 1 tbsp. vegetable oil
- 1 large onion, sliced
- 16 oz. cremini mushrooms, sliced
- Kosher salt, to taste
- black pepper, to taste
- 1 ½ lb. sirloin steak, sliced
- 2 tsp. Italian seasoning
- 16 slices provolone, chopped
- parsley leaves, chopped, to garnish

1. Preheat your outdoor Griddle by turning all its burner's knob to medium-heat setting.
2. Grease the griddle top with cooking spray.
3. Season the steak slices with salt, black pepper, Italian seasoning and place it on the hot griddle top.
4. Sauté for almost 10 minutes until brown.
5. Sear the mushrooms for 5 minutes.
6. Chop the steak, and mushrooms.
7. Mix the chopped steak and mushroom with rest of the ingredients in a bowl, except the bell peppers.
8. Divide the steak mixture into the peppers.
9. Place the peppers on the griddle top, cover with the lid and cook for 5 minutes.
10. Serve warm.

Per Serving:
Calories: 227 | Fat: 12.8g | Carbohydrates: 3.4g | Fiber: 1.3g | Sugar: 0.9g | Protein: 26g | Sodium: 159mg

CAJUN BUTTER STEAK
Prep Time: 10 mins. | Cook Time: 12 mins. | Serve: 4

- ½ cup low-sodium soy sauce
- 1/3 cup olive oil
- ¼ cup packed brown sugar
- ¼ cup bourbon
- 2 tbsp. whole-grain mustard
- 2 tsp. Cajun seasoning
- 2 garlic cloves, minced
- 1 tsp. fresh thyme leaves
- 2 lb. tri-tip steak (or a very thick cut of sirloin)
- 2 tbsp. butter, cut into tabs
- parsley leaves, chopped, to garnish

1. Boil bourbon with soy sauce, brown sugar, rest of the ingredients except steak.
2. Cook for 1 minute, mix well and allow the glaze to cool.
3. Add the steak to the glaze, mix well, cover and marinate for 1 hour in the refrigerator.
4. Preheat your outdoor Griddle by turning all its burner's knob to medium-heat setting.
5. Grease the griddle top with cooking oil.
6. Place the steak on the hot griddle top.
7. Cook for almost 6 minutes per side.
8. Garnish with parsley.
9. Serve warm.

Per Serving:
Calories: 244 | Fat: 9.3g | Carbohydrates: 28g | Fiber: 2.3g | Sugar: 3.9g | Protein: 32.1g | Sodium: 299mg

BEEF BROCCOLI KEBABS
Prep Time: 10 mins. | Cook Time: 16 mins. | Serve: 2

- 1/3 cup low-sodium soy sauce
- Juice of 2 limes
- 1 tbsp. ground ginger
- ¼ cup brown sugar
- 1 lb. sirloin steak, cut into cubes
- 2 cup broccoli florets
- 2 tbsp. olive oil
- black pepper
- Green onions, to garnish

1. Mix soy sauce, brown sugar, lime juice, ginger, and black pepper in a bowl until sugar is dissolved.
2. Stir in beef cubes, mix well and cover to marinate for 30 minutes.
3. Thread the beef and broccoli on the skewers.
4. Brush the leftover marinade over the skewers.
5. Preheat your outdoor Griddle by turning all its burner's knob to medium-heat setting.
6. Grease the griddle top with cooking spray.
7. Place the skewers on the hot griddle top.

8. Cook for almost 8 minutes per side.
9. Serve warm.

Per Serving:
Calories: 180| Fat: 5.5g | Carbohydrates: 21g | Fiber: 0.8g | Sugar: 1.4g | Protein: 26.3g | Sodium:236mg

GLAZED BEEF SKEWERS WITH SLAW

Prep Time: 10 mins. | Cook Time: 12 mins. |Serve: 4

- 1 ½ lb. eye fillet steak, cut into 5cm pieces
- 2 tbs olive oil
- Slaw
- 1/3 cup aioli
- 1/3 cup chopped dill pickled cucumber
- ½ head iceberg lettuce, shredded
- 1 carrot, shredded
- 1 green apple, cut into long matchsticks
- 1 Asian eschalot, sliced

BARBECUE SAUCE
- 1 cup barbecue sauce
- ¼ cup maple syrup
- 1 garlic clove, grated
- 2 tsp. ground allspice
- 2 tsp. ground coriander

1. Mix all the recipe ingredients for slaw in a bowl and keep it in the refrigerator until skewers are ready.
2. Mix barbecue sauce ingredient in a pan and cook to a boil
3. Allow the sauce to cool then stir in steak then mix well to coat.
4. Cover and refrigerate for 30 minutes.
5. Thread the beef on the skewers.
6. Preheat your outdoor Griddle by turning all its burner's knob to medium-heat setting.
7. Grease the griddle top with cooking spray.
8. Brush the leftover sauce over the skewers and place it on the hot griddle top.
9. Cook for almost 6 minutes per side.
10. Serve warm.

Per Serving:
Calories: 245 | Fat: 15g | Carbohydrates: 21g | Fiber: 1.3g | Sugar: 2.7g | Protein: 22.4g | Sodium:62mg

SATAY STEAK SKEWERS

Prep Time: 10 mins. | Cook Time: 10 mins. |Serve: 4

- 1 long red and green chilies, sliced
- 1/3 cup apple cider vinegar
- 4 x 5 oz. rump steaks, cubed
- 3 garlic cloves, crushed
- 2 tbsp. honey
- ¼ cup olive oil
- ½ cup crunchy peanut butter
- 1½ tbsp. Sriracha and Kecap manis
- Juice of 1 lime
- 1 tsp. fish sauce
- Micro coriander, to serve

1. Sauté garlic with oil in a suitable saucepan for 30 seconds.
2. Stir in vinegar, honey, peanut butter, Sriracha, Kecap manis, lime juice and fish sauce then mix well.
3. Cook for 1 minute until it thickens.
4. Allow this sauce to cool and toss in a steak cubes.
5. Preheat your outdoor Griddle by turning all its burner's knob to medium-heat setting.
6. Grease the griddle top with cooking spray.
7. Thread the beef cubes on the skewers.
8. Place them on the hot griddle and cook for almost 5 minutes per side.
9. Serve warm.

Per Serving:
Calories: 265 | Fat: 14.5g | Carbohydrates: 3.4g | Fiber: 0.8g | Sugar: 0.4g | Protein: 27g | Sodium: 354mg

FILET MIGNON

Prep Time: 10 mins. | Cook Time: 12 mins. |Serve: 4

- 2 tbsp. olive oil
- 4 (6-oz.) filet mignon
- Kosher salt, to taste
- black pepper, to taste
- 4 tbsp. butter
- 1 tbsp. chopped rosemary

1. Preheat your outdoor Griddle by turning all its

burner's knob to medium-heat setting.
2. Grease the griddle top with cooking oil and butter.
3. Season the steak with rosemary, black pepper and salt and place it on the hot griddle top.
4. Cook for almost 6 minutes per side.
5. Serve warm.

Per Serving:
Calories: 247 | Fat: 12.5g | Carbohydrates: 11g | Fiber: 2.3g | Sugar: 3.7g | Protein: 24.4g | Sodium: 296mg

BEEF TENDERLOIN

Prep Time: 10 mins. | Cook Time: 20 mins. | Serve: 4

- FOR BEEF
- ½ cup olive oil
- 2 tbsp. balsamic vinegar
- 2 tbsp. whole grain mustard
- 3 sprigs fresh thyme
- 3 sprigs fresh rosemary
- 1 dried bay leaf
- 2 garlic cloves, smashed
- 2 tbsp. honey
- 1 (2-lb.) beef tenderloin, rested at room temperature for 1 hour
- 1 tsp. kosher salt, to taste
- 1 tsp. black pepper
- 2 tsp. fresh rosemary, chopped
- 1 garlic clove, minced
- FOR YOGURT SAUCE
- ½ cup Greek yogurt
- ¼ cup sour cream
- 1 tsp. prepared horseradish
- Juice of ½ lemon
- Kosher salt, to taste

1. Prepare the yogurt sauce by mixing its ingredients in a bowl and keep it refrigerate until ready to serve.
2. Season the beef tenderloin with rest of the ingredients in a large bowl.
3. Cover and refrigerate for 1 hour for marination.
4. Preheat your outdoor Griddle by turning all its burner's knob to medium-heat setting.
5. Grease the griddle top with cooking spray.
6. Season the chicken and place it on the hot griddle top.
7. Cook for almost 10 minutes per side.

Per Serving:
Calories: 175 | Fat: 8.3g | Carbohydrates: 28g | Fiber: 0.5g | Sugar: 0.8g | Protein: 22.5g | Sodium: 244mg

LEMON BUTTER STEAK

Prep Time: 10 mins. | Cook Time: 17 mins. | Serve: 2

- MARINADE
- 1 lb. flank steak
- 5 tbsp. olive oil, divided
- 1 tbsp. low-sodium soy sauce
- 1 tbsp. honey
- Juice and zest of 1 lemon
- 1 tsp. thyme leaves
- FOR THE STEAK AND SPINACH
- 5 tbsp. butter, divided
- 2 garlic cloves, minced
- 2 tsp. thyme leaves
- Zest of 1 lemon
- Kosher salt, to taste
- Pinch red pepper flakes
- 6 cup baby spinach

1. Mix flank steak with rest of the marinade ingredients in a bowl.
2. Cover and refrigerate for 1 hour for marination.
3. Preheat your outdoor Griddle by turning all its burner's knob to medium-heat setting.
4. Grease the griddle top with butter.
5. Place the steak on the hot griddle top.
6. Cook for almost 6 minutes per side.
7. Add spinach and rest of the ingredients to the griddle.
8. Sauté for 5 minutes and serve the steaks with spinach mixture.
9. Enjoy.

Per Serving:
Calories: 240 | Fat: 9.3g | Carbohydrates: 4g | Fiber: 1g | Sugar: 1.8g | Protein: 34g | Sodium: 240mg

SALISBURY STEAK

Prep Time: 10 mins. | Cook Time: 15 mins. | Serve: 4

- FOR THE PATTIES
- 1 lb. ground beef
- 1 large egg
- 1/3 cup breadcrumbs
- 1 tbsp. ketchup
- 1 tbsp. Worcestershire sauce
- 1 Garlic clove, minced
- kosher salt, to taste
- black pepper, to taste
- 1 tbsp. olive oil
- FOR THE GRAVY
- 2 tbsp. unsalted butter
- 1 onion, chopped
- 2 sprigs thyme
- ½ cup Mushrooms, sliced
- 2 tbsp. all-purpose flour
- 1 tbsp. Worcestershire sauce
- 1 tbsp. tomato paste
- 1 cup beef stock
- kosher salt, to taste
- black pepper, to taste

1. Prepare the patties by mixing all its ingredients in a bowl.
2. Make 4 patties out of the meat mixture.
3. Preheat your outdoor Griddle by turning all its burner's knob to medium-heat setting.
4. Grease the griddle top with cooking spray.
5. Place the patties on the hot griddle top.
6. Cook for almost 5 minutes per side.
7. Meanwhile, prepare the sauce.
8. Sauté onion with butter and mushroom in a skillet for 5 minutes.
9. Stir in stock, tomato paste, black pepper, salt and Worcestershire sauce.
10. Mix flour with 2 tbsp. water in a bowl and pour into the gravy.
11. Cook this sauce for 5 minutes with stirring.
12. Pour the prepared gravy over the patties in a plate then serve warm.

Per Serving:
Calories: 195 | Fat: 13.3g | Carbohydrates: 13g | Fiber: 0.8g | Sugar: 1.3g | Protein: 17.4g | Sodium: 70mg

BALSAMIC STEAK SALAD WITH PEACHES
Prep Time: 10 mins. | Cook Time: 10 mins. | Serve: 2

- 1 lb. skirt steak, trimmed of fat
- ¼ cup balsamic vinegar
- 1 garlic clove, minced
- 1 tbsp. packed brown sugar
- 1 tbsp. vegetable oil
- kosher salt, to taste
- black pepper, to taste
- ¼ cup olive oil
- Juice of 1 large lemon
- 2 peaches, sliced
- 6 cup baby arugula
- 1/3 cup blue cheese, crumbled

1. Mix steak with black pepper, salt, vinegar, and garlic in a bowl
2. Preheat your outdoor Griddle by turning all its burner's knob to medium-heat setting.
3. Grease the griddle top with cooking oil.
4. Place the steak on the hot griddle top.
5. Cook for almost 5 minutes per side.
6. Toss peaches with rest of the ingredients in a bowl.
7. Slice the steak and add to the salad.
8. Serve.

Per Serving:
Calories: 426 | Fat: 18.5g | Carbohydrates: 15g | Fiber: 0.1g | Sugar: 0g | Protein: 51.4g | Sodium: 173mg

STEAK FRITE BITES
Prep Time: 10 mins. | Cook Time: 12 mins. | Serve: 2

- 1 lb. flank steak, ¼-inch thick
- 2 tbsp. olive oil
- 1 tbsp. chopped rosemary
- 1 tbsp. Dijon mustard
- 2 tbsp. Worcestershire sauce
- Kosher salt, to taste
- black pepper, to taste
- ½ (1-lb) bag frozen French fries
- Steak sauce, for serving

1. Season the flank steak with black pepper, salt, Worcestershire sauce, rosemary and oil.
2. Preheat your outdoor Griddle by turning all its burner's knob to medium-heat setting.
3. Grease the griddle top with cooking spray.
4. Place the steak on the hot griddle top.
5. Cook for almost 6 minutes per side.
6. Meanwhile, deep fry the French fries as per the packages instructions.
7. Spread the fries on the serving platter.
8. Top the fries with steak and the steak sauce.

9. Serve warm.

Per Serving:
Calories: 216 | Fat: 7.5g | Carbohydrates: 24g | Fiber: 1.1g | Sugar: 2.6g | Protein: 30.5g | Sodium:246mg

SIZZLING STEAK FAJITAS
Prep Time: 10 mins. | Cook Time: 17 mins. |Serve: 4

- ¼ cup olive oil, plus more for cooking
- Juice of 1 lime
- 1 tsp. dried oregano
- ½ tsp. ground cumin
- ½ tsp. chili powder
- 1 lb. skirt steak
- Kosher salt, to taste
- black pepper, to taste
- 1 bell pepper, sliced
- 1 large onion, sliced into half moons
- Tortillas, for serving
- Sour cream, for serving
- Cilantro, for serving
- Pico de Gallo, serving

1. Preheat your outdoor Griddle by turning all its burner's knob to medium-heat setting.
2. Grease the griddle top with cooking oil.
3. Season the steak with lime juice, cumin, oregano, chili powder, black pepper and salt and place it on the hot griddle top.
4. Cook for almost 6 minutes per side.
5. Slice the cooked steaks and add the peppers and onions to the griddle.
6. Sauté for 5 minutes.
7. Divide the steak and veggies into tortillas.
8. Top with sour cream, cilantro and Pico de Gallo.
9. Serve warm.

Per Serving:
Calories: 252 | Fat: 14.5g | Carbohydrates: 216g | Fiber: 1.4g | Sugar: 3.3g | Protein: 23.4g | Sodium: 309mg

BUTTER STEAK BITES
Prep Time: 10 mins. | Cook Time: 12 mins. |Serve: 4

- 2 lb. ribeye steak
- 4 tbsp. olive oil
- 4 tbsp. butter
- 2 large garlic clove, minced
- 1 tsp. fresh parsley leaves, minced

1. Preheat your outdoor Griddle by turning all its burner's knob to medium-heat setting.
2. Grease the griddle top with oil and butter.
3. Place the steak on the hot griddle top.
4. Top it with garlic.
5. Cook for almost 6 minutes per side.
6. Garnish with parsley.
7. Serve warm.

Per Serving:
Calories: 247 | Fat: 14.5g | Carbohydrates: 21g | Fiber: 1.8g | Sugar: 2.1g | Protein: 24.3g | Sodium:245mg

BOYFRIEND STEAK
Prep Time: 10 mins. | Cook Time: 10 mins. |Serve: 2

- Parsley BUTTER
- 1 stick butter, softened
- 1 tbsp. parsley leaves, chopped
- STEAK
- 1 tbsp. olive oil, for skillet
- 1 26- to 28-oz. bone-in rib eye or côte de boeuf
- Kosher salt, to taste
- black pepper, to taste

1. Preheat your outdoor Griddle by turning all its burner's knob to medium-heat setting.
2. Grease the griddle top with cooking oil.
3. Season the steak with black pepper and salt and place it on the hot griddle top.
4. Cook for almost 10 minutes per side until tender.
5. Mix butter with parsley and pour over the steak.
6. Slice and serve warm.

Per Serving:
Calories: 282 | Fat: 13.5g | Carbohydrates: 10.1g | Fiber:4.4g | Sugar: 4.3g | Protein: 24.3g | Sodium: 252mg

CHIMICHURRI GRILLED STEAK
Prep Time: 10 mins. | Cook Time: 18 mins. |Serve: 2

- FOR THE CILANTRO-LIME CHIMICHURRI
- ½ bunch cilantro, minced
- ¼ cup sliced chives
- 2 garlic cloves, minced
- 2 limes, zested and juiced
- ½ cup olive oil
- 1 tsp. crushed red pepper flakes

- ½ tsp. kosher salt, to taste
- ¼ tsp. black pepper
- FOR THE STEAK
- 2 tbsp. olive oil
- 1 lb. skirt steak
- kosher salt, to taste
- black pepper, to taste
- FOR THE GRILLED ASPARAGUS
- 2 tbsp. olive oil
- 1 garlic clove, minced
- Juice of 1 lemon
- 1 lb. asparagus, trimmed

1. Blend all the chimichurri ingredients in a blender until smooth.
2. Preheat your outdoor Griddle by turning all its burner's knob to medium-heat setting.
3. Grease the griddle top with cooking oil.
4. Season the steak with black pepper and salt and place on the hot griddle top.
5. Cook for almost 6 minutes per side.
6. Season the asparagus with lemon juice, garlic and oil
7. Sear them for 2-3 minutes per side.
8. Slice the steak and top it with chimichurri sauce.
9. Serve warm with asparagus.

Per Serving:
Calories: 285 | Fat: 14.4g | Carbohydrates: 15.1g | Fiber: 3.3g | Sugar: 3g | Protein: 27g | Sodium: 295mg

STEAK FAJITA SKEWERS
Prep Time: 10 mins. | Cook Time: 10 mins. |Serve: 2

- 1 lb. sirloin steak, cut into large cubes
- 1 bunch scallions, cut into thirds
- 1 pack small flour tortillas, torn into large pieces
- 4 large bell peppers, cut into large pieces
- 8 skewers, soaked in water for 20 minutes
- olive oil, for drizzling
- kosher salt, to taste
- black pepper, to taste

1. Toss steak cubes with rest of the ingredients in a large bowl.
2. Preheat your outdoor Griddle by turning all its burner's knob to medium-heat setting.
3. Grease the griddle top with cooking spray.
4. Thread the steak and veggies on the skewers and place on the hot griddle top.
5. Cook for almost 3-5 minutes per side.
6. Serve warm.

Per Serving:
Calories: 255 | Fat: 13.3g | Carbohydrates: 28g | Fiber: 0.5g | Sugar: 1.2g | Protein: 30.1g | Sodium:271mg

GRILLED SKIRT STEAK WITH GUACAMOLE
Prep Time: 10 mins. | Cook Time: 12 mins. |Serve: 2

- 1 ½ lb. skirt steak
- 2 tsp. cumin powder
- 1 tsp. coriander powder
- 2 garlic cloves, minced
- 4 tbsp. lime juice
- 3 tbsp. olive oil, divided
- 3 avocados, diced
- 2 tbsp. chopped red onion
- 2 tbsp. chopped fresh cilantro
- ½ tsp. crushed red pepper flakes
- 3/4 cup red grape tomatoes, halved
- 3/4 cup yellow grape tomatoes, halved
- kosher salt, to taste
- black pepper, to taste

1. Mash the avocado in a bow.
2. Stir in onion, cilantro, red pepper flakes, and salt in a bowl.
3. Season the steak with black pepper, salt, cumin, coriander, lime juice and garlic.
4. Preheat your outdoor Griddle by turning all its burner's knob to medium-heat setting.
5. Grease the griddle top with cooking spray.
6. Place the steak and tomatoes on the hot griddle top.
7. Cook for almost 6 minutes per side.
8. Serve the steaks with guacamole and tomatoes.

Per Serving:
Calories: 169| Fat: 8.4g | Carbohydrates: 25g | Fiber: 1.4g | Sugar: 3.6g | Protein: 17.1g | Sodium: 222mg

JAMAICAN JERK STEAK TACOS
Prep Time: 15 mins. | Cook Time: 22mins. | Serves: 4

- FOR THE JERK SEASONING
- 1 tbsp. garlic powder
- 1 tbsp. dried Italian blend seasoning
- 2 tsp. sugar
- 2 tsp. kosher salt, to taste
- 2 tsp. onion powder
- 1 tsp. ground allspice
- 1 tsp. crushed red pepper flakes
- 1 tsp. cayenne pepper

- ✓ 1 tsp. smoked paprika
- ✓ ½ tsp. black pepper
- ✓ ¼ tsp. ground cinnamon
- ✓ FOR THE TACOS
- ✓ 2 tbsp. jerk seasoning
- ✓ ¼ cup plus 2 tbsp. canola oil, divided
- ✓ 1 ½ lb. flank or skirt steak
- ✓ 10 small (taco-sized) flour tortillas
- ✓ 1 cup diced pineapple
- ✓ ½ cup diced onion
- ✓ ¼ cup chopped cilantro
- ✓ Juice of ½ lime, plus lime wedges for serving
- ✓ ¼ tsp. kosher salt, to taste
- ✓ 1 avocado, sliced
- ✓ Crumbled cotija cheese, for serving

1. Mix all the jerk seasoning ingredients in a bowl.
2. Season the steak with 2 tbsp. jerk seasoning.
3. Preheat your outdoor Griddle by turning all its burner's knob to medium-heat setting.
4. Grease the griddle top with oil.
5. Place the steak on the hot griddle top.
6. Cook for almost 6 minutes per side.
7. Add pineapple and onion to the griddle and cook for 5 minutes.
8. Slice the steak and divide in the tortillas.
9. Top them with rest of the ingredients.
10. Serve warm.

Per Serving:
Calories: 285 | Fat: 17.5g | Carbohydrates: 25g | Fiber: 3.5g | Sugar: 3g | Protein: 23.5g | Sodium: 152mg

STEAK TACO ON A STICK

Prep Time: 10 mins. | Cook Time: 15 mins. | Serve: 4

- ✓ Marinade:
- ✓ 2 garlic cloves, minced
- ✓ ½ jalapeño, chopped
- ✓ 1 cup chopped fresh cilantro
- ✓ 1 tbsp. ground cumin
- ✓ 1/3 cup lime juice
- ✓ ¼ cup vegetable oil
- ✓ ½ tsp. kosher salt, to taste
- ✓ Skewers
- ✓ 3/4 lb. sirloin steak, cut into 1" pieces
- ✓ 1 avocado, cut into chunks
- ✓ 2 ears corn, sliced into 1" thick pieces
- ✓ 1 small red onion, cut into 1" pieces
- ✓ 2 flour tortillas, cut into triangles
- ✓ Hot sauce, for serving
- ✓ Lime wedges, for serving

1. Mix the marinade ingredients in a bowl.
2. Season the steak with half of the marinade to coat well.
3. Mix the rest of the ingredients with remaining marinade.
4. Preheat your outdoor Griddle by turning all its burner's knob to medium-heat setting.
5. Thread the steak and rest of the ingredients on the skewers alternately.
6. Grease the griddle top with cooking spray.
7. Place the skewers on the hot griddle top.
8. Cook for almost 15 minutes while turning every 5 minutes.
9. Serve warm.

Per Serving:
Calories: 226 | Fat: 6.8g | Carbohydrates: 13g | Fiber: 0.3g | Sugar: 0g | Protein: 37.5g | Sodium: 79mg

GRILLED FLANK STEAK WITH POTATO

Prep Time: 10 mins. | Cook Time: 20 mins. | Serve: 2

- ✓ 1 ½ lb. small new potatoes, halved
- ✓ ¼ cup chopped chives
- ✓ 1 tbsp. Grainy mustard
- ✓ 1 tbsp. apple cider vinegar
- ✓ 3 tbsp. olive oil, divided
- ✓ kosher salt, to taste
- ✓ black pepper, to taste
- ✓ 1 ¼ lb. flank steak, cut into 2 pieces
- ✓ 1 tsp. ground coriander

1. Preheat your outdoor Griddle by turning all its burner's knob to medium-heat setting.
2. Grease the griddle top with cooking oil.
3. Season the steak with black pepper, salt, coriander, mustard and vinegar and place on the hot griddle top.
4. Cook for almost 6 minutes per side.
5. Season the potatoes with black pepper and salt.
6. Cook the potatoes for 15-20 minutes while flipping every 5 minutes.
7. Garnish with chives.
8. Serve warm.

Per Serving:
Calories: 412 | Fat: 17.5g | Carbohydrates: 13g | Fiber: 0.1g | Sugar: 0g | Protein: 52.4g | Sodium: 156mg

RIB-EYE STEAK WITH GRILLED CORN SALAD
Prep Time: 10 mins. | Cook Time: 16 mins. | Serve: 2

- 2 (10- to 12-oz.) boneless rib-eye steaks
- kosher salt, to taste
- black pepper, to taste
- 2 tbsp. butter
- FOR THE GRILLED CORN SALAD
- 2 ears of corn, husked
- ½ small red onion, chopped
- 1 large tomato, chopped
- 1 tsp. minced serrano chile
- Juice and zest of 1 lime
- 1 cup chopped cilantro

1. Preheat your outdoor Griddle by turning all its burner's knob to medium-heat setting.
2. Grease the griddle top with cooking spray.
3. Place the corn on the hot griddle top.
4. Cook for almost 3 minutes per side.
5. Cut the corn kernels and transfer to a bowl.
6. Stir in rest of the salad ingredients ten mix well.
7. Season the steak with black pepper, salt and butter.
8. Sear the steak on the griddle for 5 minutes per side.
9. Serve warm.

Per Serving:
Calories: 244 | Fat: 12.5g | Carbohydrates: 23g | Fiber: 1.5g | Sugar: 2.9g | Protein: 27g | Sodium: 220mg

BASIL GROUND BEEF
Prep Time: 10 mins. | Cook Time: 10 mins. | Serve: 2

- ½ tbsp. olive oil
- ¼ of onion, chopped
- ½ of garlic clove, minced
- ½ tsp. fresh ginger, minced
- ¼ lb. lean ground beef
- 1 tbsp. fresh basil leaves
- Salt and black pepper, to taste

1. Preheat your outdoor Griddle by turning all its burner's knob to medium-heat setting.
2. Grease the griddle top with cooking spray.
3. Add beef and rest of the ingredients on the griddle top then sauté for 10 minutes.
4. Serve warm.

Per Serving:
Calories: 285 | Fat: 12.5g | Carbohydrates: 3.1g | Fiber: 0.5g | Sugar: 1.2g | Protein: 34.8g | Sodium: 231mg

GROUND BEEF WITH CABBAGE
Prep Time: 10 mins. | Cook Time: 10 mins. | Serve: 1

- ¼ tbsp. sesame oil
- ¼ lb. lean ground beef
- ¼ tbsp. fresh ginger, minced1 garlic clove, minced
- 4 oz. cabbage, chopped
- 1 tbsp. low-sodium soy sauce
- ¼ tbsp. balsamic vinegar

1. Preheat your outdoor Griddle by turning all its burner's knob to medium-heat setting.
2. Grease the griddle top with cooking spray.
3. Add beef and rest of the ingredients on the griddle top then sauté for 10 minutes.
4. Serve warm.

Per Serving:

Calories: 274 | Fat: 10.5g | Carbohydrates: 11g | Fiber: 2.3g | Sugar: 3.3g | Protein: 36.5g | Sodium:465mg

KALE BEEF
Prep Time: 10 mins. | Cook Time: 10 mins. | Serve: 1

- ¼ lb. lean ground beef
- ½ tbsp. olive oil
- ¼ of small onion, chopped
- 1 garlic clove, minced
- ¼ cup fresh kale, chopped
- 2-3 tbsp. low-sodium beef broth
- ¼ tbsp. fresh lemon juice
- tsp. fresh parsley, chopped

1. Mix ground beef with onion and rest of the ingredients in a bowl.
2. Preheat your outdoor Griddle by turning all its burner's knob to medium-heat setting.
3. Grease the griddle top with cooking spray.
4. Spread the beef on the hot griddle top.
5. Stir and for almost 10 minutes.
6. Serve warm.

Per Serving:

Calories: 295 | Fat: 14.3g | Carbohydrates: 24g | Fiber: 0.8g | Sugar: 1.2g | Protein: 36g | Sodium: 133mg

GROUND BEEF WITH VEGGIES

Prep Time: 10 mins. | Cook Time: 15 mins. | Serve: 1

- ½ tbsp. olive oil
- ¼ of small onion, chopped
- ½ garlic clove, minced
- Salt and black pepper, to taste
- ¼ lb. lean ground beef
- 2 oz. fresh spinach
- ¼ tsp. dried oregano
- ¼ tsp. dried parsley
- tbsp. olives, pitted and sliced

1. Mix ground beef with onion and rest of the ingredients in a bowl.
2. Preheat your outdoor Griddle by turning all its burner's knob to medium-heat setting.
3. Grease the griddle top with cooking spray.
4. Spread the beef on the hot griddle top.
5. Stir and for almost 15 minutes.
6. Serve warm.

Per Serving:
Calories: 314 | Fat: 16.3g | Carbohydrates: 25g | Fiber: 2.4g | Sugar: 1g | Protein: 36.5g | Sodium: 265mg

GROUND BEEF WITH MUSHROOMS

Prep Time: 10 mins. | Cook Time: 15 mins. | Serve: 1

- ¼ lb. lean ground beef
- ½ tbsp. olive oil
- 1 garlic clove, minced
- ¼ of small onion, chopped
- 1/3 cup fresh mushrooms, sliced
- ½ tbsp. fresh basil
- tbsp. low-sodium beef broth
- ½ tbsp. fresh lemon juice
- 1 tsp. fresh parsley, chopped

1. Preheat your outdoor Griddle by turning all its burner's knob to medium-heat setting.
2. Grease the griddle top with cooking spray.
3. Add beef and rest of the ingredients on the hot griddle top.
4. Cook for almost 15 minutes.
5. Serve warm.

Per Serving:
Calories: 290 | Fat: 14.3g | Carbohydrates: 3.8g | Fiber: 0.8g | Sugar: 1.3g | Protein: 36g | Sodium: 155mg

SPICED BEEF MEATBALLS

Prep Time: 10 mins. | Cook Time: 10 mins. | Serve: 2

- ¼ lb. ground beef
- ¼ tbsp. olive oil
- ¼ tsp. dehydrated onion flakes, crushed
- 1/8 tsp. granulated garlic
- Pinch of ground cumin
- Pinch of red pepper flakes, crushed
- Salt, to taste

1. Mix ground beef with onion flakes, garlic powder, cumin and red pepper flakes in a bowl.
2. Make 1-2 inches meatballs out of this mixture.
3. Preheat your outdoor Griddle by turning all its burner's knob to medium-heat setting.
4. Grease the griddle top with cooking spray.
5. Place the meatballs on the hot griddle top.
6. Cook for almost 5 minutes per side.
7. Serve warm.

Per Serving:
Calories: 245 | Fat: 10.5g | Carbohydrates: 18g | Fiber: 0.3g | Sugar: 0.3g | Protein: 32.4g | Sodium: 230mg

SESAME-GINGER BEEF

Prep Time: 10 mins. | Cook Time: 12 mins. | Serve: 2

- 1 lb. skirt steak, sliced into ¼" strips
- kosher salt, to taste
- black pepper, to taste
- 3 tbsp. cornstarch
- 1 tsp. plus 1 tbsp. canola oil, divided
- 1 lb. green beans, trimmed
- 3 garlic cloves, minced
- 3" piece of ginger, peeled and grated
- ¼ cup soy sauce
- 1 tbsp. rice wine vinegar
- 3 tbsp. sugar
- 2 green onions, chopped
- 1 tbsp. sesame seeds

1. Preheat your outdoor Griddle by turning all its burner's knob to medium-heat setting.

2. Grease the griddle top with cooking spray.
3. Season the beef with black pepper and salt and place it on the hot griddle top.
4. Cook for almost 6 minutes per side.
5. Meanwhile, mix rest Serve warm.

Per Serving:
Calories: 262 | Fat: 12.5g | Carbohydrates: 0g | Fiber: 0g | Sugar: 0g | Protein: 34.4g | Sodium: 225mg

GRILLED STEAK SKEWERS WITH CHIMICHURRI
Prep Time: 10 mins. | Cook Time: 12 mins. |Serve: 2

- Chimichurri
- 1/3 cup Fresh basil
- 1/3 cup fresh cilantro
- 1/3 cup fresh parsley
- 1 tbsp. red wine vinegar
- Juice of ½ lemon
- 1 Garlic clove, minced
- 1 shallot, minced
- ½ tsp. crushed red pepper flakes
- Skewers
- ½ cup olive oil, divided
- kosher salt, to taste
- black pepper, to taste
- 1 red onion, cut into 1 ½" chunks
- 1 red pepper, cut into 1 ½" pieces
- 1 orange pepper, cut into 1 ½" pieces
- 1 yellow pepper, cut into 1 ½" pieces
- 1 ½ lb. sirloin steak, cut into 1 ½" chunks

1. Puree all chimichurri ingredients in a blender until smooth.
2. Season the steak with this sauce and thread with veggies alternately on the skewers.
3. Preheat your outdoor Griddle by turning all its burner's knob to medium-heat setting.
4. Grease the griddle top with cooking spray.
5. the skewers on the hot griddle top.
6. Cook for almost 6 minutes per side.
7. Serve warm with chimichurri sauce.

Per Serving:
Calories: 282 | Fat: 12.5g | Carbohydrates: 0g | Fiber: 0g | Sugar: 0g | Protein: 38.4g | Sodium: 255mg

STEAK WITH ONIONS AND POLENTA
Prep Time: 5 mins. | Cook Time: 19 mins. |Serve: 2

- 1 head broccoli, cut into florets
- kosher salt, to taste
- black pepper, to taste
- 1 ½ cup polenta, cooked
- 3 tbsp. butter
- 1 small red onion, sliced into half-moons
- 2 tbsp. brown sugar
- ¼ cup balsamic vinegar
- 1 ¼ lb. skirt steak

1. Preheat your outdoor Griddle by turning all its burner's knob to medium-heat setting.
2. Grease the griddle top with butter.
3. Season the steak, broccoli and onion with black pepper, salt, and vinegar and place them on the hot griddle top.
4. Cook steaks for almost 6 minutes per side.
5. Sauté broccoli for 7 minutes and cook onion until caramelized
6. Serve steak with the veggies and polenta.

Per Serving:
Calories: 324 | Fat: 15.1g | Carbohydrates: 10g |Fiber: 0.1g | Sugar: 0g | Protein: 43.5g | Sodium:246mg

BEEF BURGER PATTIES
Prep Time: 10 mins. | Cook Time: 10 mins. |Serve: 4

- 2 lbs. ground beef
- 2 tbsp. Worcestershire sauce
- ¾ cup onion, chopped
- ½ tsp. black pepper
- ½ tsp. salt

1. In a suitable mixing bowl, mix well all of the ingredients and stir until well blended
2. Preheat your outdoor Griddle by turning all its burner's knob to medium-heat setting.
3. Grease the griddle top with cooking spray.
4. Form patties from the mixture and cook for 5 minutes per side on the hot griddle top.
5. Enjoy.

Per Serving:
Calories: 284 | Fat: 14.5g | Carbohydrates: 15g |Fiber: 0.3g | Sugar: 0.3g | Protein: 33.3g | Sodium:246mg

BUFFALO FILET MIGNON
Prep Time: 5 mins. | Cook Time: 12 mins. |Serve: 4

- ✓ 4 (6 oz.) beef filets
- ✓ 1 tsp. garlic salt
- ✓ Italian olive oil
- ✓ 2 Roma tomatoes, sliced
- ✓ 4 oz. fresh buffalo mozzarella, cut into four slices
- ✓ 8 fresh basil leaves
- ✓ 1 tbsp. balsamic vinegar glaze, for drizzling
- ✓ ½ tsp. sea salt, to taste
- ✓ ½ tsp. fresh ground pepper

1. brush each beef fillet with olive oil on all sides and season with garlic salt.
2. Preheat your outdoor Griddle by turning all its burner's knob to medium-heat setting.
3. Grease the griddle top with cooking spray.
4. Place the steaks on the hot griddle top, and cook for 5 minutes.
5. Flip, and cook for an additional 5 minutes; top each with a mozzarella slice then cook for 2 minutes.
6. Place a few tomato slices and 2 basil leaves on top of each one.
7. Drizzle with salt, balsamic vinegar, and black pepper, and serve.

Per Serving:
Calories: 144 | Fat: 4g | Carbohydrates: 11g | Fiber: 0.4g | Sugar: 0.1g | Protein: 24.4g | Sodium: 215mg

COFFEE CRUSTED STEAK

Prep Time: 10 mins. | Cook Time: 10 mins. | Serve: 4

- ✓ ¼ cup coffee beans, ground
- ✓ ¼ cup dark brown sugar, firmly packed
- ✓ 1½ tsp. sea salt
- ✓ ⅛ tsp. ground cinnamon
- ✓ Pinch cayenne pepper
- ✓ 2½ lbs. skirt steak, diced
- ✓ 1 tbsp. olive oil

1. To make the rub, mix well the brown sugar, ground coffee beans, cinnamon, salt, and cayenne pepper in a bowl.
2. Rub the steak with oil and spice rub.
3. Preheat your outdoor Griddle by turning all its burner's knob to medium-heat setting.
4. Grease the griddle top with cooking spray.
5. Sear the steak on the hot griddle top for 5 minutes per side.
6. Slice and serve.

Per Serving:
Calories: 257 | Fat: 10.5g | Carbohydrates: 15g | Fiber: 0.1g | Sugar: 0.1g | Protein: 36.1g | Sodium:88mg

ZUCCHINI BEEF SKEWERS

Prep Time: 10 mins. | Cook Time: 8 mins. | Serve: 2

- ✓ 1 lb. beef sirloin tips
- ✓ 1 zucchini, cut into chunks
- ✓ For marinade:
- ✓ ¼ cup olive oil
- ✓ 1 jalapeno pepper
- ✓ ½ tbsp. lime juice
- ✓ 1½ tbsp. red wine vinegar
- ✓ 1 tsp. dried oregano
- ✓ 2 garlic cloves
- ✓ 1 cup cilantro

1. In a blender, mix well all marinade ingredients and blend until smooth.
2. Into the mixing bowl, pour the mixed mixture.
3. Mix in the beef tips and set aside for 30 minutes to marinate.
4. Preheat your outdoor Griddle by turning all its burner's knob to medium-heat setting.
5. Grease the griddle top with cooking spray.
6. Thread the skewers with marinated meat tips and zucchini slices alternately.
7. Cook skewers for 7-8 minutes on the hot griddle top.
8. Serve and enjoy.

Per Serving:
Calories: 285 | Fat: 17.5g | Carbohydrates: 4g | Fiber: 1.3g | Sugar: 1.5g | Protein: 25.4g | Sodium:205mg

SIMPLE JUICY NY STRIP STEAK

Prep Time: 10 mins. | Cook Time: 10 mins. | Serve: 2

- ✓ 1 (8 oz. / 227-g) NY strip steak
- ✓ 1 tbsp. olive oil
- ✓ ¼ tsp. sea salt
- ✓ ¼ tsp. fresh black pepper

1. Preheat your outdoor Griddle by turning all its burner's knob to medium-heat setting.
2. Grease the griddle top with cooking spray.
3. Pour the egg mixture onto the hot griddle top
4. Rub the steak with salt and black pepper on all sides
5. Cook the steak on the hot griddle top for 4–5

minutes per side.
6. Slice and serve warm.

Per Serving:
Calories: 172 | Fat: 4.3g | Carbohydrates: 23g | Fiber: 1.5g | Sugar: 3.3g | Protein: 26g | Sodium: 205mg

FLANK STEAK GYROS

Prep Time: 10 mins. | Cook Time: 10 mins. | Serve: 2

- 1 lb. flank steak
- 1 white onion, sliced
- 1 roma tomato, sliced
- 1 cucumber, peeled and sliced
- ¼ cup crumbled feta cheese
- 4 6-inch pita pockets
- For the marinade:
- ¼ cup olive oil
- 1 tsp. dried oregano
- 1 tsp. balsamic vinegar
- 1 tsp. garlic powder
- ½ tsp. salt and black pepper
- For the sauce:
- 1 cup plain yogurt
- 2 tbsp. fresh dill, chopped
- 1 tsp. garlic, minced
- 2 tbsp. lemon juice

1. Against the grain, cut the flank steak into thin strips.
2. In a large sealable plastic bag, mix well the marinade ingredients.
3. Add the sliced meat, seal, and shake to coat.
4. Marinate for almost 2 hours or overnight in the refrigerator.
5. Preheat your outdoor Griddle by turning all its burner's knob to medium-heat setting.
6. Grease the griddle top with cooking spray.
7. In a suitable mixing bowl, mix well the sauce ingredients and set aside.
8. Spritz the pitas with water, wrap them in foil, and warm them on the griddle top.
9. Drizzle olive oil on the hot griddle top.
10. Place the marinated flank steak on the griddle. Cook for 5 minutes per side,
11. Take the pita bread and slice them in half.
12. Place pitas on plates and fill with tomato, cucumber, onions, and beef.
13. Drizzle some yoghurt sauce over the meat and sprinkle with feta cheese.
14. Serve warm.

Per Serving:
Calories: 212 | Fat: 10.5g | Carbohydrates: 14g | Fiber: 0.3g | Sugar: 0.6g | Protein: 26g | Sodium: 215mg

SOY BEEF WITH VEGETABLES

Prep Time: 10 mins. | Cook Time: 18 mins. | Serve: 2

- Steak:
- 2(1 lb.) sirloin steaks
- 1 tbsp. garlic powder
- 4 tbsp. soy sauce
- 1 white onion, sliced
- 3 zucchinis, sliced
- 2 cups snap peas
- 4 tbsp. vegetable oil
- 3 tbsp. butter
- ½ tsp. salt and black pepper

1. Sprinkle salt, garlic powder and pepper over the steak.
2. Preheat your outdoor Griddle by turning all its burner's knob to medium-heat setting.
3. Grease the griddle top with butter.
4. Add the zucchini, onion rings, salt, black pepper and snap peas to the griddle and cook for 7 minutes.
5. Cook the steaks on the hot griddle top for 2 minutes per side.
6. Top with butter, and season with soy sauce. Continue to cook for another 4 minutes.
7. Serve warm.

Per Serving:
Calories: 289| Fat: 17.5g | Carbohydrates: 24g | Fiber: 1.4g | Sugar: 1.8g | Protein: 27.1g | Sodium:219mg

PINEAPPLE BEEF PATTIES

Prep Time: 10 mins. | Cook Time: 8 mins. | Serves: 2

- 1¼ lbs. ground beef
- 2 pineapple slices, chopped
- ¼ tsp. black pepper
- 1 garlic clove, minced
- 1 tsp. ginger, grated
- ¼ cup green onions, chopped
- ¼ cup soy sauce
- ¼ tsp. salt

1. In a suitable mixing bowl, mix well all of the ingredients and stir until well blended.
2. Preheat your outdoor Griddle by turning all its

burner's knob to medium-heat setting.
3. Grease the griddle top with cooking spray.
4. Form patties from the mixture and cook for 4 minutes per side on the hot griddle top.
5. Serve and enjoy.

Per Serving:

Calories: 192 | Fat: 6.5g | Carbohydrates: 28g | Fiber: 1.5g | Sugar: 2.2g | Protein: 26.3g | Sodium:163mg

SMOKED PAPRIKA BRISKET
Prep Time: 10 mins. | Cook Time: 6 hrs.|Serve: 8

- 1 (4 ½ lbs.) flat cut beef brisket (3 inches thick)
- For the rub:
- 1 tbsp. sea salt
- 1 tbsp. dark brown sugar
- 2 tsp. smoked paprika
- 2 tsp. chili powder
- 1 tsp. garlic powder
- 1 tsp. onion powder
- 1 tsp. black pepper
- 1 tsp. mesquite liquid smoke

1. In a small mixing dish, mix well the rub ingredients.
2. Rinse the brisket and pat it dry before rubbing it with the coffee mixture.
3. Preheat your outdoor Griddle by turning all its burner's knob to high-heat setting.
4. Grease the griddle top with cooking spray.
5. Sear for 3 to 5 minutes per side on high heat until charred.
6. Reduce to a low heat setting and cook for 6 hours.
7. Flip the brisket every 30 minutes.
8. Slice the brisket across the grain and serve.

Per Serving:
Calories: 305 | Fat: 15.5g | Carbohydrates: 24g |Fiber: 1.8g | Sugar: 2.6g | Protein: 34.8g | Sodium:285mg

STEAK AU POIVRE
Prep Time: 10 mins. | Cook Time: 12 mins. |Serve: 2

- 2 tbsp. whole black peppercorns
- 2 (4-oz.) filet mignon
- Kosher salt, to taste
- 1 tbsp. vegetable oil
- 2 tbsp. unsalted butter
- 1 small shallot, minced
- 2 tbsp. cognac or brandy
- 2 garlic cloves, minced
- 2 tsp. fresh thyme leaves
- ½ cup heavy cream

1. Sauté shallot with butter in a saucepan for 5 minutes.
2. Stir in garlic, thyme, cream and cognac then cook to a boil with stirring.
3. Season the mignon with salt
4. Preheat your outdoor Griddle by turning all its burner's knob to medium-heat setting.
5. Grease the griddle top with cooking oil.
6. Place the mignon on the hot griddle top.
7. Cook for almost 6 minutes per side.
8. Serve warm with creamy sauce on top.

Per Serving:
Calories: 216 | Fat: 10.3g | Carbohydrates: 23g |Fiber: 1.5g | Sugar: 2.9g | Protein: 25.3g | Sodium:228mg

REVERSE SEAR STEAK
Prep Time: 10 mins. | Cook Time: 12 mins. |Serve: 1

- 1 2"-thick rib eye steak (14 oz.)
- Kosher salt, to taste
- black pepper, to taste
- Canola oil
- 2 tbsp. butter
- 3 garlic cloves, crushed
- 2 sprigs rosemary
- Flaky sea salt

1. Preheat your outdoor Griddle by turning all its burner's knob to medium-heat setting.
2. Grease the griddle top with cooking spray.
3. Season the steak with rest of the ingredients and place on the hot griddle top.
4. Cook for almost 6 minutes per side.
5. Serve warm.

Per Serving:
Calories: 237 | Fat: 13g | Carbohydrates: 24g | Fiber: 2.5g | Sugar: 2.1g | Protein: 27.3g | Sodium:167mg

SMOTHERED CUBE STEAK
Prep Time: 10 mins. | Cook Time: 15 mins. |Serve: 4

- 2 lb. cube steak (4 pieces)
- 2 tsp. kosher salt, to taste

- 1 ½ tsp. black pepper
- 1 cup all-purpose flour
- 2 tsp. garlic powder
- 1 tsp. vegetable oil
- 3 tbsp. butter
- 1 yellow onion, sliced
- 1 (1-oz.) packet onion soup mix
- 1 ½ cup water

1. Preheat your outdoor Griddle by turning all its burner's knob to medium-heat setting.
2. Grease the griddle top with cooking oil.
3. Toss steak with black pepper, salt, garlic powder and coat with flour and place on the hot griddle top.
4. Cook for almost 3 minutes per side.
5. Sauté onion with butter in a pan for 3 minutes.
6. Stir in water and onion soup mix.
7. Mix well until smooth then cook for 5 minutes until it thickens.
8. Toss in seared steaks and mix well.
9. Serve warm.

Per Serving:
Calories: 300 | Fat: 17.5g | Carbohydrates: 6g | Fiber: 2.3g | Sugar: 1.6g | Protein: 26.8g | Sodium:157mg

Calories: 155 | Fat: 7.5g | Carbohydrates: 21g | Fiber: 0.4g | Sugar: 3.3g | Protein: 15.4g | Sodium:165mg

SEARED ROUND STEAK

Prep Time: 10 mins. | Cook Time: 12 mins. |Serve: 1

- 1 1"-thick round steak (10 oz.)
- Kosher salt, to taste
- black pepper, to taste
- ¼ cup olive oil
- 2 tbsp. red wine vinegar
- ½ tsp. crushed red pepper flakes
- 3/4 tsp. dried oregano
- 3 garlic cloves, divided
- 2 tbsp. vegetable oil
- 2 tbsp. butter
- 2 sprigs rosemary
- Flaky sea salt

1. Preheat your outdoor Griddle by turning all its burner's knob to medium-heat setting.
2. Grease the griddle top with cooking spray.
3. Season the steak with rest of the ingredients and place on the hot griddle top.
4. Cook for almost 6 minutes per side.
5. Serve warm.

Per Serving:

PORK RECIPES

PORK CHOPS AND HERB APPLE COMPOTE

Prep Time: 10 mins. | Cook Time: 28 mins. |Serve: 4

- 4 bone-in pork chops
- 2 honey crisp apples, peeled, chopped
- ⅓ cup orange juice
- 1 tsp. chopped fresh rosemary
- 1 tsp. chopped fresh sage
- ½ tsp. sea salt
- ½ tsp. black pepper

1. In a suitable saucepan, mix well the herbs, apples, and orange juice and cook for 12 minutes.
2. Preheat your outdoor Griddle by turning all its burner's knob to medium-heat setting.
3. Grease the griddle top with cooking spray.
4. Sprinkle salt and black pepper over the pork chops.
5. Place the pork chop on the hot griddle top and cook for 4 minutes per side.
6. Slice and serve with apple compote on top!

Per Serving:
Calories: 204 | Fat: 10g | Carbohydrates: 28g | Fiber: 0.8g | Sugar: 1.4g | Protein: 24.4g | Sodium:216mg

PEPPER HONEY VINEGAR PORK CHOPS

Prep Time: 10 mins. | Cook Time: 10 mins. |Serve: 6

- 6 pork chops, boneless
- 1 tbsp. vinegar
- 2 tbsp. olive oil
- 1 tbsp. soy sauce
- ¼ cup honey
- ½ tsp. black pepper
- ½ tsp. salt

1. Mix well the pork chops and the remaining ingredients in a zip-lock bag and mix thoroughly.
2. Shake the sealed bag well before placing it in the refrigerator for 2 hours.
3. Preheat your outdoor Griddle by turning all its burner's knob to medium-heat setting.
4. Grease the griddle top with cooking spray.
5. Pour the egg mixture onto the hot griddle top
6. Cook pork chops for 5 minutes per side on the hot griddle top.
7. Serve and enjoy.

Per Serving:
Calories: 196 | Fat: 9.3g | Carbohydrates: 5g | Fiber: 1g | Sugar: 1.7g | Protein: 32.3g | Sodium: 12mg

COUNTRY PORK RIBS

Prep Time: 10 mins. | Cook Time: 2 hrs. 15 mins. | Serve: 6

- 3 lbs. country-style pork ribs
- 1 cup ketchup
- ½ cup water
- ¼ cup onion, chopped
- ¼ cup cider vinegar
- ¼ cup light molasses
- 2 tbsp. Worcestershire sauce
- 2 tsp. chili powder
- 2 garlic cloves, minced

1. In a suitable saucepan, mix well water, ketchup, vinegar, onion, Worcestershire sauce, chili powder, and garlic; bring to a boil.
2. Cook for almost 10 to 15 minutes with occasional stirring.
3. Preheat your outdoor Griddle by turning all its burner's knob to medium-heat setting.
4. Grease the griddle top with cooking spray.
5. Pour the egg mixture onto the hot griddle top
6. Place the ribs on the hot griddle top, and cook for ½ to 2 hours, brushing with sauce.
7. Toss with the remaining sauce and serve.

Per Serving:
Calories: 226| Fat: 11g | Carbohydrates: 28g | Fiber: 1.4g | Sugar: 2.1g | Protein: 26.8g | Sodium: 206mg

GARLIC CAYENNE PORK CHOPS

Prep Time: 15 mins. | Cook Time: 10 mins. | Serve: 4

- 4 pork chops
- 1 tsp. garlic, minced
- ½ tsp. black pepper
- 2 tbsp. Worcestershire sauce
- ¼ cup soy sauce
- ¼ cup olive oil
- ¼ tsp. cayenne
- ½ tsp. salt

1. In a suitable mixing dish, mix well the pork chops and the remaining ingredients.
2. Refrigerate 2-3 hours for marination.
3. Preheat your outdoor Griddle by turning all its burner's knob to medium-heat setting.
4. Grease the griddle top with cooking spray.
5. Place pork chops on the hot griddle top and cook for 3-5 minutes per side.
6. Serve and enjoy.

Per Serving:
Calories: 327 | Fat: 13.5g | Carbohydrates: 10.1g | Fiber: 3.3g | Sugar: 4.3g | Protein: 34.4g | Sodium: 125mg

PEPPER GARLIC SOY PORK CHOPS

Prep Time: 10 mins. | Cook Time: 8 mins. | Serve: 4

- 4 to 6 pork chops
- 4 garlic cloves, chopped
- ½ cup olive oil
- ½ cup soy sauce
- ½ tsp. garlic powder
- ½ tsp. salt
- ½ black pepper
- ¼ cup butter

1. Mix well the garlic, olive oil, soy sauce, and garlic powder in a big zipper lock bag.
2. Mix pork chops with the marinade to coat.
3. Keep them aside for 30 minutes for marination.
4. Preheat your outdoor Griddle by turning all its burner's knob to medium-heat setting.
5. Grease the griddle top with 2 tbsp. olive oil and 2 tbsp. butter.
6. Place the chops on the hot griddle top and cook the chops for 4 minutes per side.
7. Serve.

Per Serving:
Calories: 247 | Fat: 10.5g | Carbohydrates: 13g | Fiber: 0.1g | Sugar: 0g | Protein: 33.3g | Sodium: 295mg

MONTREAL PORK CHOPS

Prep Time: 10 mins. | Cook Time: 14 mins. | Serve: 4

- 4 pork chops
- 2 tsp. Montreal marinade
- 2 tbsp. soy sauce
- ¼ cup olive oil

1. Toss the pork chops with the remaining ingredients in a suitable mixing bowl and refrigerate for 6 hours.
2. Preheat your outdoor Griddle by turning all its burner's knob to medium-heat setting.
3. Grease the griddle top with cooking spray.
4. Cook pork chops on the hot griddle top for 5-7 minutes per side.
5. Serve and enjoy.

Per Serving:
Calories: 222 | Fat: 9.5g | Carbohydrates: 15g | Fiber: 1.3g | Sugar: 4.3g | Protein: 24.4g | Sodium: 215mg

HONEY PORK CHOPS WITH SOY

Prep Time: 10 mins. | Cook Time: 10 mins. | Serve: 6

- 6 (4 oz.) boneless pork chops
- ¼ cup organic honey
- 1 to 2 tbsp. soy sauce
- 2 tbsp. olive oil
- 1 tbsp. rice mirin

1. Mix well the soy sauce, honey, oil, and white vinegar until blended.
2. In a big sealable plastic bag, mix well the sauce and

pork chops and refrigerate for 1 hour.
3. Preheat your outdoor Griddle by turning all its burner's knob to medium-heat setting.
4. Grease the griddle top with cooking spray.
5. Sear the pork chop for 4 to 5 minutes per side.
6. Serve and enjoy.

Per Serving:
Calories: 284 | Fat: 17.5g | Carbohydrates: 4g | Fiber: 1.3g | Sugar: 2g | Protein: 26.5g | Sodium:206mg

SESAME BOSTON BUTT PORK
Prep Time: 10 mins. | Cook Time: 8 mins. |Serve: 10

- 1 (5 lbs.) Boston butt pork
- For the marinade:
- 2 tbsp. garlic, minced
- 1 large piece ginger, peeled and chopped
- 1 cup hoisin sauce
- ¾ cup fish sauce
- ⅔ cup honey
- ⅔ cup Shaoxing
- ½ cup chili oil
- ⅓ cup oyster sauce
- ⅓ cup sesame oil
- For the glaze:
- ¾ cup dark brown sugar
- 1 tbsp. light molasses

1. In a blender, puree the marinade, reserving 1 ½ cup for the glaze, then cover and chill.
2. Pour the remaining marinade into a large plastic bag that can be sealed.
3. Place the pork shoulder in the bag and marinate for 8 hours in the refrigerator.
4. Remove the pork from the marinade and drain any excess.
5. Whisk the glaze ingredients, reserving the marinade, until the sugar is dissolved.
6. Preheat your outdoor Griddle by turning all its burner's knob to medium-heat setting.
7. Grease the griddle top with cooking spray.
8. Sear pork for 4 minutes per side while basting with glaze.
9. Transfer to a cutting board and slice 14" thick against the grain then serve.

Per Serving:
Calories: 280 | Fat: 9.5g | Carbohydrates: 11g | Fiber: 2.3g | Sugar: 4.3g | Protein: 35.4g | Sodium:180mg

GARLIC FLANK STEAK WITH OREGANO
Prep Time: 10 mins. | Cook Time: 10 mins. |Serve: 2

- 1 lb. flank steak
- 1 white onion, sliced
- 1 Roma tomato, sliced
- 1 cucumber, peeled and sliced
- ¼ cup crumbled feta cheese
- 4 6-inch pita pockets
- For the marinade:
- ¼ cup olive oil
- 1 tsp. dried oregano
- 1 tsp. balsamic vinegar
- 1 tsp. garlic powder
- Salt and black pepper, to taste
- For the sauce:
- 1 cup plain yogurt
- 2 tbsp. fresh dill, chopped
- 1 tsp. garlic, minced
- 2 tbsp. lemon juice

1. Against the grain, cut the flank steak into thin strips.
2. In a suitable sealable plastic bag, mix well the marinade ingredients.
3. Add the sliced meat, seal, and turn to coat.
4. Marinate for 2 hours or overnight in the refrigerator.
5. In a small mixing dish, mix well the sauce ingredients and put aside.
6. Preheat your outdoor Griddle by turning all its burner's knob to medium-heat setting.
7. Grease the griddle top with cooking spray.
8. Spritz the pitas with water, wrap them in foil, and warm them on the griddle top.
9. Remove this meat from the marinade and place it on the griddle.
10. Cook for almost 5 minutes per side until golden.
11. Take the pitas rounds out of the oven and slice them in half.
12. Stuff the pitas with tomato, cucumber, onions, and beef and arrange on plates.
13. Drizzle some yoghurt sauce over the meat and sprinkle with feta cheese.
14. Serve warm

Per Serving:
Calories: 22 | Fat: 14.5g | Carbohydrates: 11g | Fiber: 3.4g | Sugar: 4.3g | Protein: 27.4g | Sodium:225mg

CUBAN PORK CHOPS

Prep Time: 10 mins. | Cook Time: 10 mins. | Serve: 4

- 4 pork chops
- 4 garlic cloves, smashed
- 2 tbsp. olive oil
- ⅓ cup lime juice
- ¼ cup water
- 1 tsp. ground cumin
- Salt and black pepper, to taste

1. Preheat your outdoor Griddle by turning all its burner's knob to medium-heat setting.
2. Grease the griddle top with cooking spray.
3. Cook the pork chops on the hot griddle top until browned on both side.
4. In a suitable mixing bowl, beat the garlic, water, and lime juice until smooth.
5. While the pork chops are cooking, baste them with the lime juice mixture.
6. Garnish with more sauce, salt and black pepper.
7. Serve warm

Per Serving:
Calories: 297 | Fat: 10.5g | Carbohydrates: 3.8g | Fiber: 1.1g | Sugar: 2.3g | Protein: 40.4g | Sodium: 275mg

GARLIC PEPPER PORK CHOPS

Prep Time: 10 mins. | Cook Time: 12 mins. | Serve: 4

- 4 pork chops, boneless
- For rub:
- ½ tsp. ground ginger
- ½ tsp. ground cumin
- 2 tbsp. brown sugar
- ½ tsp. dry mustard
- 1 tsp. black pepper
- 1 tsp. garlic powder
- 1 tbsp. sugar
- 1½ tbsp. paprika

1. In a suitable mixing dish, mix well the pork chops and rub ingredients.
2. Preheat your outdoor Griddle by turning all its burner's knob to medium-heat setting.
3. Grease the griddle top with cooking spray.
4. Cook pork chops for 6 minutes per side on the hot griddle top.
5. Serve and enjoy.

Per Serving:
Calories: 333 | Fat: 17.5g | Carbohydrates: 23g | Fiber: 1.4g | Sugar: 0.8g | Protein: 31.4g | Sodium: 265mg

DIJON PORK MUSHROOMS SKEWERS

Prep Time: 10 mins. | Cook Time: 14 mins. | Serve: 4

- 1½ lbs. pork loin, cut into 1-inch cubes
- 2 cups mushrooms
- 2 cups cherry tomatoes
- 2 cups onion, cut into pieces
- 2 cups bell peppers, cut into pieces
- For marinade:
- ½ cup vinaigrette
- ¼ cup Dijon mustard
- ½ tsp. black pepper
- ½ tsp. salt

1. In a suitable mixing dish, mix well the pork cubes and marinade ingredients; and set aside for 30 minutes.
2. Thread the skewers with mushrooms, marinated pork cubes, tomatoes, onion, and bell peppers alternately.
3. Preheat your outdoor Griddle by turning all its burner's knob to medium-heat setting.
4. Grease the griddle top with cooking spray.
5. Cook the prepared pork skewers for 7 minutes per side on the hot griddle top.
6. Serve and enjoy.

Per Serving:
Calories: 210 | Fat: 7.8g | Carbohydrates: 11g | Fiber: 0g | Sugar: 0g | Protein: 32.1g | Sodium: 225mg

PAPRIKA CINNAMON PORK TENDERLOIN

Prep Time: 10 mins. | Cook Time: 20 mins. | Serve: 4

- 2 (1 lb.) pork tenderloins
- 1 tsp. ground cinnamon
- 1 tsp. ground cilantro
- 1 tsp. ground cumin
- 1 tsp. paprika
- 1 tsp. sea salt
- 2 tbsp. olive oil
- For creamy harissa sauce:
- 1 cup Greek yogurt (8 oz.)
- 1 tbsp. fresh lemon juice
- 1 tbsp. olive oil
- 1 tsp. harissa sauce

✓ 1 garlic clove, minced

1. In a small mixing dish, mix well all of the ingredients for the harissa sauce and set aside.
2. Mix the coriander, cinnamon, paprika, cumin, salt, and olive oil in a suitable mixing bowl.
3. Season the pork tenderloins with the seasonings; cover and refrigerate for 30 minutes.
4. Preheat your outdoor Griddle by turning all its burner's knob to medium-heat setting.
5. Grease the griddle top with cooking spray.
6. Cook tenderloins for 10 minutes per side until browned.
7. Slice and serve with a creamy harissa sauce.

Per Serving:
Calories: 334 | Fat: 17.5g | Carbohydrates: 11g | Fiber: 2.4g | Sugar: 1.5g | Protein: 34.3g | Sodium: 235mg

PORK CHOPS WITH ORANGE MARINADE
Prep Time: 10 mins. | Cook Time: 20 mins. | Serve: 4

✓ 4 ½-inch-thick bone-in pork chops
✓ 3 tbsp. olive oil
✓ Kosher salt, to taste and black pepper
✓ For the marinade:
✓ 1 habanero chili, seeded, chopped fine
✓ 2 garlic cloves, minced
✓ ½ cup fresh orange juice
✓ 2 tbsp. brown sugar
✓ 1 tbsp. apple cider vinegar

1. In a big sealable plastic bag, mix well the marinade ingredients.
2. Use a fork to pierce the pork chops all over, then place them in the bag, seal it, and turn to coat.
3. Marinate for 30 minutes.
4. Pat the pork chops dry after removing them from the marinade.
5. Preheat your outdoor Griddle by turning all its burner's knob to medium-heat setting.
6. Grease the griddle top with cooking spray.
7. Cook for almost 10 minutes per side on the hot griddle top.
8. Serve.

Per Serving:
Calories: 300 | Fat: 14.5g | Carbohydrates: 21g | Fiber: 1.8g | Sugar: 2g | Protein: 31.8g | Sodium: 265mg

THYME GARLIC PORK PATTIES
Prep Time: 10 mins. | Cook Time: 10 mins. | Serve: 2

✓ 1 lb. ground pork
✓ ⅛ tsp. red pepper, crushed
✓ ¾ tsp. black pepper
✓ ½ tsp. onion powder
✓ 1 tsp. garlic powder
✓ ⅛ tsp. ground nutmeg
✓ ½ tsp. dried thyme
✓ ¾ tsp. ground sage
✓ ¾ tsp. fennel seeds
✓ ½ tsp. salt

1. In a suitable mixing bowl, mix well all of the ingredients and stir until well blended.
2. Preheat your outdoor Griddle by turning all its burner's knob to medium-heat setting.
3. Grease the griddle top with cooking spray.
4. Form patties from the mixture and cook for almost 5 minutes per side on the hot griddle top.
5. Serve and enjoy.

Per Serving:
Calories: 202 | Fat: 4.5g | Carbohydrates: 24g | Fiber: 1.4g | Sugar: 2.6g | Protein: 31.4g | Sodium: 265mg

GARLIC MUSTARD PORK CHOPS
Prep Time: 10 mins. | Cook Time: 16 mins. | Serve: 4

✓ 4 pork chops
✓ 1 tsp. dried rosemary
✓ ⅛ tsp. chili flakes
✓ ½ tsp. black pepper
✓ 1 tsp. garlic, minced
✓ 2 tbsp. Dijon mustard
✓ 3 tbsp. olive oil
✓ ½ cup balsamic vinegar
✓ ¾ tsp. salt

1. Place the pork chops in a zip-lock bag with the remaining ingredients.
2. Refrigerate for 4 hours after sealing the bag and shaking it firmly.
3. Preheat your outdoor Griddle by turning all its burner's knob to medium-heat setting.
4. Grease the griddle top with cooking spray.
5. Place the marinated pork chops on the hot griddle top and cook for 6-8 minutes per side.
6. Enjoy.

Per Serving:
Calories: 252 | Fat: 10.5g | Carbohydrates: 11g | Fiber: 3.3g | Sugar: 4.3g | Protein: 27.4g | Sodium:205mg

LEMON PORK TENDERLOIN
Prep Time: 10 mins. | Cook Time: 20 mins. |Serve: 2

- 1 lb. pork tenderloin
- 1 tbsp. olive oil
- 2 tsp. dried oregano
- ¾ tsp. lemon pepper
- 1 tsp. garlic powder
- ¼ cup parmesan cheese, grated
- 3 tbsp. olive tapenade

1. Season the pork tenderloin with olive oil, oregano, lemon pepper, and garlic powder on the working surface.
2. Wrap the pork in a plastic sheet and refrigerate for 1 hour.
3. Slit the tenderloin in half horizontally to spread it like a butterfly.
4. Place the tenderloin on a plastic sheet and spread tapenade and cheese on top.
5. Slowly roll the pork to seal the tapenade inside.
6. Tie together in 2-inch intervals using thread.
7. Preheat your outdoor Griddle by turning all its burner's knob to medium-heat setting.
8. Grease the griddle top with cooking spray.
9. Sear tenderloin on the griddle top for 20 minutes and flip once cooked halfway though.
10. Remove the tenderloin from the griddle and place it on a chopping board.
11. Cover with foil and set aside for 10 minutes.
12. Remove the string and slice the meat into 14-inch thick pieces to serve.

Per Serving:

Calories: 197 | Fat: 9.5g | Carbohydrates: 10g | Fiber: 0.3g | Sugar: 0.4g | Protein: 25.1g | Sodium: 235mg

GRILLED CEVAPI SKEWERS WITH PICKLES
Prep Time: 10 mins. | Cook Time: 10 mins. |Serve: 4

- 12 cevapi sausages
- 2 tbs olive oil
- 8 Lebanese flatbreads
- 2 white onions, cut into wedges

1. Preheat your outdoor Griddle by turning all its burner's knob to medium-heat setting.
2. Grease the griddle top with cooking spray.
3. Place the sausages on the griddle top.
4. Cook for almost 5 minutes per side.
5. Serve warm in flatbread with onion.

Per Serving:
Calories: 205 | Fat: 14.3g | Carbohydrates: 4g | Fiber: 2.1g | Sugar: 0.8g | Protein: 17.3g | Sodium:167mg

PORK AND PINEAPPLE SKEWERS
Prep Time: 10 mins. | Cook Time: 20 mins. |Serve: 6

- 6 boneless pork rashers
- ½ whole pineapple, peeled, diced
- 2 tbs sunflower oil
- 4 spring onions, chopped
- 1/3 cup hoisin sauce
- 1/3 cup rice wine vinegar

1. Mix pork with pineapple and rest of the ingredients in a bowl.
2. Cover and marinate for almost 1 hour in the refrigerator.
3. Sear the pork and pineapple on the hot griddle top.
4. Cook the pineapple for 3-5 minutes per side.
5. Sear the pork spare ribs for 10 minutes per side.
6. Serve warm.

Per Serving:
Calories: 242 | Fat: 12.4g | Carbohydrates: 21g |Fiber: 1.4g | Sugar: 1.7g | Protein: 28.8g | Sodium:133mg

MAPLE CARAMEL PORK BELLY SKEWERS
Prep Time: 10 mins. | Cook Time: 12 mins. |Serve: 6

- 1 cup maple syrup
- 1 tbs black peppercorns
- 2 garlic cloves, chopped
- 1/3 cup fish sauce
- Juice of 3 limes
- 3 lbs. pork belly, skin removed, cut into 2cm cubes
- 1/3 cup toasted cashews, chopped

1. Mix fish sauce, maple syrup, black pepper, and lime juice in a bowl.
2. Thread the pork cubes on the skewers and dip

them in maple sauce.
3. Preheat your outdoor Griddle by turning all its burner's knob to medium-heat setting.
4. Grease the griddle top with cooking spray.
5. Place the skewers on the hot griddle top.
6. Cook for almost 6 minutes per side.
7. Brush the remaining maple mixture over the skewers
8. Drizzle cashews on top.
9. Serve warm.

Per Serving:
Calories: 215 | Fat: 9.3g | Carbohydrates: 28g | Fiber: 1.4g | Sugar: 2.1g | Protein: 27g | Sodium: 300mg

HOT DOG SKEWERS

Prep Time: 10 mins. | Cook Time: 10 mins. | Serve: 2

- SAUCE
- ¼ cup barbecue sauce
- 1 ½ tbsp. ketchup
- 1 tbsp. soy sauce
- 1 tsp. rice wine vinegar
- ½ tsp. chili powder
- FOR SKEWERS
- 1 hot dogs, quartered
- 3 cup pineapple, diced
- 1 red bell pepper, diced
- 1 green bell pepper, diced
- 1 small red onion, diced

1. Thread hot dogs, pineapple, red bell pepper, green bell pepper and red onion on the skewers alternately.
2. Mix all the recipe ingredients for the sauce in a bowl.
3. Preheat your outdoor Griddle by turning all its burner's knob to medium-heat setting.
4. Grease the griddle top with cooking spray.
5. Season the skewers with the sauce and place them on the hot griddle top.
6. Cook for almost 5 minutes per side.
7. Serve warm with remaining sauce.

Per Serving:
Calories: 174 | Fat: 8g | Carbohydrates: 21g | Fiber: 0.8g | Sugar: 1.7g | Protein: 19.8g | Sodium: 245mg

MISO GLAZED PORK FILLET

Prep Time: 10 mins. | Cook Time: 10 mins. | Serves: 1

- 1 lb. lean pork fillet
- 1 tbsp. toasted sesame seeds
- Marinade
- 2 tbsp. white miso paste
- 2 tbsp. honey
- 2 tbsp. Japanese mirin or rice wine vinegar
- 1 tsp. toasted sesame oil
- 1 tbsp. fresh ginger, peeled and grated
- 1 garlic clove, peeled and chopped

1. Mix all the marinade ingredients in a bowl.
2. Add pork, mix well and refrigerate overnight.
3. Preheat your outdoor Griddle by turning all its burner's knob to medium-heat setting.
4. Grease the griddle top with cooking spray.
5. Place the pork on the hot griddle top.
6. Cook for almost 5 minutes per side.
7. Serve warm.

Per Serving:
Calories: 222 | Fat: 7.4g | Carbohydrates: 23g | Fiber: 1.1g | Sugar: 0.2g | Protein: 34.8g | Sodium: 114mg

PORK FILLET SALTIMBOCCA

Prep Time: 10 mins. | Cook Time: 16 mins. | Serves: 4

- 4 pork fillet medallions, trimmed
- 8 sage leaves
- 4 slices Parma ham
- 1 tbsp. olive oil
- 10 1/2 oz. new potatoes, boiled and halved
- 2 tbsp. plain flour
- 1/2 cup marsala wine
- 1/3 cup hot chicken stock
- Juice of ½ lemon
- 10g butter
- To serve:
- sugar snap peas

1. Wrap the pork medallion with the ham and Preheat your outdoor Griddle by turning all its burner's knob to medium-heat setting.
2. Grease the griddle top with cooking oil.
3. Place pork on the hot griddle top.
4. Cook for almost 6 minutes per side.
5. Sear the potatoes on the griddle for 5 minutes per side.
6. Meanwhile, sauté flour with butter in a saucepan for 1 minute.
7. Stir in stock and mix until lump-free.
8. Add wine, mix and cook for 5 minutes.

9. Pour this sauce over the pork and potatoes and serve warm.

Per Serving:
Calories: 222 | Fat: 9.5g | Carbohydrates: 13g | Fiber: 0.1g | Sugar: 0g | Protein: 31.4g | Sodium: 91mg

PIRI PIRI PORK MEDALLIONS

Prep Time: 10 mins. | Cook Time: 14 mins. |Serves: 4

Marinated pork
- 4 pork loin medallions, fat removed
- 3 tbsp. sweet chilli sauce
- Grated zest and juice of 1 lime
- 2 garlic cloves, peeled and grated
- 1 tbsp. ground coriander
- 1 tbsp. ground cumin

Serve
- 16 sweet potato wedges
- 3 1/2 oz. bag mixed salad leaves
- 5 oz. soured cream and chive dip
- 3 1/2 oz. bag mixed salad leaves

1. Mix pork with its marinade ingredients in a bowl.
2. Cover and refrigerate for 1 hour.
3. Preheat your outdoor Griddle by turning all its burner's knob to medium-heat setting.
4. Grease the griddle top with cooking spray.
5. Place pork on the hot griddle top.
6. Cook for almost 5-7 minutes per side.
7. Serve warm with your favorite sides.

Per Serving:
Calories: 255 | Fat: 13g | Carbohydrates: 3.1g | Fiber: 1.3g | Sugar: 1.2g | Protein: 32.4g | Sodium:115mg

PORK FILLET WITH GREEN VEGETABLE SALAD

Prep Time: 10 mins. | Cook Time: 10 mins. |Serve: 2

- 7 oz. pork fillet
- Zest and juice of 1 lemon
- 1 tsp. ground paprika
- 2 garlic cloves, peeled sliced
- 1 tsp. rapeseed or olive oil

Yogurt and Mint Dressing:
- 5 tbsp. fat-free Greek yogurt
- Zest and juice of ½ lemon
- 2-3 tbsp. chopped mint

Salad:
- 3 1/2 oz. green beans, trimmed and blanched
- 3 1/2 oz. Brussel sprouts, shredded
- 3 1/2 oz. cauliflower rice, cooked and cooled
- Juice of ½ lemon
- chopped mint, to garnish

1. Mix all the salad ingredients in a bowl and keep it aside.
2. Whisk the mint dressing ingredients in a bowl and pour over the salad.
3. Season the pork with rest of the ingredients.
4. Preheat your outdoor Griddle by turning all its burner's knob to medium-heat setting.
5. Grease the griddle top with cooking spray.
6. Place pork on the hot griddle top.
7. Cook for almost 6 minutes per side.
8. Serve warm with the prepared salad.

Per Serving:
Calories: 252 | Fat: 11.3g | Carbohydrates: 3.4g | Fiber: 1g | Sugar: 0.3g | Protein: 32.1g | Sodium: 225mg

PORK FILLET WITH FRAGRANT PILAU RICE

Prep Time: 10 mins. | Cook Time: 16 mins. |Serve: 4

- 7 oz. Whole pork fillet, cut into thin medallions
- 1 tsp. oil
- 7 oz. mushrooms, thickly sliced
- 1 red onion, peeled and sliced
- 1 cinnamon stick, broken in half
- 1 tsp. ground coriander
- 1 tbsp. cardamon pods, crushed
- 7 oz. easy cook long grain rice
- Zest of 1 lemon
- 450ml vegetable stock
- 2 spring onions, chopped
- 2 tbsp. chopped coriander

1. Preheat your outdoor Griddle by turning all its burner's knob to medium-heat setting.
2. Grease the griddle top with cooking spray.
3. Place pork medallion on the hot griddle top.
4. Cook for almost 6 minutes per side.
5. Meanwhile, mix rice, stock and rest of the ingredients in a saucepan and until rice turn soft.
6. Top the cooked rice with pork medallion.
7. Serve warm.

Per Serving:
Calories: 290| Fat: 15g | Carbohydrates: 3.4g | Fiber: 1g | Sugar: 1.3g | Protein: 31.4g | Sodium: 254mg

CAJUN PORK FILLET WITH SWEET POTATOES
Prep Time: 10 mins. | Cook Time: 32 mins. |Serve: 2

- 1 lb. lean pork fillet
- 2 tbsp. Cajun spice mix
- 2 lbs. sweet potatoes, peeled and cubed
- 2 spring onions chopped
- 2 tbsp. fromage frais
- 1x1 lb. can pineapple rings
- 1 tsp. runny honey
- Black pepper, to taste

1. Mix sweet potatoes and rest of the ingredients in a bowl.
2. Preheat your outdoor Griddle by turning all its burner's knob to medium-heat setting.
3. Grease the griddle top with cooking spray.
4. place the pork on the hot griddle top.
5. Cook for almost 6 minutes per side.
6. Sauté onion and sweet potatoes on the griddle for 10 minutes.
7. Sear the pineapple for 5 minutes per side.
8. Serve the pork with veggies and pineapple.
9. Serve warm.

Per Serving:
Calories: 264 | Fat: 13.5g | Carbohydrates: 23g |Fiber: 1.3g | Sugar: 0.8g | Protein: 25.4g | Sodium:265mg

PORK FILLET WITH CREAMY WINE SAUCE
Prep Time: 10 mins. | Cook Time: 22 mins. |Serve: 2

- 7 oz. lean pork fillet, cut into medallions
- 1 tbsp. oil
- 1 garlic clove, peeled and chopped
- 25g dried prunes, chopped
- 1/2 cup white wine
- 4 tbsp. crème fraiche
- 2 tbsp. parsley leaves, chopped

1. Preheat your outdoor Griddle by turning all its burner's knob to medium-heat setting.
2. Grease the griddle top with cooking spray.
3. Place the pork on the hot griddle top.
4. Cook for almost 6 minutes per side.
5. Sauté garlic with oil and prunes in a saucepan for 5 minutes.
6. Stir in wine, crème fraiche and parsley, mix well and cook for 5 minutes.
7. Serve pork with the sauce.

Per Serving:
Calories: 292 | Fat: 13.5g | Carbohydrates: 21g |Fiber: 1.4g | Sugar: 2g | Protein: 35.4g | Sodium: 225mg

PORK WITH CHILLI SAUCE
Prep Time: 10 mins. | Cook Time: 10 mins. |Serve: 1

- 1 lb. lean pork fillet, scored
- 3 tbsp. sweet chilli sauce
- Zest and juice of 1 lime
- 1 tbsp. parsley leaves, chopped
- 2 garlic cloves, peeled and crushed
- 1 tbsp. ground coriander
- 1 tbsp. ground cumin

1. Mix sweet chilli sauce with rest of the seasoning in a bowl.
2. Add pork to the sauce, mix well, cover and refrigerate for 1 hour.
3. Preheat your outdoor Griddle by turning all its burner's knob to medium-heat setting.
4. Grease the griddle top with cooking spray.
5. Place the pork on the hot griddle top.
6. Cook for almost 7 minutes per side.
7. Serve warm with leftover marinade.

Per Serving:
Calories: 154 | Fat: 7.3g | Carbohydrates: 24g | Fiber: 0.5g | Sugar: 1.3g | Protein: 16.4g | Sodium:165mg

PORK FILLET WITH CHORIZO
Prep Time: 10 mins. | Cook Time: 15 mins. |Serve: 4

- 12 oz. pork fillet, sliced
- 1 oz. chorizo sausage, sliced
- 1 tbsp. olive oil
- 3 garlic cloves, peeled and crushed
- 1 red onion, peeled and sliced
- 1 red pepper, deseeded and sliced
- 2 tbsp. smoked paprika
- 1 x 14 oz. can chopped tomatoes
- Black pepper, to taste

1. Preheat your outdoor Griddle by turning all its burner's knob to medium-heat setting.
2. Grease the griddle top with cooking spray.
3. Sauté pork with chorizo and rest of the ingredients on the hot griddle top.
4. Cook for almost 10-15 minutes until brown.
5. Serve warm.

Per Serving:
Calories: 290 | Fat: 12.5g | Carbohydrates: 3.8g | Fiber: 1.3g | Sugar: 1.2g | Protein: 35.4g | Sodium: 245mg

SALTIMBOCCA ALLA ROMANA
Prep Time: 10 mins. | Cook Time: 15 mins. | Serve: 6

- saltimbocca
- 7 oz pork fillet, sliced into 6 diagonally
- 6 sage leaves
- 6 slices prosciutto
- 1 oz plain flour
- 1 tbsp. olive oil
- Sea salt and black pepper, to taste

Green beans
- 1 garlic clove, crushed
- 5 ½ oz cherry tomatoes, halved
- 7 oz French beans
- 2 oz white wine

1. Place the pork fillet on the working surface and top each with on prosciutto slice, and sage leaves.
2. Roll and seal the pork with a toothpick.
3. Rub the pork rolls with flour, black pepper and salt.
4. Preheat your outdoor Griddle by turning all its burner's knob to medium-heat setting.
5. Grease the griddle top with cooking oil.
6. Place pork roll on the hot griddle top.
7. Cook for almost 5 minutes per side.
8. Add green beans and rest of the ingredients to one side of the griddle and cook for 5 minutes.
9. Serve pork with green beans.

Per Serving:
Calories: 227 | Fat: 11.1g | Carbohydrates: 28g | Fiber: 1.3g | Sugar: 1.3g | Protein: 25.3g | Sodium: 265mg

STICKY SOY AND GINGER PORK
Prep Time: 10 mins. | Cook Time: 13 mins. | Serve: 2

Marinade
- 1 ½ in fresh ginger, peeled and grated
- 4 tbsp. soy sauce
- 2 garlic cloves, minced
- 2 tbsp. sweet chilli sauce
- 3 tbsp. honey

Pork
- 1 large pork fillet
- 4 spring onions, thin strips
- 1 red chilli, sliced
- 2 tbsp. chopped fresh coriander
- salt and black pepper, to taste
- steamed rice or cooked noodles, to serve

1. Mix pork with the marinade ingredients in a bowl.
2. Cover and refrigerate for 1 hour.
3. Preheat your outdoor Griddle by turning all its burner's knob to medium-heat setting.
4. Grease the griddle top with cooking spray.
5. place pork, and onions on the hot griddle top.
6. Cook for almost 6 minutes per side.
7. Add coriander, black pepper, salt and red chilli.
8. Sauté for 1 minute then add to the rice.
9. Serve warm.

Per Serving:
Calories: 380 | Fat: 17.5g | Carbohydrates: 8g | Fiber: 2.4g | Sugar: 3.3g | Protein: 34.3g | Sodium: 265mg

PORK STUFFED WITH APRICOTS
Prep Time: 10 mins. | Cook Time: 25 mins. | Serve: 4

- stuffing
- 1 knob of butter
- 1 tbsp. sunflower oil
- 1 large banana (long) shallot, chopped
- 2 garlic cloves, crushed
- 1 eating apple, such as Gala
- 2 ½ oz ready-to-eat dried apricots, quartered
- 1 ¾ oz sultanas
- 3 balls stem ginger in syrup, drained, chopped
- 2 ½ oz fresh white breadcrumbs
- 1 tsp. ground ginger
- 1 lemon, grated zest and juice
- 3 tbsp. parsley leaves, chopped
- 1 tbsp. chopped fresh thyme leaves
- 1 tsp. flaked sea salt
- black pepper, to taste
- 1 tbsp. ginger syrup
- For the pork
- 2 (1 lb. 2 oz) pork fillets (tenderloin)
- 16 rindless smoked streaky bacon rashers, sliced
- sunflower oil, for greasing
- sauce
- 3 ½ oz ginger wine
- 3 ½ oz double cream
- 1 tsp. corn flour

1. Mix all the stuffing ingredients in a saucepan and cook for 20 minutes.

2. Divide the stuffing on the pork fillets.
3. Roll the pork and wrap it with bacon.
4. Preheat your outdoor Griddle by turning all its burner's knob to medium-heat setting.
5. Grease the griddle top with cooking spray.
6. Place pork on the hot griddle top.
7. Cook for almost 6-10 minutes per side until tender.
8. Mix the wine, cream and corn flour in a saucepan and cook for 5 minutes with stirring.
9. Pour the sauce over the pork.
10. Serve warm.

Per Serving:
Calories: 270 | Fat: 12.5g | Carbohydrates: 13g | Fiber: 2.1g | Sugar: 3.5g | Protein: 27.4g | Sodium:365mg

CHILLI-GLAZED STICKY RIBS

Prep Time: 10 mins. | Cook Time: 27 mins. |Serve: 4

- ribs
- 2 racks pork spare ribs, cut into pieces
- 1 tsp. black peppercorns
- 3 bay leaves
- small bunch flatleaf parsley
- 1 onion, chopped
- 1 carrot, cut into chunks
- For the sauce
- 6 oz tomato ketchup
- 5 oz chipotle chilli ketchup
- 3½ oz dark soy sauce
- 6 oz dark muscovado sugar
- 4 tbsp. teriyaki sauce

1. Prepare the glaze by mixing all the ingredients in a saucepan and cook for 2-3 minutes.
2. Dip the ribs in the glaze to coat.
3. Preheat your outdoor Griddle by turning all its burner's knob to medium-heat setting.
4. Grease the griddle top with cooking spray.
5. Place the ribs on the hot griddle top.
6. Cook for almost 5-7 minutes per side.
7. Add the veggies to the griddle and cook for 5-10 minutes until tender.
8. Pour the leftover glaze over the cooked ribs and veggies.
9. Serve warm.

Per Serving:
Calories: 340 | Fat: 14.5g | Carbohydrates: 11g | Fiber: 1.4g | Sugar: 3.3g | Protein: 38.1g | Sodium:265mg

CHINESE FIVE-SPICE SPARE RIBS

Prep Time: 10 mins. | Cook Time: 25 minutes|Serve: 2

Spareribs
- 1½ lb. pork spareribs
- 1 pint groundnut oil
- For the marinade
- 1 tbsp. Shaoxing rice wine
- 1 tbsp. light soy sauce
- 1 tbsp. Chinese black rice vinegar
- 2 tsp. sesame oil
- 1 tbsp. corn flour

For the sauce
- 2 tbsp. chopped garlic
- 2 tsp. five-spice powder
- 3 tbsp. chopped spring onions
- 3 tbsp. Chinese rock sugar
- 3 tbsp. Shaoxing rice wine
- 5 oz chicken stock
- 1½ tbsp. light soy sauce
- 2 tbsp. dried grated orange peel
- 3 oz Chinese black rice vinegar

1. Prepare ribs marinade by mixing all its ingredients in a large pan.
2. Add spare ribs, mix well and refrigerate overnight.
3. Preheat your outdoor Griddle by turning all its burner's knob to medium-heat setting.
4. Grease the griddle top with cooking spray.
5. Place the spareribs on the hot griddle top.
6. Cook for almost 5-10 minutes per side until tender.
7. Meanwhile, prepare it sauce by mixing all its ingredients in a saucepan then cook for 5 minutes.
8. Pour the sauce over the spare ribs and serve warm.

Per Serving:
Calories: 219| Fat: 14.5g | Carbohydrates: 3.3g |Fiber: 1.3g | Sugar: 1.7g | Protein: 18.4g | Sodium:129mg

MEXICAN PORK TENDERLOIN

Prep Time: 10 mins. | Cook Time: 35 mins. |Serve: 4

- 700 g piece pork tenderloin, trimmed
- olive oil
- MARINADE
- 2 red onions
- 6 garlic cloves
- 2 dried chipotle chilies

- 1 ancho chilli
- ½ a bunch of fresh coriander
- 1 tsp. ground cumin
- ½ tsp. sweet smoked paprika
- 3 sprigs of fresh thyme
- 2 tbsp. red wine vinegar
- 1 tbsp. tomato purée
- 2 tbsp. dark brown sugar
- ½ an orange
- RAINBOW SALAD
- 1 corn on the cob
- ¼ of a white cabbage
- 2 tbsp. white vinegar
- 6 mixed radishes
- 2 carrots
- 3 little gem hearts

1. Mix the rainbow salad ingredients in a bowl and keep It aside.
2. Prepare the marinade by mixing all its ingredients in a saucepan.
3. Cook this marinade for 5 minutes then allow it to cool
4. Add steak to this marinade, mix well to coat and refrigerate for 12 hours.
5. Preheat your outdoor Griddle by turning all its burner's knob to medium-heat setting.
6. Grease the griddle top with cooking oil.
7. Place the tenderloin on the hot griddle top.
8. Cook for almost 30 minutes while flipping every 5 minutes.
9. Slice and serve with rainbow salad.

Per Serving:

Calories: 165 | Fat: 8g | Carbohydrates: 18g | Fiber: 0.3g | Sugar: 0.1g | Protein: 21.4g | Sodium: 125mg

HONEY MUSTARD ROASTED PORK FILLET
Prep Time: 10 mins. | Cook Time: 20 mins. | Serve: 2

- 1 large pork fillet
- ¼ cup seeded mustard
- 4 tbsp. honey
- 1 lemon, zested and juiced
- 1 tbsp. olive oil

1. Season pork fillet with mustard, honey, lemon juice, and zest.
2. Cover and marinate the pork for 30 minutes.
3. Preheat your outdoor Griddle by turning all its burner's knob to medium-heat setting.
4. Grease the griddle top with cooking spray.
5. Place pork on the hot griddle top.
6. Cook for almost 10 minutes per side.
7. Serve warm.

Per Serving:
Calories: 260 | Fat: 8g | Carbohydrates: 21g | Fiber: 1.4g | Sugar: 3g | Protein: 35.8g | Sodium: 239mg

LAMB RECIPES

GREEK LAMB CHOPS

Prep Time: 10 mins. | Cook Time: 12 mins. | Serve: 8

- ¼ cup olive oil
- Juice of 1 lemon
- 2 tsp. dried oregano
- 4 garlic cloves minced
- 1 tsp. salt
- ½ tsp. black pepper
- 8 lamb chops
- 1 tbsp. olive oil for cooking

1. Preheat your outdoor Griddle by turning all its burner's knob to medium-heat setting.
2. Grease the griddle top with cooking spray.
3. Season the lamb chops with rest of the ingredients and place them on the hot griddle top.
4. Cook for almost 6 minutes per side.
5. Serve warm.

Per Serving:
Calories: 232 | Fat: 10.3g | Carbohydrates: 14g | Fiber: 2.3g | Sugar: 3.6g | Protein: 27.4g | Sodium:219mg

LAMB CHOPS SIZZLED WITH GARLIC

Prep Time: 10 mins. | Cook Time: 12 mins. | Serve: 8

- 8 ½-inch-thick lamb loin chops (2 lbs.)
- Salt and pepper
- dried thyme
- 3 tbsp. olive oil
- 10 small garlic cloves (halved)
- 3 tbsp. water
- 2 tbsp. fresh lemon juice
- 2 tbsp. minced parsley
- crushed red pepper

1. Preheat your outdoor Griddle by turning all its burner's knob to medium-heat setting.
2. Grease the griddle top with cooking spray.
3. Season the lamb chops with rest of the ingredients and place them on the hot griddle top.
4. Cook for almost 6 minutes per side.
5. Serve warm.

Per Serving:
Calories: 215 | Fat: 7.3g | Carbohydrates: 15g | Fiber: 0.3g | Sugar: 0.1g | Protein: 34.4g | Sodium:233mg

GARLIC BUTTER LAMB CHOPS

Prep Time: 10 mins. | Cook Time: 12 mins. | Serve: 5

- 5 lamb loin chops
- kosher salt, to taste
- black pepper, to taste
- 2 tbsp. grass-fed butter, melted
- 3 garlic cloves - minced
- 1 tsp. fresh thyme, chopped

1. Preheat your outdoor Griddle by turning all its burner's knob to medium-heat setting.
2. Grease the griddle top with cooking spray.
3. Season the lamb chops with rest of the ingredients and place them on the hot griddle top.
4. Cook for almost 6 minutes per side.
5. Serve warm.

Per Serving:
Calories: 284 | Fat: 12.5g | Carbohydrates: 25g | Fiber: 1.3g | Sugar: 3.3g | Protein: 33.8g | Sodium:265mg

ROSEMARY LAMB CHOPS

Prep Time: 10 mins. | Cook Time: 12 mins. | Serve: 4

- ✓ 2 lbs. lamb loin or rib chops thick cut
- ✓ 4 garlic cloves minced
- ✓ 1 tbsp. fresh rosemary chopped
- ✓ 1 ¼ tsp. kosher salt, to taste
- ✓ ½ tsp. black pepper
- ✓ zest of 1 lemon
- ✓ ¼ cup olive oil

1. Preheat your outdoor Griddle by turning all its burner's knob to medium-heat setting.
2. Grease the griddle top with cooking spray.
3. Season the lamb chops with rest of the ingredients and place them on the hot griddle top.
4. Cook for almost 6 minutes per side.
5. Serve warm.

Per Serving:
Calories: 227 | Fat: 12.5g | Carbohydrates: 25g | Fiber: 4.3g | Sugar: 1.2g | Protein: 18.4g | Sodium:42mg

SPICY LAMB CHOPS

Prep Time: 10 mins. | Cook Time: 12 mins. |Serves: 6

- ✓ 2 large garlic cloves, crushed
- ✓ 1 tbsp. fresh rosemary leaves
- ✓ 1 tsp. fresh thyme leaves
- ✓ Pinch cayenne pepper
- ✓ Coarse sea salt
- ✓ 2 tbsp. olive oil
- ✓ 6 lamb chops, about 3/4-inch thick

1. Preheat your outdoor Griddle by turning all its burner's knob to medium-heat setting.
2. Grease the griddle top with cooking spray.
3. Season the lamb chops with rest of the ingredients and place them on the hot griddle top.
4. Cook for almost 6 minutes per side.
5. Serve warm.

Per Serving:
Calories: 195 | Fat: 7.4g | Carbohydrates: 14g | Fiber: 0.3g | Sugar: 0.1g | Protein: 29.8g | Sodium:119mg

LAMB KOFTA FLATBREADS

Prep Time: 10 mins. | Cook Time: 10 mins. |Serves: 2

- ✓ 8 oz. ground lamb
- ✓ 2 tsp. rose harissa , plus extra to serve
- ✓ 8 oz. red cabbage
- ✓ 2 whole-meal tortillas , or flatbreads
- ✓ 2 tbsp. cottage cheese

1. Mix lamb with rose harissa, and cheese in a bowl.
2. Make 1-2 inches meatballs out of this mixture.
3. Preheat your outdoor Griddle by turning all its burner's knob to medium-heat setting.
4. Grease the griddle top with cooking spray.
5. Place the meatballs on the hot griddle top.
6. Cook for almost 5 minutes per side.
7. Spread the lamb meatballs, and cabbage on the tortillas.
8. Serve warm.

Per Serving:
Calories: 244 | Fat: 7.8g | Carbohydrates: 11g | Fiber: 3.3g | Sugar: 2.1g | Protein: 31.3g | Sodium:157mg

TAHINI BBQ LAMB CHOPS

Prep Time: 10 mins. | Cook Time: 35 mins. |Serve: 7

- ✓ 14 lamb chops
- ✓ 3 1/2 oz. baby red chard
- ✓ 4 plums , halved and stones removed
- ✓ **TAHINI BBQ SAUCE**
- ✓ 5¼ oz tahini paste
- ✓ 1 clove of garlic , peeled and minced
- ✓ 2 salted anchovies , chopped
- ✓ 1 tsp. pul biber chilli flakes
- ✓ 2 tbsp. pomegranate molasses
- ✓ 3½ oz water
- ✓ 1 tsp. flaky sea salt
- ✓ **SPICED PLUM SAUCE**
- ✓ 6 plums , cut into eighths and stones removed
- ✓ 1¾ oz sugar
- ✓ 1 clove of garlic
- ✓ 1 whole dried chilli,
- ✓ 1 tsp. Szechuan pepper
- ✓ 1 bay leaf
- ✓ 3 tbsp. pomegranate molasses
- ✓ ½ tsp. flaky sea salt
- ✓ 1 tbsp. red wine vinegar

1. Preheat your outdoor Griddle by turning all its burner's knob to medium-heat setting.
2. Grease the griddle top with cooking spray.
3. Place the meatballs on the hot griddle top.
4. Cook the lamb chops for almost 5-10 minutes per side.
5. Meanwhile, prepared the plum sauce by mixing all its ingredients in a saucepan.
6. Cook this sauce for 15 minutes while stirring.
7. Brush the sauce over the lamb racks during the last

10 minutes of cooking.
8. Mix all the tahini sauce ingredients in a bowl.
9. Serve the lamb chops with the tahini and plum sauce.

Per Serving:
Calories: 277 | Fat: 9.5g | Carbohydrates: 18g | Fiber: 0g | Sugar: 0.8g | Protein: 44.4g | Sodium: 275mg

SPICY RACK OF LAMB
Prep Time: 10 mins. | Cook Time: 50 mins. | Serves: 8

- 1 x 8 -bone rack of lamb , French trimmed
- 2 sprigs of fresh rosemary
- 4 garlic cloves
- 1 tsp. Worcestershire sauce
- 1 tbsp. Dijon mustard

1. Season the lamb rack with rosemary, garlic, Worcestershire sauce, and mustard.
2. Cover and marinate in the refrigerator for 12 hours.
3. Preheat your outdoor Griddle by turning all its burner's knob to medium-heat setting.
4. Grease the griddle top with cooking oil.
5. Place the rack on the hot griddle top.
6. Cook for almost 40-50 minutes until tender while flipping every 5-10 minutes.
7. Serve warm.

Per Serving:
Calories: 365 | Fat: 18.5g | Carbohydrates: 10g | Fiber: 0g | Sugar: 0.1g | Protein: 40.1g | Sodium:265mg

STUFFED LEG OF LAMB
Prep Time: 10 mins. | Cook Time: 50 mins. | Serve: 4

- 4 oz. stale rustic bread
- 50 ml Prosecco
- olive oil
- 1 lemon
- 4 garlic cloves
- 1 dried red chilli
- 1 bunch of fresh mint
- 4 anchovy fillets in oil
- 1 tbsp. baby capers in brine
- 1 large butterflied leg of lamb , boned

1. Season the lamb leg with red chili and top it with lemon juice, garlic cloves, mint, prosecco, bread, anchovy and capers.
2. Roll the lamb leg and tie a butchers twine.
3. Preheat your outdoor griddle by turning all its burner's knob to medium-heat setting.
4. Grease the griddle top with cooking spray.
5. Place the lamb leg on the griddle top for almost 50 minutes while fillping every 10 per side.
6. Serve warm.

Per Serving:
Calories: 275 | Fat: 14.5g | Carbohydrates: 15g | Fiber: 0.1g | Sugar: 1.2g | Protein: 29.3g | Sodium:250mg

GUNPOWDER LAMB
Prep Time: 10 mins. | Cook Time: 50 mins. | Serve: 4

- 1 x 4 ½ lbs. butterflied leg of lamb
- 1-2 fresh mixed-colour chilies

GUNPOWDER SPICE PASTE
- 2 dried red chilies
- 2 tsp. ground turmeric
- 2 tsp. fenugreek seeds
- 2 tsp. coriander seeds
- 2 tsp. cayenne pepper
- 2 garlic cloves
- 2 tbsp. red wine vinegar
- 1 tbsp. vegetable oil

1. Mix all the recipe ingredients for gunpowder spice paste in a bowl.
2. Rub the gunpowder paste liberally over the lamb.
3. Cover and refrigerate for overnight.
4. Preheat your outdoor Griddle by turning all its burner's knob to medium-heat setting.
5. Grease the griddle top with cooking spray.
6. Cook the lamb for almost 40-50 minutes while flipping every 10 minutes.
7. Serve warm.

Per Serving:
Calories: 335 | Fat: 17.5g | Carbohydrates: 8g | Fiber: 1.4g | Sugar: 5g | Protein: 29.8g | Sodium:265mg

SAGANAKI LAMB SKEWERS
Prep Time: 10 mins. | Cook Time: 12 mins. | Serve: 4

- 3 garlic cloves
- 5 oz. kefalotyri cheese
- 2 medium eggplant
- 1 iceberg lettuce

- ✓ 1 tbsp. coriander seeds
- ✓ 2 tsp. dried oregano
- ✓ 2 lemons
- ✓ 4 tbsp. olive oil
- ✓ 1 ½ lb. lamb neck fillet , in 2cm chunks
- ✓ 12 fresh bay leaves

PICKLED CABBAGE
- ✓ ½ a large cabbage
- ✓ 2 onions
- ✓ 400 ml cider vinegar
- ✓ 4 oz. granulated sugar
- ✓ 1 bay leaf
- ✓ 1 tbsp. juniper berries

1. Mix the lamb chunks with rest of the skewers ingredients in a bowl.
2. Cover and refrigerate for 1 hour for marination.
3. Meanwhile, mix the pickled cabbage ingredients in a bowl.
4. Cover and keep it refrigerate until skewers are ready.
5. Preheat your outdoor Griddle by turning all its burner's knob to medium-heat setting.
6. Grease the griddle top with cooking spray.
7. Cook the skewers for almost 6 minutes per side.
8. Serve warm with pickled cabbage.

Per Serving:
Calories: 276 | Fat: 17.8g | Carbohydrates: 14g | Fiber: 0.8g | Sugar: 0.3g | Protein: 26.8g | Sodium:237mg

CRUSTED LAMB RACK

Prep Time: 10 mins. | Cook Time: 50 mins. |Serve: 4

- ✓ 6 tbsp. runny honey
- ✓ olive oil
- ✓ 2 oz. whole or flaked almonds
- ✓ 1 bunch of fresh mixed herbs
- ✓ 1 handful of breadcrumbs
- ✓ 2 racks of lamb
- ✓ 2 tbsp. Dijon mustard

1. Season the lamb racks with mustard, honey, and herbs.
2. Preheat your outdoor Griddle by turning all its burner's knob to medium-heat setting.
3. Grease the griddle top with cooking spray.
4. Place the lamb on the griddle and cook for almost 15 minutes per side until tender.
5. Drizzle breadcrumbs on both the two sides of the lamb and press them with a spatula during the last 10 minutes of cooking.
6. Garnish the lamb rack with almonds.
7. Serve warm.

Per Serving:
Calories: 355 | Fat: 20.5g | Carbohydrates: 5g | Fiber: 1.3g | Sugar: 2.5g | Protein: 21.1g | Sodium:395mg

HERBY LAMB KEBABS

Prep Time: 10 mins. | Cook Time: 12 mins. |Serves: 4

- ✓ 1 ½ lb. lean lamb , such as cannon, loin, leg
- ✓ 2 large red onions
- ✓ 8 oz. ripe cherry tomatoes
- ✓ ½ a bunch of fresh mint
- ✓ 10 ½ oz. yoghurt
- ✓ 1 lemon
- ✓ olive oil
- ✓ MARINADE
- ✓ 1 large handful of garlic leaves
- ✓ 2 big pinches of fennel seeds
- ✓ 1 lemon
- ✓ olive oil

1. Mix the marinade ingredients in a large bowl.
2. Toss in lamb then mix well.
3. Make 1-2 inches sized meatballs out of this mixture.
4. Preheat your outdoor Griddle by turning all its burner's knob to medium-heat setting.
5. Grease the griddle top with cooking oil.
6. Thread the lamb meatballs and veggies on the skewers alternately.
7. Place the skewers on the hot griddle top.
8. Cook for almost 6 minutes per side while seasoning with mint, lemon and rosemary.
9. Serve warm yogurt.

Per Serving:
Calories: 344 | Fat: 21.5g | Carbohydrates: 3.5g | Fiber: 0.4g | Sugar: 0.2g | Protein: 20.5g | Sodium: 225mg

LAMB CHOPS WITH RATATOUILLE

Prep Time: 10 mins. | Cook Time: 10 mins. |Serve: 8

- ✓ 2 garlic cloves
- ✓ 2 onions
- ✓ 2 sticks of celery
- ✓ 2 courgettes

- ✓ 1 eggplant
- ✓ 2 ripe tomatoes
- ✓ 1 sprig of fresh thyme
- ✓ olive oil
- ✓ 1 tbsp. caper berries
- ✓ 1 handful black olives
- ✓ 8 lamb chops

1. Preheat your outdoor Griddle by turning all its burner's knob to medium-heat setting.
2. Grease the griddle top with cooking spray.
3. Place the chops on the hot griddle top.
4. Around rest of the ingredients around the chops
5. Cook the chops for almost 6 minutes per side.
6. Spread the eggplant mixture on the griddle top and cook for 10 minutes.
7. Serve chops with vegetables.

Per Serving:
Calories: 247 | Fat: 10g | Carbohydrates: 15g | Fiber: 0.5g | Sugar: 0.8g | Protein: 37.4g | Sodium:162mg

LAMB BOTI KABAB

Prep Time: 1 mins. | Cook Time: 10 mins. | Serve: 4

- ✓ 2 lb. boneless lamb leg, cut into cubes
- ✓ unsalted butter
- ✓ MARINADE
- ✓ 5 garlic cloves
- ✓ 3cm piece of ginger
- ✓ ½ a lime
- ✓ 5 oz. Greek yoghurt
- ✓ 50 ml sunflower oil
- ✓ 2/3 oz. papaya paste
- ✓ ½ oz. deggi mirch
- ✓ 1 tsp. garam masala
- ✓ 1 tsp. red chilli powder
- ✓ 1 pinch of cumin seeds
- ✓ 1 pinch of ground cumin

1. Blend all the marinade ingredients in a blender.
2. Season the lamb cubes with the marinade, cover and refrigerate for 30 minutes.
3. Preheat your outdoor Griddle by turning all its burner's knob to medium-heat setting.
4. Grease the griddle top with butter.
5. Place lamb cubes on the hot griddle top.
6. Cook for almost 5 minutes per side.
7. Serve warm.

Per Serving:
Calories: 185 | Fat: 4.1g | Carbohydrates: 18g | Fiber: 0.3g | Sugar: 0.2g | Protein: 35.4g | Sodium:265mg

QUICK LAMB KEBABS

Prep Time: 10 mins. | Cook Time: 10 mins. | Serves: 4

- ✓ 2 garlic cloves
- ✓ 1 tsp. dried oregano
- ✓ olive oil
- ✓ 4 lamb steaks, diced
- ✓ 2 red peppers
- ✓ 8 fresh bay leaves
- ✓ 2 lemons
- ✓ a few sprigs of fresh flat-leaf parsley

1. Thread the lamb cubes on the skewers. Blend garlic, oregano, oil, bay leaves, lemon juice in a blender.
2. Preheat your outdoor Griddle by turning all its burner's knob to medium-heat setting.
3. Grease the griddle top with cooking spray.
4. Season the lamb skewers with the garlic mixture and place on the hot griddle top.
5. Cook for almost 5 minutes per side.
6. Serve warm.

Per Serving:
Calories: 490 | Fat: 21.5g | Carbohydrates: 15g | Fiber: 0.4g | Sugar: 0g | Protein: 56.8g | Sodium: 40mg

MOROCCAN LAMB CHOPS

Prep Time: 10 mins. | Cook Time: 12 mins. | Serves: 8

- ✓ 8 lean lamb cutlets
- ✓ 1 tsp. dried mint
- ✓ 1 tsp. mild smoked paprika
- ✓ ½ a lemon
- ✓ olive oil
- ✓ 1 tbsp. fennel seeds
- ✓ 1 tbsp. cumin seeds
- ✓ 5 oz. blanched almonds
- ✓ 5 oz. quality houmous
- ✓ 2 tbsp. harissa paste
- ✓ COLESLAW
- ✓ 2 carrots
- ✓ ½ a celeriac
- ✓ ¼ of a small red cabbage
- ✓ ½ an onion
- ✓ 1 bunch of fresh coriander
- ✓ 6 tbsp. natural yoghurt
- ✓ 1 lime

1. Mix all the coleslaw ingredients in a bowl.
2. Toss lamb cutlets with rest of the ingredients in a bowl.
3. Cover and refrigerate for 30 minutes.
4. Preheat your outdoor Griddle by turning all its burner's knob to medium-heat setting.
5. Grease the griddle top with cooking oil.
6. Place the lamb cutlets on the hot griddle top.
7. Cook for almost 6 minutes per side.
8. Serve warm with coleslaw.

Per Serving:
Calories: 480 | Fat: 20.5g | Carbohydrates: 14g | Fiber: 0.4g | Sugar: 0g | Protein: 56.8g | Sodium: 84mg

SPICED LAMB LOLLIPOPS

Prep Time: 10 mins. | Cook Time: 10 mins. | Serve: 8

- 8 quality lamb cutlets, French-trimmed
- 3 tbsp. cumin seeds, toasted and ground
- 1 thumb-sized piece ginger, grated
- 3 tbsp. olive oil
- 5 oz. blanched almonds
- ½ tsp. black pepper
- ½ tsp. cloves
- ½ stick cinnamon
- ½ tsp. cardamom
- 1 tsp. butter
- 2 garlic cloves, sliced
- 1 tsp. ground turmeric
- 1 red onion, sliced
- 5 oz. tinned chopped tomatoes
- 250 ml fat-free natural yoghurt

1. Beat yogurt with rest of the ingredients except lamb in a large bowl
2. Lamb cutlets, mix, cover and refrigerate for 1 hour.
3. Preheat your outdoor Griddle by turning all its burner's knob to medium-heat setting.
4. Grease the griddle top with cooking spray.
5. Place the lamb cutlets on the hot griddle and cook for almost 6 minutes per side.
6. Cook the leftover marinade in a saucepan and cook for 5 minutes with stirring.
7. Serve the lamb cutlets with its sauce.

Per Serving:
Calories: 337 | Fat: 16.5g | Carbohydrates: 11g | Fiber: 0.5g | Sugar: 0.2g | Protein: 46.4g | Sodium:290mg

LAMB CUTLETS WITH CORIANDER POTATOES

Prep Time: 10 mins. | Cook Time: 14 mins. | Serve: 8

- 8 lamb cutlets
- 4 tbsp. olive oil
- sea salt
- 1 tbsp. black pepper
- 1 dried chilli, sliced
- 1 small handful fresh thyme leaves
- 2 lb. waxy red potatoes
- 2 tbsp. coriander seeds
- ½ tsp. ground cinnamon
- 1 small glass red wine
- 1 large cabbage, shredded
- 1 lemon, juice of
- olive oil

1. Preheat your outdoor Griddle to high heat.
2. In a bowl, add the garlic, rosemary, salt and black pepper and mix well.
3. Coat the lamb chop with the herb mixture generously.
4. Place the chop onto the hot side of grill and cook for about 2 minutes per side.
5. Now, move the chop onto the cooler side of the griddle and cook for about 6-7 minutes.
6. Serve hot.

Per Serving:
Calories: 322 | Fat: 12.5g | Carbohydrates: 10g | Fiber: 0.4g | Sugar: 0g | Protein: 45.4g | Sodium:265mg

SPICY BARBECUED LEG OF LAMB

Prep Time: 10 mins. | Cook Time: 40 mins. | Serve: 4

- 3 sticks lemon grass
- 5 cm piece fresh root ginger, peeled and chopped
- 5 garlic cloves, peeled and chopped
- 6 lime leaves
- 1 good pinch ground cumin
- 1 lemon, zest and juice of
- sea salt, to taste
- black pepper, to taste
- 1 quality leg of lamb, boned and butterflied
- a few sprigs fresh mint, leaves picked and chopped
- fat-free natural yoghurt
- 1 lemon
- rocket, to serve

1. Mix all the recipe ingredients except the lamb in a

large bowl.
2. Place the lamb in the marinade, mix well and cover to refrigerate for 1 hour.
3. Preheat your outdoor Griddle by turning all its burner's knob to medium-heat setting.
4. Grease the griddle top with cooking spray.
5. Place the lamb on the hot griddle top.
6. Cook for almost 30-40 minutes while flipping every 5 minutes.
7. Serve warm.

Per Serving:
Calories: 415 | Fat: 21.5g | Carbohydrates: 15g | Fiber: 0.3g | Sugar: 0g | Protein: 50.8g | Sodium: 310mg

LAMB CHOP WITH VEGGIES
Prep Time: 10 mins. | Cook Time: 10 mins. | Serve: 1

- 1 (4-oz.) lamb loin chop
- ¼ tbsp. fresh basil leaves
- ¼ tbsp. fresh mint leaves
- ¼ tbsp. fresh rosemary leaves
- ½ of garlic clove, peeled
- ½ tbsp. olive oil, divided
- ¼ of zucchini, sliced
- ¼ cup cherry tomatoes

1. Blend garlic with oil and herbs in a blender.
2. Preheat your outdoor Griddle by turning all its burner's knob to medium-heat setting.
3. Grease the griddle top with cooking spray.
4. Place lamb chops and veggies on the griddle top.
5. Add herbs mixture on top and cook the chops and veggies for 5-10 minutes until tender.
6. Serve warm.

Per Serving:
Calories: 294 | Fat: 15.4g | Carbohydrates: 24g | Fiber: 1.4g | Sugar: 2.1g | Protein: 33g | Sodium: 94mg

ROSEMARY LAMB BITES
Prep Time: 10 mins. | Cook Time: 12 mins. | Serve: 1

- ½ garlic clove, minced
- ¼ tbsp. fresh rosemary, minced Salt and black pepper, to taste
- ¼ lb. boneless leg of lamb, cut into bite-sizedpieces
- 1 tsp. olive oil

1. Preheat your outdoor Griddle by turning all its burner's knob to medium-heat setting.
2. Grease the griddle top with cooking oil.
3. Season the lamb with black pepper, rosemary, salt, and garlic and place them on the hot griddle top.
4. Cook for almost 6 minutes per side.
5. Serve warm.

Per Serving:
Calories: 255 | Fat: 13.1g | Carbohydrates: 10g | Fiber: 0.4g | Sugar: 0g | Protein: 33g | Sodium: 242mg

GROUND LAMB WITH PEAS
Prep Time: 10 mins. | Cook Time: 15 mins. | Serve: 1

- ½ tbsp. olive oil
- ¼ of medium onion, chopped
- 1 (¼-inch) piece fresh ginger, minced
- 1 garlic clove, minced
- ¼ tsp. ground coriander
- ¼ tsp. ground cumin
- 1/8 tsp. ground turmeric
- ¼ lb. lean ground lamb
- 3 tbsp. tomato, chopped
- ¼ cup fresh green peas, shelled
- ½ tbsp. fat-free Greek yogurt, whipped
- 1 tsp. fresh cilantro, chopped
- Salt and black pepper, to taste

1. Mix ground lamb with rest of the recipe ingredients in a large bowl.
2. Preheat your outdoor Griddle by turning all its burner's knob to medium-heat setting.
3. Grease the griddle top with cooking oil.
4. Spread the lamb mixture on the hot griddle top and cook for 10-15 minutes with stirring with a spatula.
5. Serve warm.

Per Serving:
Calories: 325 | Fat: 14.5g | Carbohydrates: 10g | Fiber: 2.8g | Sugar: 4.7g | Protein: 34.4g | Sodium:252mg

LAMB KOFTAS
Prep Time: 10 mins. | Cook Time: 12 mins. | Serve: 1

- ¼ lb. lean ground lamb
- ½ tbsp. fat-free plain Greek yogurt
- ½ tbsp. onion, grated
- ½ tsp. garlic, minced
- ½ tbsp. fresh cilantro, minced

- ¼ tsp. ground coriander
- ¼ tsp. ground cumin
- 1/8 tsp. ground turmeric
- Salt and black pepper, to taste
- ½ tbsp. olive oil

1. Blend lamb ground with onion and rest of the ingredients in a food processor.
2. Make 1-2 inches sized meatballs out of this mixture.
3. Preheat your outdoor Griddle by turning all its burner's knob to medium-heat setting.
4. Grease the griddle top with cooking spray.
5. Place the meatballs on the hot griddle top.
6. Cook for almost 6 minutes per side.
7. Serve warm.

Per Serving:
Calories: 282 | Fat: 14.5g | Carbohydrates: 18g | Fiber: 0.3g | Sugar: 0.7g | Protein: 32.5g | Sodium:120mg

SIZZLING LAMB WITH CUCUMBER DIP
Prep Time: 10 mins. | Cook Time: 12 mins. |Serve: 8

- LAMB & MARINADE
- 1 heaped tsp. coriander seeds
- 1 level tsp. cumin seeds
- 1 generous pinch turmeric
- 2 bird's-eye chilies, stalks removed, sliced
- 2 garlic cloves, peeled and sliced
- olive oil
- 8 quality long lamb cutlets
- SPICED NUTS
- 50 g blanched almonds
- 50 g shelled pistachios
- 1 tbsp. sesame seeds
- 1 pinch ground cumin
- CUCUMBER DIP
- ½ cucumber
- 1 handful fresh mint leaves
- 3 1/2 oz. fat-free natural yoghurt
- ½ lemon

1. Mix lamb with its marinade ingredients in a bowl.
2. Cover and refrigerate for 30 minutes.
3. Mix well and thread the lamb on the skewers.
4. Preheat your outdoor Griddle by turning all its burner's knob to medium-heat setting.
5. Grease the griddle top with cooking spray.
6. Place the skewers on the hot griddle top.
7. Cook for almost 6 minutes per side.
8. Meanwhile, mix spied nuts mixture in a bowl.
9. Mix cucumber dip ingredients in a bowl
10. Drizzle spiced nuts on top of the lamb.
11. Serve warm with cucumber dip.

Per Serving:
Calories: 176 | Fat: 11g | Carbohydrates: 3.4g | Fiber: 1.3g | Sugar: 1.8g | Protein: 15.8g | Sodium:365mg

MOROCCAN-STYLE LAMB BURGERS
Prep Time: 10 mins. | Cook Time: 25 mins. |Serve: 4

- 1 1/2 lb. quality lamb shoulder, minced
- olive oil
- 6 burger buns
- 6 tbsp. yoghurt
- 1 heaped tbsp. harissa paste
- 1 lemon
- olive oil
- ½ a bunch of fresh mint
- DRY RUB
- ½ tsp. cumin seeds
- 1 tsp. ground coriander
- 1 tsp. Ras El Hanout
- 1-2 tsp. sweet smoked paprika

1. Grind the dry rub ingredients in a grinder.
2. Mix the lamb minced with the dry rub, lemon juice and rest of the ingredients in a bowl.
3. Make 6 patties out of this mixture.
4. Preheat your outdoor Griddle by turning all its burner's knob to medium-heat setting.
5. Grease the griddle top with cooking spray.
6. Place the patties on the hot griddle top.
7. Cook for almost 6 minutes per side.
8. Place the lamb patties in the buns.
9. Sear the burgers for almost 2 minutes per side.
10. Serve warm.

Per Serving:
Calories: 268| Fat: 11.4g | Carbohydrates: 23g |Fiber: 1.3g | Sugar: 1.1g | Protein: 36.8g | Sodium:265mg

FISH AND SEAFOOD RECIPES

YUMMY GROUPER

Prep Time: 10 mins. | Cook Time: 10 mins. | Serve: 6

- 1 (3-lbs.) whole grouper, scaled and gutted
- Oil and salt, for coating

1. Preheat your outdoor Griddle by turning all its burner's knob to medium-heat setting.
2. Grease the griddle top with cooking spray.
3. Season the whole grouper with salt and oil.
4. Sear the fish for 5 minutes per side on the hot griddle top.
5. Serve warm.

Per Serving:
Calories: 280| Fat: 18g | Carbohydrates: 28g | Fiber: 1.4g | Sugar: 0.8g | Protein: 19.5g | Sodium: 229mg

WHITEFISH WITH MAYONNAISE

Prep Time: 10 mins. | Cook Time: 10 mins. | Serve: 4

Roasted Garlic Mayo
- 3 egg yolks
- 1 tbsp. lemon or lime juice
- 1¾ cups oil
- 2 tbsp. roasted garlic
- 2 tsp. salt

Beer-Battered Fish
- 4 tbsp. cooking oil
- 1½ cups all-purpose flour
- 1 tsp. ancho chili powder
- 1 tsp. salt
- ½ tsp. baking soda
- 1 (12-oz.) can dark beer
- 2 lbs. boneless whitefish fillets

1. Preheat your outdoor Griddle by turning all its burner's knob to medium-heat setting.
2. Grease the griddle top with cooking oil.
3. Blend the egg yolks with lemon juice then drip in the oil slowly and continue blending for 5 minutes.
4. In a suitable mixing bowl, mix well the salt, chili powder, flour, and baking soda.
5. While mixing, slowly pour in the beer and whisk until smooth.
6. Season the fish fillets with salt and black pepper, then dredge them in plain flour.
7. Dip the fish in the beer batter then fry in the oil for 5 minutes per side.
8. Serve with a dollop of garlic mayonnaise.
9. Serve hot.

Per Serving:
Calories: 197 | Fat: 10.5g | Carbohydrates: 10.1g | Fiber: 0.5g | Sugar: 1g | Protein: 13.4g | Sodium: 218mg

GARLIC FISH WITH CILANTRO

Prep Time: 10 mins. | Cook Time: 10 mins. | Serve: 6

- 4 garlic cloves, minced
- 1 white onion, quartered
- 1 jalapeño chile, stemmed, halved
- 1 (3- lbs.) whole fish, scaled and gutted
- Salt, to taste
- 1 bunch cilantro leaves
- Juice of 2 limes

1. Preheat your outdoor Griddle by turning all its burner's knob to medium-heat setting.
2. Grease the griddle top with cooking oil.
3. Add the garlic, onion, and jalapeno and cook for 3 minutes then transfer to a plate.
4. Make cuts on top of the fish and season with black pepper, salt and oil.
5. Place the fish on the hot griddle top and cook for 5 minutes per side.
6. Blend cilantro, lime juice, garlic, onion, and jalapeno in a food processor until smooth.
7. Serve the fish with the sauce.

Per Serving:
Calories: 254 | Fat: 15.8g | Carbohydrates: 18g | Fiber: 0.1g | Sugar: 0.1g | Protein: 27.8g | Sodium: 225mg

CHILLS AMBERJACK

Prep Time: 10 mins. | Cook Time: 10 mins. | Serve: 2

- 1½ lbs. boneless amberjack fillets
- 1½ cups oil
- 1 tsp. salt
- 4 guajillo chiles, toasted, stemmed, and seeded

1. Use oil and salt to coat the amberjack.
2. Preheat your outdoor Griddle by turning all its burner's knob to medium-heat setting.
3. Grease the griddle top with cooking spray.
4. Place the fillets on the hot griddle top and cook for 5 minutes per side.
5. In a blender, mix well the 1½ cup oil, chiles, and 1 tsp. salt and blend until smooth.
6. Strain the liquid and pour it over the fish to completely cover it.
7. Serve immediately or keep refrigerated, covered.

Per Serving:
Calories: 315 | Fat: 17.5g | Carbohydrates: 21g | Fiber: 0.4g | Sugar: 0.7g | Protein: 31.5g | Sodium: 284mg

LEMONY CUMIN RAINBOW TROUT

Prep Time: 10 mins. | Cook Time: 10 mins. | Serve: 4

- Citrus Vinaigrette
- 1½ tbsp. cumin seeds
- 3 oranges, juiced
- 3 lemons, juiced
- 1½ cups oil
- 3 tbsp. honey
- ¼ cup vinegar
- ½ shallot, grated
- 1½ tsp. salt
- ½ tsp. Mexican oregano
- Fish
- 4 (12 oz.) whole rainbow trout
- Oil and salt, for coating

1. Roast the cumin on a skillet over medium heat for about 2 minutes.
2. In a spice grinder or blender, grind until extremely fine and set aside.
3. Mix all the vinaigrette ingredients in a bowl.
4. Add fish fillets, rub well and marinate for 30 minutes.
5. Preheat your outdoor Griddle by turning all its burner's knob to medium-heat setting.
6. Grease the griddle top with cooking oil.
7. Place the fish on the hot griddle top and cook for 5 minutes per side.
8. Serve warm.

Per Serving:
Calories: 370 | Fat: 20.5g | Carbohydrates: 25g | Fiber: 0.8g | Sugar: 1.2g | Protein: 36.8g | Sodium: 365mg

SHRIMP WITH PINEAPPLE SAUCE

Prep Time: 10 mins. | Cook Time: 6 mins. | Serve: 4

- Fermented Pineapple–Peanut Sauce
- 1 cup roasted unsalted peanuts
- 10 dried chiles de árbol, seeded
- 1 cup oil
- 2 tbsp. honey
- 1 tbsp. salt
- 1 ripe pineapple, cored, and cut into small chunks
- 2 lbs. unpeeled jumbo shrimp
- Oil and salt, for coating

1. Blend the chilies, peanuts, honey, oil, and salt until smooth in a blender.
2. Preheat your outdoor Griddle by turning all its burner's knob to medium-heat setting.
3. Grease the griddle top with cooking spray.
4. Dip the shrimp in the sauce and sear for 2-3 minutes on per side on the hot griddle top.
5. Serve with remaining sauce and pineapple chunks

Per Serving:
Calories: 254 | Fat: 19g | Carbohydrates: 21g | Fiber: 1.1g | Sugar: 1.9g | Protein: 15.4g | Sodium: 265mg

SNAPPER CEVICHE

Prep Time: 10 mins. | Cook Time: 11 mins. | Serve: 2

- ✓ Marinade
- ✓ 1 cucumber
- ✓ 1 cup lime juice
- ✓ 1 jalapeño chile, stemmed
- ✓ ½ cup basil leaves
- ✓ 1 tsp. salt

Pickled Onions:
- ✓ 8 spring onions, white and green parts
- ✓ Oil, for coating
- ✓ 1 tsp. salt
- ✓ 1 tsp. sugar
- ✓ Vinegar, for pickling

Cucumber
- ✓ 1 cucumber
- ✓ Oil and salt, for coating
- ✓ 1½ lbs. boneless snapper or any other whitefish
- ✓ Salt, to taste
- ✓ ½ cup basil leaves, chopped
- ✓ 1 celery stalk, sliced

1. Blend lime juice, cucumber, basil, jalapeno, and salt in a blender and puree until smooth.
2. Push the mixture through a cheesecloth over a large bowl then discard solids.
3. Preheat your outdoor Griddle by turning all its burner's knob to High-heat setting.
4. Grease the griddle top with cooking oil.
5. Toss the greens with the oil and salt and cook for 1 minute over high heat, then chop.
6. Slice the white onions and mix with sugar, 1 tsp. salt, and vinegar in a suitable mixing bowl.
7. Season the fish with salt and marinade thoroughly.
8. Sear the fish on the hot griddle top for 5 minutes per side.
9. In a suitable mixing bowl, mix well the onion greens, drained pickled onions, basil, cucumber, and celery.
10. Serve.

Per Serving:
Calories: 246 | Fat: 10.5g | Carbohydrates: 23g | Fiber: 0.1g | Sugar: 3.3g | Protein: 34.4g | Sodium: 365mg

HONEY TUNA STEAKS

Prep Time: 5 mins. | Cook Time: 10 mins. | Serve: 2

- ✓ 2 tbsp. salt
- ✓ 2 tsp. cayenne pepper
- ✓ 2 tsp. sweet paprika
- ✓ 1 tsp. ground white pepper
- ✓ 1 tsp. celery salt
- ✓ 1 tbsp. peeled and grated fresh ginger
- ✓ 1 large garlic clove, grated
- ✓ 2 tbsp. oil
- ✓ 1 tbsp. honey
- ✓ 2 (12-oz.) tuna steaks, about 1½ inches thick
- ✓ Oil, for drizzling
- ✓ Lemon wedges, for serving

1. In a suitable mixing bowl, mix the cayenne, salt, white pepper, paprika, ginger, celery salt, garlic, oil, and honey.
2. Coat the tuna with the wet rub, rub well, then chill for 60 minutes uncovered.
3. Preheat your outdoor Griddle by turning all its burner's knob to medium-heat setting.
4. Grease the griddle top with cooking oil.
5. Place the tuna steaks on the hot griddle top and cook for 3-5 minutes per side.
6. Slice and serve.

Per Serving:
Calories: 210 | Fat: 14g | Carbohydrates: 11g | Fiber: 0g | Sugar: 0g | Protein: 23g | Sodium: 205mg

SWEET POTATO SNAPPER CEVICHE

Prep Time: 5 mins. | Cook Time: 12 mins. | Serve: 2

- ✓ 1 small fennel bulb, with fronds attached
- ✓ 1 tsp. salt
- ✓ 1 tbsp. sugar
- ✓ Vinegar, for pickling
- ✓ ¼ cup oil
- ✓ ¼ cup honey
- ✓ 1 large sweet potato, sliced
- ✓ 5 limes, sliced
- ✓ 2 oranges, sliced
- ✓ 2 mandarins, sliced
- ✓ 1 grapefruit, sliced
- ✓ 1½ lbs. boneless snapper
- ✓ ½ small red onion, sliced
- ✓ 2 plum tomatoes, diced
- ✓ ½ Granny Smith apple, peeled, cut into matchstick
- ✓ ¼ cup chopped cilantro leaves

1. Toss the salt, fennel, sugar, and vinegar in a bowl to coat the fennel.

2. In a suitable mixing bowl, mix well the oil and honey.
3. Toss in the sweet potato in the oil-honey mixture to coat it completely then drain.
4. Preheat your outdoor Griddle by turning all its burner's knob to medium-heat setting.
5. Grease the griddle top with cooking oil.
6. Season the sweet potatoes with salt and sear for about 5 minutes per side until caramelized.
7. Transfer to a bowl with tongs, then cover securely with plastic wrap
8. Set aside 2 limes and half the rest of the fruit.
9. Brush the cut sides with the remaining oil–honey mixture and cook over medium heat, for almost 2 minutes.
10. Mix fish with salt and citrus juice thoroughly.
11. Mix well the drained pickled fennel, sweet potato, tomato, onion, cilantro, apple, and 2 tsp. fennel fronds in a suitable mixing bowl.
12. Serve.

Per Serving:
Calories: 290 | Fat: 17.5g | Carbohydrates: 15g | Fiber: 0.4g | Sugar: 0.1g | Protein: 33.3g | Sodium: 235mg

CLAM AND SHRIMP BOUILLABAISSE

Prep Time: 10 mins. | Cook Time: 16 mins. | Serve: 2

- 1 large tomato
- ½ small fennel bulb, with fronds attached
- ¼ cup oil
- ½ white onion, minced
- 4 garlic cloves, sliced
- 2-inch piece fresh ginger, peeled and sliced
- 2 tbsp. tarragon leaves, chopped
- 6 basil leaves, chopped
- 4 cups fish stock
- Salt and black pepper, to taste
- ½ lb. small hard-shell clams, scrubbed
- ½ lb. large shrimp
- 1½ lbs. boneless whitefish fillets
- Tarragon–Garlic Toasts
- 6 tbsp. oil
- 3 tbsp. minced garlic
- Generous pinch of salt
- ¼ cup minced tarragon leaves
- 8 (½-inch-thick) slices French bread

1. Preheat your outdoor Griddle by turning all its burner's knob to medium-heat setting.
2. Grease the griddle top with cooking oil.
3. Place the tomato on the hot griddle top and cook it until it is blackened. Set aside
4. Add the onion, garlic, ginger, and minced fennel to griddle and cook for about 5 minutes then transfer the tomatoes and mash lightly.
5. Add 2 tbsp. of the fennel fronds, basil, fish stock, the tarragon, and salt and black pepper.
6. Place the clams on the hot griddle top, cover, and cook until the shells open.
7. Place the shrimp and fish directly on the hot griddle top and cook for 2-3 minutes per side.
8. Cook until the garlic begins to turn golden brown, then add the garlic and salt.
9. Toast the bread slices over medium heat until golden brown.
10. Brush the slices thickly with oil. With the bouillabaisse, serve right away.

Per Serving:
Calories: 287 | Fat: 17.5g | Carbohydrates: 14g | Fiber: 0.1g | Sugar: 0.3g | Protein: 33g | Sodium: 244mg

PAPRIKA SHRIMP WITH HONEY LIME

Prep Time: 10 mins. | Cook Time: 6 mins. | Serve: 4

- Rub:
- 1 tbsp. coriander seeds
- 1 tbsp. whole allspice berries
- ½ tbsp. cumin seeds
- 1 tsp. black peppercorns
- 1 tsp. ground cloves
- 1 tsp. sweet paprika
- 1 tsp. cayenne pepper
- Zest of 2 limes
- 1 tbsp. salt
- 16 jumbo shrimp, peeled and deveined
- Honey, as needed
- 4 limes, halved, for serving

1. Roast the allspice, coriander, cumin, and peppercorns in a suitable skillet for 3 minutes.
2. In a spice grinder, grind the paprika, cloves, lime zest, cayenne, roasted spices and salt to a fine powder.
3. Preheat your outdoor Griddle by turning all its burner's knob to medium-heat setting.
4. Grease the griddle top with cooking oil.
5. Liberally coat the shrimp with the spice mixture, lime juice and honey.
6. Sear the skewers for 3 minutes per side.
7. Serve warm

Per Serving:
Calories: 292 | Fat: 17.5g | Carbohydrates: 15g | Fiber: 0.3g | Sugar: 0.3g | Protein: 33.3g | Sodium: 233mg

ORANGE LOBSTER CORN SALAD
Prep Time: 10 mins. | Cook Time: 12 mins. | Serve: 4

- 4 ears of corn, shucked
- 4 spring onions, chopped
- Oil, for coating
- Salt, to taste
- 4 large lobster tails meat (8 oz.)
- 1 serrano chile, stemmed and sliced into rounds
- 3 celery stalks, sliced
- ½ cup basil leaves, chopped
- ¼ cup dill, chopped
- ¼ cup mint leaves, chopped
- ½ cup celery leaves, chopped
- Citrus–Brown Butter Vinaigrette
- 2 oranges, juiced
- 2 limes, juiced
- Oil and honey, for coating
- ½ cup 1 stick butter

1. Preheat your outdoor Griddle by turning all its burner's knob to medium-heat setting.
2. Grease the griddle top with cooking spray.
3. Pour the egg mixture onto the hot griddle top
4. Mix the corn and spring onions with the oil and salt.
5. Cook over medium heat for about 4 minutes then transfer to a plate.
6. Season the lobster flesh with salt and oil and cook for 2 minutes per side on the hot griddle top.
7. Transfer the lobster meat to a bowl.
8. Remove the kernels and add to the lobster.
9. Stir in rest of the ingredients to the lobster.
10. Cut the oranges and limes in half, mix with the oil and honey.
11. Cook for 3 minutes or until charred, then transfer to a plate.
12. Meanwhile, in a suitable saucepan, melt the butter until it turns a light brown color.
13. Remove the pan from the heat and add the lemon juice.
14. Whisk, then season with more honey and salt.
15. Serve the lobster salad with a generous amount of vinaigrette

Per Serving:
Calories: 255 | Fat: 15.5g | Carbohydrates: 14g | Fiber: 0.3g | Sugar: 0.6g | Protein: 28.3g | Sodium: 465mg

SALMON FILLETS WITH BROCCOLINI
Prep Time: 10 mins. | Cook Time: 12 mins. | Serve: 4

- 2 (6-oz.) salmon fillets, skin removed
- 2 tbsp. butter, unsalted
- 2 basil leaves, minced
- 1 garlic clove, minced
- 6 oz. broccolini
- 2 tsp. olive oil
- Sea salt, to taste

1. In a suitable mixing bowl, mix well the butter, basil, and garlic. Form into a ball and store in the fridge.
2. Season the salmon fillets with salt and put aside.
3. Toss broccolini with a tsp. of salt and a drizzle of olive oil in a suitable mixing dish to coat, then set aside.
4. Preheat your outdoor Griddle by turning all its burner's knob to medium-heat setting.
5. Grease the griddle top with cooking oil.
6. Pour the egg mixture onto the hot griddle top
7. Cook the salmon on the hot griddle top for 12 minutes per side then transfer to a plate.
8. Add the broccolini to the griddle, and cook for almost 6 minutes.
9. Serve salmon with a serving of broccolini and a slice of basil butter.
10. Enjoy.

Per Serving:
Calories: 324 | Fat: 18.5g | Carbohydrates: 23g | Fiber: 1g | Sugar: 0.5g | Protein: 33.4g | Sodium: 275mg

SPICED SNAPPER WITH SALSA
Prep Time: 10 mins. | Cook Time: 10 mins. | Serve: 4

- 2 red snappers, cleaned
- Sea salt, to taste
- ⅓ cup tandoori spice
- Olive oil, plus more for grill
- Olive oil, for drizzling
- Lime wedges, for serving
- For the Salsa:
- 1 ripe but firm mango, peeled and chopped
- 1 small red onion, sliced
- 1 bunch cilantro, chopped
- 3 tbsp. fresh lime juice

1. In a suitable mixing bowl, combine onion, mango, lime juice, cilantro, oil and a pinch of salt.
2. Make slashes on top of the fish fillet and season with spices, oil and salt.
3. Preheat your outdoor Griddle by turning all its burner's knob to medium-heat setting.
4. Grease the griddle top with cooking oil.
5. Cook the fish for 5 minutes per side on the hot griddle top.
6. Garnish with mango salad and lime wedges.
7. Serve.

Per Serving:
Calories: 290 | Fat: 17.5g | Carbohydrates: 18g | Fiber: 0.5g | Sugar: 0.2g | Protein: 33.3g | Sodium: 231

LIME CORN TILAPIA WITH CILANTRO

Prep Time: 10 mins. | Cook Time: 15 mins. | Serve: 4

- ✓ 4 fillets tilapia
- ✓ 2 tbsp. honey
- ✓ 4 limes, sliced
- ✓ 2 ears corn, shucked
- ✓ 2 tbsp. fresh cilantro leaves
- ✓ ¼ cup olive oil
- ✓ Kosher salt, to taste, to taste
- ✓ black pepper, to taste

1. Cut 4 foil squares about 12" long.
2. Place a piece of tilapia on top of each piece of foil.
3. Preheat your outdoor Griddle by turning all its burner's knob to medium-heat setting.
4. Grease the griddle top with cooking spray.
5. Pour the egg mixture onto the hot griddle top
6. Drizzle olive oil, salt, black pepper, honey, lime, corn, and cilantro over the tilapia.
7. Cook for 15 minutes on the hot griddle top.
8. Serve.

Per Serving:
Calories: 285 | Fat: 17.5g | Carbohydrates: 13g | Fiber: 0.1g | Sugar: 0g | Protein: 33.1g | Sodium: 315mg

SPINACH HALIBUT WITH OLIVES

Prep Time: 10 mins. | Cook Time: 11 mins. | Serve: 4

- ✓ 4 (6-oz.) halibut fillets
- ✓ ⅓ cup olive oil
- ✓ 4 cups baby spinach
- ✓ ¼ cup lemon juice
- ✓ 2 oz. pitted black olives, halved
- ✓ 2 tbsp. flat leaf parsley, chopped
- ✓ 2 tsp. fresh dill, chopped
- ✓ Lemon wedges, to serve

1. In a suitable mixing bowl, toss the spinach with the lemon juice and leave aside.
2. Preheat your outdoor Griddle by turning all its burner's knob to medium-heat setting.
3. Grease the griddle top with cooking spray.
4. Pour the egg mixture onto the hot griddle top
5. Brush each side of the salmon with olive oil and cook on the hot griddle for 3-4 minutes per side
6. Add the remaining oil and spinach then cook for 3 minutes.
7. Toss in olives and remaining herbs, then serve with lemon wedges and the fish.

Per Serving:
Calories: 285 | Fat: 17.5g | Carbohydrates: 13g | Fiber: 0.1g | Sugar: 0g | Protein: 33.1g | Sodium: 315mg

PARSLEY GARLIC SWORDFISH SKEWERS

Prep Time: 5 mins. | Cook Time: 8 mins. | Serve: 2

- ✓ 1 (½-lb.) skinless swordfish fillet
- ✓ 2 tsp. lemon zest
- ✓ 3 tbsp. lemon juice
- ✓ ½ cup parsley leaves, chopped
- ✓ 2 tsp. garlic, minced
- ✓ ¾ tsp. sea salt
- ✓ ¼ tsp. black pepper
- ✓ 2 tbsp. olive oil
- ✓ ½ tsp. red pepper flakes
- ✓ 3 lemons, cut into slices

1. Blend parsley, lemon zest, ¼ tsp. salt, garlic, and pepper black in a small bowl.
2. Mix well the swordfish pieces with the reserved lemon juice, red pepper flakes, olive oil, and the remaining salt in a suitable mixing bowl.
3. Thread swordfish and lemon slices onto metal skewers alternately.
4. Preheat your outdoor Griddle by turning all its burner's knob to medium-heat setting.
5. Grease the griddle top with cooking spray.
6. Pour the egg mixture onto the hot griddle top
7. Grill skewers for 4 minutes per side.
8. Arrange the skewers on a plate and top with gremolata.

9. Finish with a drizzle of olive oil and serve.

Per Serving:
Calories: 197 | Fat: 7.5g | Carbohydrates: 0g | Fiber: 0g | Sugar: 0g | Protein: 33.4g | Sodium: 265mg

GARLIC LIME LOBSTER TAILS
Prep Time: 10 mins. | Cook Time: 6 mins. | Serve: 4

- 4 lobster tails, cut in half lengthwise
- 3 tbsp. olive oil
- Lime wedges, to serve
- Sea salt and black pepper, to taste
- For the Lime Basil Butter:
- 1 stick butter, softened
- ½ bunch basil, chopped
- 1 lime, zested and juiced
- 2 garlic cloves, minced
- ¼ tsp. red pepper flakes

1. In a suitable mixing dish, mix well the basil butter ingredients.
2. Preheat your outdoor Griddle by turning all its burner's knob to medium-heat setting.
3. Drizzle olive oil over the lobster tail halves and season with salt and black pepper.
4. Place the lobster tails on the hot griddle top.
5. Cook for 3 minutes or until opaque, then flip and cook for another 3 minutes.
6. In the last minute of cooking, add a dollop of lime basil butter.
7. Serve with the lime wedges.

Per Serving:
Calories: 180 | Fat: 8.5g | Carbohydrates: 10g | Fiber: 0.4g | Sugar: 0.2g | Protein: 25.4g | Sodium: 235mg

CHILI OIL CRAB LEGS
Prep Time: 10 mins. | Cook Time: 10 mins. | Serve: 8

- 4 lbs. king crab legs
- 2 tbsp. chili oil

1. Preheat your outdoor Griddle by turning all its burner's knob to medium-heat setting.
2. Grease the griddle top with cooking spray.
3. Brush the crab legs on both the two sides with chili oil and set them on the hot griddle top.
4. Cook them for 5 minutes per side.

5. Arrange on plates and serve with a dollop of drawn butter.

Per Serving:
Calories: 244 | Fat: 9g | Carbohydrates: 11g | Fiber: 2.5g | Sugar: 4g | Protein: 32.4g | Sodium: 285mg

MUSTARD CRAB PANKO CAKES
Prep Time: 10 mins. | Cook Time: 10 mins. | Serve: 2

- 1 lb. lump crab meat
- ½ cup panko breadcrumbs
- ⅓ cup mayonnaise
- 1 egg, beaten
- 2 tbsp. Dijon mustard
- 2 tsp. Worcestershire sauce
- ½ tsp. paprika
- ½ tsp. salt
- ¼ tsp. black pepper
- 3 tbsp. vegetable oil

1. Mix well the breadcrumbs, crab, egg, mayonnaise, paprika, mustard Worcestershire sauce, salt, and pepper in a suitable mixing bowl.
2. Roll the crab mixture into four large balls and flatten them.
3. Preheat your outdoor Griddle by turning all its burner's knob to medium-heat setting.
4. Grease the griddle top with cooking oil.
5. Fry the crab cakes for 5 minutes per side until golden brown and crispy.
6. Serve right away.

Per Serving:
Calories: 156 | Fat: 6g | Carbohydrates: 13g | Fiber: 0g | Sugar: 0g | Protein: 26.4g | Sodium: 265mg

GARLIC PEPPER SHRIMP WITH PARSLEY
Prep Time: 10 mins. | Cook Time: 6 mins. | Serve: 2

- 1½ lbs. uncooked jumbo shrimp, peeled and deveined
- For the Marinade:
- 2 tbsp. fresh parsley
- 1 bay leaf, dried
- 1 tsp. chili powder
- 1 tsp. garlic powder
- ¼ tsp. cayenne pepper
- ¼ cup olive oil

- ¼ tsp. salt
- ⅛ tsp. black pepper

1. In a food processor, mix well all marinade ingredients and pulse until smooth.
2. Pour the marinade into a big mixing bowl.
3. Toss in the shrimp and toss to coat; chill for 30 minutes, covered.
4. Preheat your outdoor Griddle by turning all its burner's knob to medium-heat setting.
5. Grease the griddle top with cooking spray.
6. Pour the egg mixture onto the hot griddle top
7. Skewer the shrimp on metal skewers.
8. Cook, flipping once, for 5 to 6 minutes, or until shrimp are opaque pink.
9. Serve right away.

Per Serving:
Calories: 155 | Fat: 7.5g | Carbohydrates: 21g | Fiber: 0.4g | Sugar: 3.3g | Protein: 15.4g | Sodium:165mg

SHRIMP SKEWERS WITH PINEAPPLE
Prep Time: 10 mins. | Cook Time: 6 mins. |Serve: 2

- 1½ lbs. uncooked jumbo shrimp, peeled and deveined
- ½ cup light coconut milk
- 1 tbsp. cilantro, chopped
- 4 tsp. Tabasco red sauce
- 2 tsp. soy sauce
- ¼ cup orange juice
- ¼ cup lime juice
- ¾ lb. pineapple, cut into 1 inch chunks
- Olive oil, for grilling

1. Beat the coconut milk, cilantro, orange juice, Tabasco sauce, soy sauce, and lime juice in a suitable mixing bowl.
2. Toss in the shrimp to coat them.
3. Cover and marinate for 1 hour in the refrigerator.
4. Alternate threading shrimp and pineapple onto metal skewers.
5. Heat the griddle to medium heat and brush it with the oil.
6. Preheat your outdoor Griddle by turning all its burner's knob to medium-heat setting.
7. Grease the griddle top with cooking spray.
8. Pour the egg mixture onto the hot griddle top
9. Cook, flipping once, for 5 to 6 minutes, or until shrimp are opaque pink.
10. Serve right away.

Per Serving:
Calories: 296 | Fat: 16.5g | Carbohydrates: 24g |Fiber: 2.4g | Sugar: 0.5g | Protein: 35.4g | Sodium:215mg

CAJUN SHRIMP SAUSAGE SKEWERS
Prep Time: 10 mins. | Cook Time: 6 mins. |Serve: 2

- 1 lb. shrimp, peeled and deveined
- 4 andouille sausages, sliced into ½" thick rounds
- ¼ cup melted butter
- 1 tbsp. lemon zest
- Juice of 1 lemon (2 tbsp.)
- 1 tbsp. chopped thyme
- 1 tsp. smoked paprika
- 1 tsp. garlic powder
- ¼ tsp. cayenne
- Kosher salt, to taste
- black pepper
- 2 tbsp. parsley leaves, chopped, to garnish

1. Mix shrimp, and sausages with zest, lemon juice, thyme, paprika, garlic powder, cayenne, salt, black pepper and parsley in a suitable bowl.
2. Thread the shrimp and sausages on the skewers alternately.
3. Grease the griddle top with butter.
4. Preheat your outdoor Griddle by turning all its burner's knob to medium-heat setting.
5. Place the shrimp skewers on the griddle top and cook for 3 minutes per side.
6. Serve warm.

Per Serving:
Calories: 207 | Fat: 8.5g | Carbohydrates: 14g | Fiber: 0.3g | Sugar: 0.2g | Protein: 33g | Sodium: 285mg

MEDITERRANEAN SALMON SKEWERS
Prep Time: 5 mins. | Cook Time: 4 mins. |Serve: 2

- 1 lb. salmon fillets, preferably wild, cut into 2" pieces
- 3 lemons, sliced
- olive oil, for brushing
- kosher salt, to taste
- black pepper
- Torn fresh dill, to garnish

1. Season the salmon pieces with black pepper and salt.

2. Grease the griddle top with olive oil.
3. Preheat your outdoor Griddle by turning all its burner's knob to medium-heat setting.
4. Thread the salmon pieces and lemon slice on the skewers alternately.
5. Place the salmon lemon skewers on the griddle top and cook for 2 minutes per side.
6. Garnish with dill and serve warm.

Per Serving:
Calories: 252 | Fat: 8.5g | Carbohydrates: 0g | Fiber:0g | Sugar: 0g | Protein: 41.3g | Sodium: 208mg

CAJUN SHRIMP KEBABS
Prep Time: 10 mins. | Cook Time: 4 mins. |Serves: 2

- 1 lb. shrimp
- 2 tbsp. olive oil
- 1 tsp. kosher salt, to taste
- 1 tsp. cayenne
- 1 tsp. paprika
- 1 tsp. garlic powder
- 1 tsp. onion powder
- 1 tsp. oregano
- 2 lemons, sliced crosswise

1. Mix shrimp with cayenne and rest of the ingredients in a mixing bowl.
2. Grease the griddle top with olive oil.
3. Thread the seasoned shrimp on the skewers.
4. Preheat your outdoor Griddle by turning all its burner's knob to medium-heat setting.
5. Place the Cajun shrimp skewers on the griddle top and cook for 2 minutes per side.
6. Serve warm.

Per Serving:
Calories: 190 | Fat: 9.5g | Carbohydrates: 14g | Fiber: 0.3g | Sugar: 0.2g | Protein: 24g | Sodium: 216mg

HALIBUT PARCEL
Prep Time: 10 mins. | Cook Time: 20 mins. |Serve: 1

- ¼ of onion, chopped
- ¼ of tomato, chopped
- 1 oz. kalamata olives, pitted
- 1 tbsp. capers
- ½ tbsp. olive oil
- ¼ tbsp. fresh lemon juice
- Salt and black pepper, to taste
- 1 (5-oz.) halibut fillet
- ¼ tbsp. Greek seasoning

1. Toss tomato, onion, capers, olives, oil, salt lemon juice, and black pepper in a suitable bowl.
2. Place a large piece of aluminum sheet on the working surface.
3. Rub the halibut fillet with Greek seasoning and place them on the aluminum sheet.
4. Top the fillet with the tomato-caper mixture and fold the aluminum to pack the fish.
5. Grease the griddle top with olive oil.
6. Preheat your outdoor Griddle by turning all its burner's knobs to medium low-heat setting.
7. Place the halibut parcel on the griddle top and cook for 15-20 minutes until fish is done
8. Serve warm.

Per Serving:
Calories: 267 | Fat: 12.5g | Carbohydrates: 21g |Fiber: 3g | Sugar: 1.7g | Protein: 30.8g | Sodium: 365mg

HALIBUT WITH VEGGIES
Prep Time: 10 mins. | Cook Time: 10 mins. |Serve: 2

- 2 tsp. olive oil
- 4 tbsp. yellow onion, minced
- ¼ cup zucchini, chopped
- 1 small garlic clove, minced
- ½ tsp. fresh basil, chopped
- 3 tbsp. tomato, chopped
- Salt and black pepper, to taste
- 1 (6-oz.) halibut fillet

1. Season the halibut with black pepper and salt.
2. Grease the griddle top with olive oil.
3. Preheat your outdoor Griddle by turning all its burner's knob to medium-heat setting.
4. Place the halibut on the griddle top and spread the veggies around it.
5. Drizzle black, salt and basil over the veggies.
6. Cook for 5 minutes then flip the halibut and veggies.
7. Continue cooking for 5 minutes then serve warm.

Per Serving:
Calories: 245 | Fat: 8.5g | Carbohydrates: 3.5g | Fiber: 1g | Sugar: 1.9g | Protein: 36.4g | Sodium: 249mg

SIMPLE TUNA

Prep Time: 5 mins. | Cook Time: 6 mins. | Serve: 1

- ✓ 1 (6-oz.) tuna steak
- ✓ ¼ tbsp. olive oil
- ✓ Salt and black pepper, to taste

1. Rub the tuna with black pepper and salt then leave for 5 minutes.
2. Grease the griddle top with olive oil.
3. Preheat your outdoor Griddle by turning all its burner's knob to medium-heat setting.
4. Place the seasoned tun on the griddle top and cook for 3 minutes per side.
5. Serve warm.

Per Serving:
Calories: 206 | Fat: 5g | Carbohydrates: 0g | Fiber:0g | Sugar: 0g | Protein: 39.8g | Sodium: 220mg

THYME TUNA

Prep Time: 10 mins. | Cook Time: 8 mins. | Serve: 1

- ✓ ½ tbsp. fresh lemon juice
- ✓ ¼ tbsp. olive oil
- ✓ ½ tsp. fresh thyme, minced
- ✓ ½ of garlic clove, minced
- ✓ Salt and black pepper, to taste
- ✓ 1 (6-oz.) tuna steak

1. Rub lemon juice, thyme, garlic, black pepper and salt over the tuna steak.
2. Grease the griddle top with olive oil.
3. Preheat your outdoor Griddle by turning all its burner's knob to medium-heat setting.
4. Place the tuna steak on the griddle top and cook for 3-4 minutes per side.
5. Serve warm.

Per Serving:
Calories: 215 | Fat: 5.1g | Carbohydrates: 10g | Fiber: 0.3g | Sugar: 0.2g | Protein: 40g | Sodium: 222mg

LEMONY TUNA

Prep Time: 10 mins. | Cook Time: 8 mins. | Serve: 1

- ✓ ½ tbsp. olive oil
- ✓ ½ tbsp. fresh lemon juice
- ✓ ¼ tsp. lemon zest, grated
- ✓ ¼ tsp. dried dill
- ✓ Salt and black pepper, to taste1 (6-oz.) tuna steak

1. Rub the tuna steak with black pepper, salt, dill, lemon zest, and lemon juice.
2. Grease the griddle top with olive oil.
3. Preheat your outdoor Griddle by turning all its burner's knob to medium-heat setting.
4. Place the tun steak on the griddle top and cook for 3-4 minutes per side.
5. Serve warm.

Per Serving:
Calories: 242 | Fat: 8.5g | Carbohydrates: 14g | Fiber: 0.1g | Sugar: 0.2g | Protein: 39.8g | Sodium:223mg

SPICY TUNA

Prep Time: 10 mins. | Cook Time: 8 mins. | Serve: 1

- ✓ 1/8 tsp. dried oregano
- ✓ 1/8 tsp. paprika
- ✓ 1/8 tsp. cayenne pepper
- ✓ 1/8 tsp. fennel seeds, crushed
- ✓ Salt and black pepper, to taste
- ✓ 1 (5-oz.) tuna steak
- ✓ ½ tbsp. olive oil

1. Mix oregano, paprika, cayenne pepper, fennel seeds, black pepper and salt in a bowl.
2. Rub the spice mixture over the tuna steak liberally.
3. Grease the griddle top with olive oil.
4. Preheat your outdoor Griddle by turning all its burner's knob to medium-heat setting.
5. Place the tuna steak on the griddle top and cook for 3-4 minutes per side.
6. Serve warm.

Per Serving:
Calories: 212 | Fat: 8.1g | Carbohydrates: 15g | Fiber: 0.3g | Sugar: 0.1g | Protein: 33.3g | Sodium:209mg

TUNA WITH CHIMICHURI

Prep Time: 10 mins. | Cook Time: 30 mins. | Serve: 1

- ✓ ¼ cup fresh parsley
- ✓ 1 garlic clove, chopped
- ✓ 1 tbsp. olive oil
- ✓ 1 tbsp. fresh lemon juice
- ✓ 1/8 tsp. red pepper flakes
- ✓ Salt and black pepper, to taste
- ✓ 1 (6-oz.) tuna steak

1. Puree parsley with garlic, lemon juice, red pepper flakes, black pepper and salt in a blender for 1 minute.
2. Grease the griddle top with olive oil.
3. Preheat your outdoor Griddle by turning all its burner's knob to medium-heat setting.
4. Place the tuna on the griddle top and spread the ½ of the chimichurri sauce over it.
5. Flip and cook for 3 minutes.
6. Flip again and brush ½ of the chimichurri sauce on top.
7. Cook for another 3 minutes then serve warm.

Per Serving:

Calories: 314 | Fat: 14.5g | Carbohydrates: 24g |Fiber: 0.5g | Sugar: 0.5g | Protein: 40.4g | Sodium:177mg

SIMPLE MACKEREL

Prep Time: 10 mins. | Cook Time: 10 mins. |Serve: 1

- ✓ 1 (6-oz.) mackerel fillet
- ✓ ½ tbsp. olive oil
- ✓ Salt and black pepper, to taste

1. Season the mackerel fillet with black pepper and salt.
2. Grease the griddle top with olive oil.
3. Preheat your outdoor Griddle by turning all its burner's knob to medium-heat setting.
4. Place the mackerel on the griddle top.
5. Cook for 5 minutes per side.
6. Serve warm.

Per Serving:
Calories: 330| Fat: 17.5g | Carbohydrates: 0g | Fiber: 0g | Sugar: 0g | Protein: 29.8g | Sodium: 265mg

HERBED SEA BASS

Prep Time: 10 mins. | Cook Time: 20 mins. |Serves: 2

- ✓ 1 (1¼-lb.) whole sea bass, gutted, gilled, scaledand fins removed
- ✓ Salt and black pepper, to taste
- ✓ 3 fresh bay leaves
- ✓ 1 fresh thyme sprig
- ✓ 1 fresh parsley sprig
- ✓ 1 fresh rosemary sprig1 tbsp. olive oil
- ✓ 1 tbsp. fresh lemon juice

1. Rub the inside and outside of the seabass fish with black pepper and salt.
2. Wrap it with a plastic sheet and refrigerate for 1 hour.
3. Place the seabass on a suitable-sized aluminum sheet and top it with the herbs, oil and lemon juice.
4. Wrap the sheet over to pack the fish.
5. Preheat your outdoor Griddle by turning all its burner's knob to medium-heat setting.
6. Place the seabass parcel on the griddle top and cook for 10 minutes per side.
7. Unwrap and serve warm.

Per Serving:
Calories: 344 | Fat: 8.4g | Carbohydrates: 18g | Fiber: 0.4g | Sugar: 0.2g | Protein: 56g | Sodium: 80mg

LEMONY TROUT

Prep Time: 10 mins. | Cook Time: 20 mins. |Serves: 4

- ✓ 1 (1½-lb.) wild-caught trout, gutted and cleaned
- ✓ Salt and black pepper, to taste
- ✓ ½ of lemon, sliced
- ✓ 1 tbsp. fresh dill, minced
- ✓ 1 tbsp. olive oil
- ✓ ½ tbsp. fresh lemon juice

1. Place the trout on a suitable-sized aluminum sheet and top it with the lemon slices, black pepper, salt, dill, oil, and lemon juice.
2. Wrap the sheet over to pack the fish.
3. Preheat your outdoor Griddle by turning all its burner's knob to medium-heat setting.
4. Place the trout parcel on the griddle top and cook for 10 minutes per side.
5. Unwrap and serve warm.

Per Serving:
Calories: 355 | Fat: 18g | Carbohydrates: 15g | Fiber: 0.1g | Sugar: 0g | Protein: 45.1g | Sodium:155mg

SPICED SHRIMP

Prep Time: 10 mins. | Cook Time: 8 mins. |Serve: 2

- ✓ ¼ tbsp. olive oil
- ✓ ¼ lb. medium shrimp, peeled and deveined
- ✓ ¼ tsp. dry mustard
- ✓ ¼ tsp. dried thyme
- ✓ ¼ tsp. dried oregano
- ✓ ¼ tsp. cayenne pepper

- ¼ tsp. paprika
- ¼ tsp. ground cumin
- Salt and black pepper, to taste

1. Mix shrimp with black pepper, salt, cumin, paprika, cayenne, oregano, thyme, and mustard in a suitable bowl.
2. Cover and marinate these shrimp for 15 minutes.
3. Grease the griddle top with olive oil.
4. Preheat your outdoor Griddle by turning all its burner's knob to medium-heat setting.
5. Place the shrimp on the griddle top and cook for 3-4 minutes per side.
6. Serve warm.

Per Serving:
Calories: 174 | Fat: 6g | Carbohydrates: 13g | Fiber: 0.5g | Sugar: 0.2g | Protein: 26.3g | Sodium: 233mg

LEMONY SCALLOPS

Prep Time: 10 mins. | Cook Time: 7 mins. |Serve: 1

- ½ tbsp. olive oil
- ¼ lb. medium scallop, peeled and deveined
- 1 small garlic clove, minced
- ¼ of lemon, sliced thinly
- 1/8 tsp. red pepper flakes, crushed
- Salt, to taste
- 1 tbsp. water
- ¼ tbsp. fresh lemon juice
- 1 tsp. fresh parsley, chopped

1. Mix scallops with lemon juice, parsley, water, red pepper flakes, salt.
2. Grease the griddle top with olive oil.
3. Preheat your outdoor Griddle by turning all its burner's knob to medium-heat setting.
4. Place the shrimp on the griddle top and cook for 2-3 minutes per side.
5. Serve warm.

Per Serving:
Calories: 175 | Fat: 8.5g | Carbohydrates: 13g | Fiber: 0.3g | Sugar: 0.1g | Protein: 24.4g | Sodium:165mg

GARLICKY SHRIMP

Prep Time: 10 mins. | Cook Time: 6 mins. |Serve: 1

- ½ tbsp. olive oil
- ¼ lb. medium shrimp, peeled and deveined
- 1 large garlic clove, minced
- Salt and black pepper, to taste

1. Toss shrimp with black pepper, salt, and garlic in a bowl.
2. Cover and marinate for 15 minutes.
3. Grease the griddle top with olive oil.
4. Preheat your outdoor Griddle by turning all its burner's knob to medium-heat setting.
5. Place the shrimp on the griddle top and cook for 2-3 minutes per side.
6. Serve warm.

Per Serving:
Calories: 172 | Fat: 8.4g | Carbohydrates: 10g | Fiber: 0.1g | Sugar: 0g | Protein: 24.5g | Sodium: 212mg

SOY SAUCE SHRIMP

Prep Time: 10 mins. | Cook Time: 6 mins. |Serve: 1

- ½ tbsp. olive oil
- 1 garlic clove, minced
- ¼ lb. raw jumbo shrimp, peeled and deveined
- 1 tbsp. low-sodium soy sauce
- Black pepper, to taste

1. Mix shrimp with black pepper, soy sauce, and garlic in a bowl and marinate for 15 minutes.
2. Grease the griddle top with olive oil.
3. Preheat your outdoor Griddle by turning all its burner's knob to medium-heat setting.
4. Place the scallops on the griddle top and cook for 2-3 minutes per side.
5. Serve warm.

Per Serving:
Calories: 152 | Fat: 7g | Carbohydrates: 21g | Fiber: 0.1g | Sugar: 3.1g | Protein: 21.5g | Sodium: 365mg

SHRIMP IN ORANGE SAUCE

Prep Time: 10 mins. | Cook Time: 11 mins. |Serve: 1

For Sauce
- 1 tbsp. fresh orange juice1-2 drops liquid stevia
- ½ tbsp. low-sodium soy sauce
- ¼ tbsp. balsamic vinegar

For Shrimp
- ¼ lb. shrimp, peeled and deveined1/8 tbsp. arrowroot powder
- ½ tbsp. olive oil1 small garlic clove, minced

- ¼ tsp. fresh ginger, minced

1. Grease the griddle top with olive oil.
2. Preheat your outdoor Griddle by turning all its burner's knob to medium-heat setting.
3. Mix shrimp with ginger, garlic, and arrowroot powder in a bowl to coat well.
4. Place the shrimp on the griddle top and cook for 2-3 minutes per side.
5. Mix the orange juice, vinegar, stevia and soy sauce in a saucepan and cook for 5 minutes on medium heat until it thickens.
6. Toss the cooked shrimp to the sauce then mix well.
7. Serve warm.

Per Serving:
Calories: 210 | Fat: 7.5g | Carbohydrates: 28g | Fiber: 0g | Sugar: 1.8g | Protein: 26.5g | Sodium: 365mg

VEGETARIAN RECIPES

BURGERS WITH MUSHROOMS AND ARUGULA
Prep Time: 10 mins. | Cook Time: 15 mins. | Serve: 4

- 4 (5-inch) Portobello mushroom caps, gills removed
- 1 large red onion, sliced
- 3 tbsp. 1 tsp. olive oil
- Salt and black pepper, to taste
- 2 garlic cloves, minced
- 2 tsp. minced fresh thyme
- 2 oz. goat cheese, crumbled
- 4 hamburger buns
- 1 cup baby arugula
- ¼ tsp. balsamic vinegar
- 1 tomato, cored and sliced thin

1. Score the top of each mushroom cap in a crosshatch pattern with the tip of a sharp knife. Season onion rounds with salt, black pepper and 1 tbsp. oil.
2. In a bowl, beat garlic, 2 tbsp. oil, salt, thyme, and ¼ tsp. black pepper.
3. Preheat your outdoor Griddle by turning all its burner's knob to medium-heat setting.
4. Grease the griddle top with cooking spray.
5. Add onion and mushroom on the hot griddle top and cook until soft.
6. Split the hamburger buns and cook for about 5 minutes.
7. In a suitable mixing bowl, toss the arugula with 1 tsp. oil, salt and black pepper to taste.
8. Divide vinegar, mushroom caps, arugula, tomato, and onion in the buns.
9. Serve.

Per Serving:
Calories: 282 | Fat: 17.1g | Carbohydrates: 3.4g | Fiber: 0.3g | Sugar: 0.2g | Protein: 27.8g | Sodium: 165mg

ASPARAGUS WITH BUTTER
Prep Time: 10 mins. | Cook Time: 10 mins. | Serve: 2

- 1½ lbs. thick asparagus spears, trimmed
- 3 tbsp. butter, melted
- Salt and black pepper, to taste

1. Preheat your outdoor Griddle by turning all its burner's knob to medium-heat setting.
2. Grease the griddle top with cooking spray.
3. Drizzle melted butter over asparagus and season with salt and black pepper.
4. Arrange asparagus on the hot griddle top and cook for 10 minutes.
5. Serve warm.

Per Serving:

Calories: 244 | Fat: 8.5g | Carbohydrates: 13g | Fiber: 2.1g | Sugar: 0.4g | Protein: 29g | Sodium: 219mg

PEPPER BUTTERNUT SQUASH
Prep Time: 10 mins. | Cook Time: 13 mins. | Serve: 2

- 1 small butternut squash (2 lbs.), peeled, seeded, and sliced
- Salt and black pepper, to taste
- 3 tbsp. olive oil

1. Add squash slice to a pot filled with boiling water and cook for 3 minutes then drain.
2. Preheat your outdoor Griddle by turning all its burner's knob to medium-heat setting.
3. Grease the griddle top with cooking oil.
4. Place squash slices on the hot griddle top and cook 5 minutes per side while seasoning with black pepper and salt.
5. Serve warm.

Per Serving:
Calories: 225 | Fat: 8.3g | Carbohydrates: 8g | Fiber:

1.3g | Sugar: 2.3g | Protein: 27.5g | Sodium: 265mg

CABBAGE WITH THYME AND LEMON
Prep Time: 10 mins. | Cook Time: 14 mins. |Serve: 2

- Salt and black pepper, to taste
- 1 cup vinaigrette
- 1 (2-lb.) head green cabbage, cut into wedges
- 1 tbsp. minced fresh thyme
- 2 tsp. minced shallot
- 2 tsp. honey
- 1 tsp. Dijon mustard
- ½ tsp. grated lemon zest
- 2 tbsp. juice
- 6 tbsp. olive oil

1. Season cabbage wedges evenly with 1 tsp. salt and set aside for 45 minutes.
2. In a suitable mixing bowl, mix well the shallot, thyme, honey, lemon zest and juice, mustard, and ¼ tsp. black pepper.
3. Whisk in the oil slowly until it is all incorporated.
4. Preheat your outdoor Griddle by turning all its burner's knob to medium-heat setting.
5. Grease the griddle top with cooking oil.
6. Brush half of the vinaigrette on one cut side of the cabbage wedges.
7. Place cabbage on a hot griddle top, and cook for 7 minutes
8. Brush the tops of the wedges with the remaining vinaigrette; flip and cook for 7 minutes.
9. Serve and enjoy.

Per Serving:
Calories: 212 | Fat: 9g | Carbohydrates: 28g | Fiber:1g | Sugar: 1.6g | Protein: 7g | Sodium: 248mg

BROCCOLI RICE WITH HERBS
Prep Time: 10 mins. | Cook Time: 17 mins. |Serve: 4

- 6 large tomatillos, peeled and rinsed
- Oil, for coating
- 1 white onion, chopped
- 2 cups cilantro, leaves
- 1 tbsp. roasted garlic
- 2 tsp. salt
- 1½ cups water
- 2 cups white rice
- 1 bunch scallions, bases trimmed
- 1 head broccoli, cut in half
- 1 cup basil leaves, chopped
- 1 cup parsley leaves, chopped

1. Preheat your outdoor Griddle by turning all its burner's knob to medium-heat setting.
2. Grease the griddle top with cooking oil.
3. Toss the tomatillos with oil to coat them and cook over for about 5 minutes on the hot griddle top.
4. Blend the onion, tomatillos, garlic, 1 cup cilantro, salt, and water in a blender until smooth.
5. Transfer this mixture to a pan and place on the hot griddle top.
6. Add the rice and cook, for 3 minutes, or until toasted and transparent.
7. Toss in the tomatillo puree and mix well.
8. Cook for 10 to 12 minutes, or until liquid has been absorbed.
9. Cook for another 5 minutes, covered.
10. Remove from the griddle with the cover on and set aside to steam until ready to serve.
11. Toss the scallions and broccoli in enough oil to coat and cook over medium heat until charred.
12. Add broccoli and rest of the ingredients to the rice.
13. Serve warm.

Per Serving:
Calories: 202 | Fat: 9g | Carbohydrates: 28g | Fiber: 0.1g | Sugar: 0.2g | Protein: 2.1g | Sodium: 235mg

EGGPLANT WITH MOLE
Prep Time: 10 mins. | Cook Time: 29 mins. |Serve: 4

- For the Mole:
- ¼ cup coriander seeds
- 4 cloves
- 1 cinnamon stick
- 1 cup unsalted peanuts
- ½ cup raw pumpkin seeds (pepitas)
- ½ cup raw sunflower seeds
- 5 chipotle chiles, seeded
- 4 guajillo chiles, seeded
- 3 Passilla chiles, seeded
- 2 ancho chiles, seeded
- 2 oz. dark chocolate
- Others
- 1 tsp. dried oregano
- 1 head roasted garlic; cloves removed
- 1 white or red onion, quartered
- 3 ripe plantains, unpeeled
- ½ ripe pineapple, cored
- ¾ cup apple juice

- ¼ cup apple cider vinegar
- ½ cup honey
- Salt, to taste
- 3 large globe eggplants
- Oil, for coating.

1. Toast the mole ingredients in a skillet for 1-2 minutes then transfer to a bowl.
2. Preheat your outdoor Griddle by turning all its burner's knob to medium-heat setting.
3. Grease the griddle top with cooking spray.
4. Sear onions, pineapple and plantains on the hot griddle top for 3-4 minutes per side.
5. Add mole, honey, apple juice, vinegar and seasoning to the fruits and cook for 15 minutes on low heat.
6. Cut the eggplants in half, brush with oil and cook for 3 minutes per side.
7. Serve the eggplants with the mole mixture.
8. Enjoy.

Per Serving:
Calories: 160 | Fat: 7.8g | Carbohydrates: 25g | Fiber: 0g | Sugar: 0g | Protein: 9.1g | Sodium: 238mg

GARLIC EGGPLANT WITH MINT YOGURT
Prep Time: 10 mins. | Cook Time: 10 mins. |Serve: 4

- 6 tbsp. olive oil
- 5 garlic cloves, minced
- ⅛ tsp. red pepper flakes
- ½ cup plain whole-milk yogurt
- 3 tbsp. minced fresh mint
- 1 tsp. grated lemon zest plus 2 tsp. juice
- 1 tsp. ground cumin
- Salt and black pepper, to taste
- 2 lbs. eggplant, sliced into ¼-inch-thick rounds

1. In a microwave-safe bowl, heat the garlic, oil, and pepper flakes for 2 minutes then strain.
2. Mix yoghurt, 1 tbsp. garlic oil, lemon zest and juice, mint, cumin, and ¼ tsp. salt in a bowl. Season eggplant with remaining garlic oil, salt and black pepper.
3. Preheat your outdoor Griddle by turning all its burner's knob to medium-heat setting.
4. Grease the griddle top with cooking spray.
5. Pour the egg mixture onto the hot griddle top
6. Half of the eggplant should be placed on the hot griddle top. Cook for 5 minutes per side.
7. Repeat with the remaining eggplant on a dish.

8. Drizzle with yoghurt sauce and top with garlic mixture.
9. Serve.

Per Serving:
Calories: 164 | Fat: 7.8g | Carbohydrates: 13g | Fiber: 0.1g | Sugar: 0g | Protein: 1.3g | Sodium: 238mg

GARLICKY LEMON MUSHROOMS
Prep Time: 10 mins. | Cook Time: 12 mins. |Serve: 4

- ½ cup olive oil
- 3 tbsp. lemon juice
- 6 garlic cloves, minced
- ¼ tsp. salt
- 4 Portobello mushrooms, stemmed

1. Mix well the lemon juice, oil, garlic, and salt in a ziplock bag.
2. Toss in the mushrooms, seal the bag, shake well and marinate for 30 minutes.
3. Preheat your outdoor Griddle by turning all its burner's knob to medium-heat setting.
4. Grease the griddle top with cooking spray.
5. Pour the egg mixture onto the hot griddle top
6. Cut four 12-inch squares of aluminum foil sheet.
7. Remove the mushrooms from the marinade and lay them, on a foil square.
8. Seal the edges of the foil around each mushroom.
9. Place foil packets on griddle top, sealed side up, and cook for 12 minutes.
10. Unwrap mushrooms with tongs and set on griddle for 60 seconds.
11. Serve.

Per Serving:
Calories: 170 | Fat: 8g | Carbohydrates: 25g | Fiber: 0.4g | Sugar: 0.5g | Protein: 1.8g | Sodium: 246mg

GARLIC BELL PEPPERS
Prep Time: 10 mins. | Cook Time: 15 mins. |Serve: 4

- ¼ cup olive oil
- 3 garlic cloves, peeled and smashed
- Salt and black pepper, to taste
- 6 red bell peppers
- 1 tbsp. sherry vinegar

1. Mix well the garlic, oil, ¼ tsp. black pepper and ½ tsp. salt.

2. Cut the stems of peppers, remove the cores and seeds.
3. Place the peppers in a bowl and toss them with oil.
4. Wrap aluminum foil around the bowl securely.
5. Preheat your outdoor Griddle by turning all its burner's knob to medium-heat setting.
6. Grease the griddle top with cooking spray.
7. Place the peppers on the hot griddle top and cook, for 15 minutes.
8. In a suitable dish, mix well the garlic, vinegar and juices.
9. Remove the cooked peppers from the griddle and place them in a separate bowl, carefully covered with foil. Allow 5 minutes for the peppers to steam.
10. Scrape the charred skin off each pepper with a spoon.
11. Quarter the peppers lengthwise and toss with the vinaigrette in a suitable mixing bowl.
12. Serve with a pinch of salt and black pepper to taste.

Per Serving:
Calories: 217 | Fat: 9.3g | Carbohydrates: 15g | Fiber: 0.4g | Sugar: 0.3g | Protein: 2.8g | Sodium: 225mg

ROSEMARY RED POTATOES
Prep Time: 10 mins. | Cook Time: 10 mins. | Serve: 4

- ¼ cup olive oil
- 9 garlic cloves, minced
- 1 tsp. chopped fresh rosemary
- Salt and black pepper, to taste
- 2 lbs. small red potatoes, halved
- 2 tbsp. chopped fresh chives

1. Preheat your outdoor Griddle by turning all its burner's knob to medium-heat setting.
2. Grease the griddle top with cooking spray.
3. Toss potatoes with garlic, rosemary and rest of the ingredients in a bowl.
4. Sear the potatoes for 5 minutes per side.

5. Serve and enjoy.

Per Serving:
Calories: 227 | Fat: 14.3g | Carbohydrates: 3.4g | Fiber: 1.1g | Sugar: 1.7g | Protein: 2.4g | Sodium: 96mg

GARLICY YUKON GOLD POTATO HOBO PACKS
Prep Time: 10 mins. | Cook Time: 10 mins. | Serve: 4

- 2 lbs. Yukon Gold potatoes, unpeeled
- 1 tbsp. olive oil
- 2 garlic cloves, peeled and chopped
- 1 tsp. minced fresh thyme
- 1 tsp. salt
- ½ tsp. black pepper

1. Halve each potato lengthwise, then cut each into eight wedges.
2. Microwave potatoes in large bowl, covered, for 7 minutes. Drain thoroughly.
3. Toss the potatoes wedges in a bowl with the oil, garlic, thyme, salt, and pepper.
4. Cut four sheets of heavy-duty aluminum foil into 14 by 10-inch rectangles.
5. Spread one-quarter of the potato mixture over half of the foil, fold foil and crimp edges tightly to seal.
6. Preheat your outdoor Griddle by turning all its burner's knob to medium-heat setting.
7. Grease the griddle top with cooking spray.
8. Place hobo packs on the hot griddle top and cook, for 10 minutes.
9. Serve.

Per Serving:
Calories: 202 | Fat: 9.8g | Carbohydrates: 13g | Fiber: 0.5g | Sugar: 1.4g | Protein: 4.4g | Sodium: 220mg

BASIL WINE ZUCCHINI AND EGGPLANT SALAD
Prep Time: 10 mins. | Cook Time: 12 mins. | Serve: 4

- 3 tbsp. white wine vinegar
- 3 garlic cloves, minced
- 1½ tsp. Dijon mustard
- Salt and black pepper, to taste
- 6 tbsp. olive oil
- 3 (8-oz. / 227-g) zucchini, halved lengthwise
- 1 red onion, sliced into ½-inch-thick rounds
- 1 red bell pepper, stemmed, seeded, and halved lengthwise

- 1 lb. eggplant, sliced into ½-inch-thick rounds
- 3 tbsp. chopped fresh basil
- 1 tbsp. minced fresh parsley

1. In a suitable mixing bowl, mix well the garlic, vinegar, ½ tsp. salt, mustard, and ½ tsp. black pepper.
2. Whisk in the oil slowly until. Set aside 2 tsp. of salad dressing.
3. Toss the zucchini, onion, and bell pepper with the remaining dressing.
4. Preheat your outdoor Griddle by turning all its burner's knob to medium-heat setting.
5. Grease the griddle top with cooking oil.
6. Sear eggplant and all the veggies on the hot griddle top for 5-6 minutes per side
7. Toss veggies with leftover dressing, black pepper, salt, basil, and parsley in 1-inch pieces.
8. Serve.

Per Serving:
Calories: 197 | Fat: 9g | Carbohydrates: 23g | Fiber: 0.3g | Sugar: 0.1g | Protein: 6g | Sodium: 232mg

TOMATO AND ZUCCHINI RATATOUILLE
Prep Time: 10 mins. | Cook Time: 35 mins. |Serve: 4

- 1 red onion, sliced
- 2 lbs. eggplant, sliced
- 1½ lbs. zucchini, sliced
- 2 bell peppers, halved, half cut into thirds
- 1 lb. tomatoes, cored and halved
- ¼ cup olive oil
- Salt and black pepper, to taste
- 3 tbsp. sherry vinegar
- ¼ cup fresh basil, chopped
- 1 tbsp. fresh thyme, minced
- 1 garlic clove, minced to paste

1. Toss the eggplant, onion, bell peppers, zucchini, and tomatoes with oil, salt and black pepper on a baking sheet.
2. In a suitable mixing bowl, combine ¼ cup oil, basil, vinegar, thyme, and garlic.
3. Preheat your outdoor Griddle by turning all its burner's knob to medium-heat setting.
4. Grease the griddle top with cooking oil.
5. Cook onions for 12 minutes, eggplant and squash for 10 minutes, peppers for 9 minutes, and tomatoes for 5 minutes on a griddle.
6. Allow the veggies to cool then chop.
7. Serve warm.

Per Serving:
Calories: 274 | Fat: 21.g | Carbohydrates: 15g | Fiber: 1.3g | Sugar: 0.9g | Protein: 6.5g | Sodium:241mg

GARLIC GINGER TOFU WITH CILANTRO
Prep Time: 10 mins. | Cook Time: 20 mins. |Serve: 2

- Glaze
- ⅓ cup soy sauce
- ⅓ cup water
- ⅓ cup sugar
- ¼ cup mirin
- 1 tbsp. fresh ginger, grated
- 2 garlic cloves, minced
- 2 tsp. cornstarch
- 1 tsp. Asian chili-garlic sauce
- Tofu
- 28 oz. firm tofu, sliced
- 2 tbsp. vegetable oil
- Salt and black pepper, to taste
- ¼ cup fresh cilantro, minced

1. Preheat your outdoor Griddle by turning all its burner's knob to low-heat setting.
2. Grease the griddle top with cooking oil.
3. Mix water, soy sauce, mirin, sugar, garlic, ginger, cornstarch, and chili-garlic sauce in a bowl.
4. Cook this sauce for almost 10 minutes on low heat with stirring.
5. Season tofu with oil, black pepper and salt.
6. Place the tofu on the hot griddle top and cook for 5 minutes per side.
7. Pour the prepared glaze on top.
8. Serve and enjoy.

Per Serving:
Calories: 225 | Fat: 9.4g | Carbohydrates: 6g | Fiber: 1.4g | Sugar: 2g | Protein: 9.3g | Sodium: 222mg

SALTY PLANTAINS
Prep Time: 10 mins. | Cook Time: 8 mins. |Serve: 2

- ✓ 2 large ripe plantains, peeled and sliced
- ✓ 2 tbsp. vegetable oil
- ✓ Salt, to taste

1. Preheat your outdoor Griddle by turning all its burner's knob to medium-heat setting.
2. Grease the griddle top with cooking spray.
3. Place plantains in a suitable mixing bowl.
4. Season with oil and salt, and then sear on griddle top for 4 minutes per side.
5. Serve.

Per Serving:
Calories: 125 | Fat: 09g | Carbohydrates: 13g | Fiber: 1.3g | Sugar: 0.9g | Protein: 2.5g | Sodium:241mg

ZUCCHINI AND CAULIFLOWER SKEWERS
Prep Time: 10 mins. | Cook Time: 10 mins. |Serve: 2

- ✓ 4 large zucchini, diced
- ✓ 1 head cauliflower, cut into florets
- ✓ 8 skewers, soaked
- ✓ olive oil, for drizzling
- ✓ kosher salt, to taste
- ✓ black pepper
- ✓ ¼ cup crumbled feta

1. Toss zucchini, cauliflower, black pepper, and salt in a bowl.
2. Thread the cauliflower and zucchini on the skewers alternately.
3. Grease the griddle top with olive oil.
4. Preheat your outdoor Griddle by turning all its burner's knob to medium-heat setting.
5. Place the skewers on the griddle top and cook for 5 minutes per side.
6. Garnish with feta cheese and serve warm.

Per Serving:
Calories: 241| Fat: 12.5g | Carbohydrates: 25g |Fiber: 1.1g | Sugar: 1.8g | Protein: 4.4g | Sodium:280mg

TATER TOT SKEWERS
Prep Time: 10 mins. | Cook Time: 10 mins. |Serve: 2

- ✓ 1 lb. frozen tater tots, defrosted
- ✓ 12 slices bacon
- ✓ 1 cup shredded Cheddar
- ✓ 2 tbsp. chives
- ✓ Ranch dressing, for serving

1. Cut the bacon slices into 3 pieces and wrap each tater tot with bacon.
2. Thread the tater tots on the skewers in a way that the bacon are sealed around the tater tots.
3. Grease the griddle top with olive oil.
4. Preheat your outdoor Griddle by turning all its burner's knob to medium-heat setting.
5. Place the tater tots on the griddle top and cook for 5 minutes per side.
6. Drizzle cheddar and chives on top
7. Serve warm with ranch dressing.

Per Serving:
Calories: 277 | Fat: 2.3g | Carbohydrates: 5g | Fiber:1g | Sugar: 1.5g | Protein: 31.4g | Sodium: 265mg

GRILLED RANCH POTATOES
Prep Time: 10 mins. | Cook Time: 6 mins. |Serve: 4

- ✓ 2 lb. baby potatoes, halved
- ✓ ¼ tbsp. olive oil
- ✓ Juice of ½ a lemon
- ✓ ½ packet ranch seasoning
- ✓ kosher salt, to taste
- ✓ black pepper
- ✓ Ranch dressing, for drizzling
- ✓ Chopped fresh chives, to garnish

1. Add potatoes to a pot filled with boiling water and cook until they are just soft.
2. Mix the potatoes with lemon juice, black pepper, salt, and ranch seasoning in a bowl.
3. Grease the griddle top with olive oil.
4. Preheat your outdoor Griddle by turning all its burner's knob to medium-heat setting.
5. Place the potatoes on the griddle top and cook for

2-3 minutes per side.
6. Serve warm with chive and ranch dressing on top.

Per Serving:

Calories: 235 | Fat: 10.4g | Carbohydrates: 6g | Fiber: 1.3g | Sugar: 1.5g | Protein: 7.8g | Sodium:345mg

ZUCCHINI MUSHROOM KABOBS
Prep Time: 18 mins. | Cook Time: 10 mins. |Serve: 2

- 2 medium zucchini, cut into half-moons
- 1 (10-oz.) package baby bella mushrooms, halved
- 1 medium red onion, cut into wedges
- 2 small lemons, cut into eighths
- 3 tbsp. olive oil
- 1 garlic clove, grated
- 1 tsp. chopped thyme, oregano, or rosemary
- Pinch crushed red pepper flakes
- Kosher salt, to taste
- black pepper

1. Mix zucchini, mushrooms, onion, lemons, garlic, thyme, red pepper flakes, black pepper and salt in a bowl.
2. Thread the veggies on the skewers, alternately.
3. Grease the griddle top with olive oil.
4. Preheat your outdoor Griddle by turning all its burner's knob to medium-heat setting.
5. Place the skewers on the griddle top and cook for 5 minutes per side.
6. Serve warm.

Per Serving:
Calories: 244 | Fat: 14.3g | Carbohydrates: 7g | Fiber: 2.1g | Sugar: 3.3g | Protein: 3.4g | Sodium:214mg

TORTELLINI SKEWERS
Prep Time: 10 mins. | Cook Time: 6 mins. |Serve: 2

- Kosher salt, to taste
- 9 oz. fresh cheese tortellini
- 8 oz. mozzarella balls, halved
- 2 tbsp. olive oil
- 1 tbsp. red wine vinegar
- ¼ tp. dried oregano
- Large pinch red pepper flakes
- 4 oz. sliced salami rounds, halved if large
- 1 cup pesto sauce pesto sauce, for dipping

1. Cook cheese tortellini as per the package's instructions.
2. Drain and mix them with vinegar, oregano, and red pepper flakes
3. Thread tortellini and salami on the skewers alternately.
4. Grease the griddle top with olive oil.
5. Preheat your outdoor Griddle by turning all its burner's knob to medium-heat setting.
6. Place the skewers on the griddle top and cook for 3 minutes per side.
7. Serve warm with pesto sauce.

Per Serving:
Calories: 226 | Fat: 5.4g | Carbohydrates: 25g | Fiber: 0.8g | Sugar: 1.6g | Protein: 38.4g | Sodium:295mg

GRILLED BRUSSELS SPROUTS
Prep Time: 10 mins. | Cook Time: 6 mins. |Serve: 4

- 1 lb. brussels sprouts, halved
- 3 tbsp. olive oil
- ¼ cup balsamic vinegar
- 1 tbsp. honey
- 1 tbsp. grainy mustard
- ½ tsp. crushed red pepper flakes
- Kosher salt, to taste
- ½ cup Parmesan, grated , to garnish

1. Mix honey with vinegar, mustard, salt and red pepper flakes in a bowl.
2. Thread the Brussel sprouts on the skewers.
3. Grease the griddle top with olive oil.
4. Preheat your outdoor Griddle by turning all its burner's knob to medium-heat setting.
5. Place the skewers on the griddle top and cook for 2-3 minutes per side.
6. Brush the honey mixture over the brussels sprouts on the both the two sides.
7. Cook for another 3 minutes per side.
8. Garnish with parmesan cheese.
9. Serve warm.

Per Serving:
Calories: 202 | Fat: 8.8g | Carbohydrates: 24g | Fiber: 0.4g | Sugar: 3.2g | Protein: 2.5g | Sodium:265mg

BANG BANG CAULIFLOWER KEBABS
Prep Time: 10 mins. | Cook Time: 15 mins. |Serve: 4

- 2 small heads cauliflower, cut into florets
- ¼ cup sweet chili sauce
- 3 tbsp. olive oil
- 1 tbsp. Sriracha
- ½ tsp. chili flakes
- 3 garlic cloves, minced
- Juice of 1 lime
- Kosher salt, to taste
- 1 green onion, sliced
- 1 tsp. toasted sesame seeds.

1. Season cauliflower florets with salt and chili flakes.
2. Grease the griddle top with olive oil.
3. Preheat your outdoor Griddle by turning all its burner's knob to medium-heat setting.
4. Place the cauliflower florets on the griddle top and cook for 5 minutes per side.
5. Mix sweet chili sauce, Sriracha, garlic, lime juice and salt in a saucepan then cook to a boil.
6. Toss in the cauliflower florets then mix well.
7. Garnish with sesame seeds
8. Serve warm

Per Serving:
Calories: 305 | Fat: 7.5g | Carbohydrates: 10.1g | Fiber: 3.1g | Sugar: 7g | Protein: 1.8g | Sodium: 161mg

Per Serving:
Calories: 304 | Fat: 7.1g | Carbohydrates: 11g | Fiber: 2.4g | Sugar: 7g | Protein: 0.4g | Sodium: 5mg

CORN ON THE COB
Prep Time: 10 mins. | Cook Time: 10 mins. |Serve: 6

- ½ cup (1 stick) unsalted butter
- 1 tsp. kosher salt, to taste
- 1 tsp. black pepper
- 6 ears of corn

1. Brush the butter over the corn cobs and drizzle salt and black pepper over them.
2. Grease the griddle top with butter.
3. Preheat your outdoor Griddle by turning all its burner's knob to medium-heat setting.
4. Place the corn cobs on the griddle top and cook for 5 minutes per side.
5. Serve.

Per Serving:
Calories: 336 | Fat: 11.4g | Carbohydrates: 3.8g | Fiber: 1g | Sugar: 2.5g | Protein: 6.3g | Sodium: 222mg

VEGGIE GRIDDLE CAKES
Prep Time: 10 mins. | Cook Time: 10 mins. |Serve: 4

- 2 eggs
- ½ cup vanilla fat-free yogurt
- 1 ¼ cups biscuit baking mix
- 1 tbsp. vegetable oil
- 1 onion, diced
- ½ cup chopped green bell pepper
- ½ cup chopped red bell pepper
- 1 tsp. chopped fresh parsley
- 1 small tomato, diced

1. Beat eggs with yogurt, and baking mix in a bowl until smooth.
2. Stir in onion, bell pepper, tomatoes and parsley.
3. Mix well and make 4-6 patties out of this mixture.
4. Grease the griddle top with olive oil.
5. Preheat your outdoor Griddle by turning all its burner's knob to medium-heat setting.
6. Place the patties on the griddle top and cook for 5 minutes per side.
7. Serve.

CAULIFLOWER WEDGES WITH HERB TARATOR
Prep Time: 10 mins. | Cook Time: 10 mins. |Serve: 4

- Tarator
- ¼ cp sliced or slivered almonds
- 2 garlic cloves, grated
- 1 cup chopped dill
- ½ cup mint leaves
- ½ cup tahini
- ⅓ cup fresh lemon juice
- Kosher salt, to taste, pepper
- Cauliflower and assembly
- 1 small cauliflower (1½ lb.)
- ¼ cup olive oil (for drizzling)
- ½ tsp. ground coriander
- ½ tsp. ground cumin
- ½ tsp. turmeric
- Handful of tender herbs

1. Mix all the tarator ingredients in a bowl and keep it aside.
2. Cut the cauliflower into wedges and mix them with coriander, cumin, turmeric and herbs in a bowl.

3. Grease the griddle top with olive oil.
4. Preheat your outdoor Griddle by turning all its burner's knob to medium-heat setting.
5. Place the wedges on the griddle top and cook for 5 minutes per side.
6. Serve the cauliflower wedges with tarator sauce.

Per Serving:
Calories: 362 | Fat: 13.5g | Carbohydrates: 25g | Fiber: 1.5g | Sugar: 3.8g | Protein: 1.4g | Sodium: 180mg

CARROTS WITH AVOCADO AND MINT
Prep Time: 10 mins. | Cook Time: 10 mins. | Serve: 4

- 1 tsp. cumin seeds
- 3 Tbsp. fresh lemon juice
- 2 tsp. honey
- ¼ cup plus 2 Tbsp. olive oil
- 1 serrano chile, seeds removed if desired, sliced
- 1 (1") piece ginger, peeled, grated
- Kosher salt, to taste
- 1½ lb. medium carrots, halved
- 2 avocados, cut into large pieces
- ½ cup mint leaves

1. Season carrots with honey, lemon juice, and salt.
2. Grease the griddle top with olive oil.
3. Preheat your outdoor Griddle by turning all its burner's knob to medium-heat setting.
4. Place the carrots on the griddle top and cook for 5 minutes per side.
5. Add mint and rest of the carrots and serve.

Per Serving:
Calories: 272 | Fat: 5.5g | Carbohydrates: 23g | Fiber: 2.4g | Sugar: 2.8g | Protein: 1g | Sodium: 162mg

EGGPLANT WITH TAHINI-YOGURT SAUCE
Prep Time: 10 mins. | Cook Time: 30 mins. | Serve: 4

- 2 lb. assorted small eggplant, sliced
- 2 heads of garlic
- 1 cup plain whole-milk Greek yogurt
- 1 tbsp. tahini
- Kosher salt, to taste
- 1 lemon, halved
- Sumac (for serving)

1. Grease the griddle top with olive oil.
2. Preheat your outdoor Griddle by turning all its burner's knob to medium-heat setting.
3. Place the eggplant on the griddle top and cook for 5 minutes per side.
4. Cook the garlic heads on the griddle top for 20 minutes on low heat.
5. Allow the garlic to cool then peel.
6. Blend garlic with yogurt and rest of the ingredients in a blender.
7. Pour the garlic sauce over the seared eggplant.
8. Serve.

Per Serving:
Calories: 240 | Fat: 17.5g | Carbohydrates: 6g | Fiber: 3.3g | Sugar: 1g | Protein: 7g | Sodium: 224mg

CARIBBEAN JERK VEGETABLES
Prep Time: 10 mins. | Cook Time: 10 mins. | Serve: 4

Jerk Seasoning
- 1 tbsp. of onion powder
- 1 tbsp. of ground allspice
- 1 tsp. of five-spice powder
- 1 tsp. of ground ginger
- 1 tsp. of ground nutmeg
- ½ tsp. of garlic powder
- ½ tsp. of cayenne pepper
- 1 tbsp. of dried thyme
- salt and pepper, to taste

Vegetables
- 1 zucchini, sliced
- 1 yellow zucchini squash, thickly sliced
- 1 bunch of asparagus, tough ends removed
- 1 cup of sliced mushrooms
- 1 red bell pepper, sliced
- 1 orange bell pepper, sliced
- 2 tbsp. of olive oil

1. Mix all the jerk seasoning in a large bowl.
2. Toss in all the veggies and mix well to coat.
3. Grease the griddle top with olive oil.
4. Preheat your outdoor Griddle by turning all its burner's knob to medium-heat setting.
5. Place the veggies on the griddle top and cook for 5 minutes per side.
6. Toss the veggies together.
7. Serve.

Per Serving:
Calories: 280 | Fat: 7.3g | Carbohydrates: 24g | Fiber: 1g | Sugar: 2.2g | Protein: 0.8g | Sodium: 161mg

BACON GREEN BEANS WITH PECANS
Prep Time: 10 mins. | Cook Time: 10 mins. | Serve: 4

- ✓ 1 bag fresh green beans
- ✓ 5-6 strips thick cut bacon
- ✓ ¼ cup bourbon
- ✓ ½ cup honey glazed pecans
- ✓ ½ cup raisins
- ✓ ¼ cup brown sugar
- ✓ 1-2 tbsp. unsalted butter
- ✓ pinch kosher salt, to taste
- ✓ Pinch Coarse Pepper

1. Mix bourbon, sugar, salt and black pepper in a bowl.
2. Grease the griddle top with butter.
3. Preheat your outdoor Griddle by turning all its burner's knob to medium-heat setting.
4. Place the wrapped green beans and bacon on the griddle top and cook for 5 minutes per side.
5. Chop the green beans and bacon into pieces.
6. Pour the prepared bourbon sauce, pecans and craisins then mix well.
7. Serve.

Per Serving:
Calories: 296 | Fat: 7.4g | Carbohydrates: 13g | Fiber: 3g | Sugar: 2g | Protein: 2.1g | Sodium: 165mg

LEEK POTATO SALAD
Prep Time: 10 mins. | Cook Time: 16 mins. | Serve: 4

- ✓ 2 lb. new red potatoes, boiled and halved
- ✓ Kosher salt, to taste and pepper
- ✓ 2 medium leeks, halved
- ✓ 3 tbsp. 2 tsp. olive oil
- ✓ 1 tbsp. grated lemon zest
- ✓ ¼ tsp. red pepper flakes
- ✓ 2 tbsp. cider vinegar
- ✓ 2 tbsp. whole-grain mustard

1. Toss leeks with potatoes, lemon zest, red pepper flakes, vinegar and mustard in a bowl.
2. Grease the griddle top with olive oil.
3. Preheat your outdoor Griddle by turning all its burner's knob to medium-heat setting.
4. Place the veggies on the griddle top and cook for 6-8 minutes per side.
5. Serve.

Per Serving:
Calories: 385 | Fat: 16.5g | Carbohydrates: 24g | Fiber: 1.5g | Sugar: 2.8g | Protein: 5.5g | Sodium: 251mg

GREEN BEANS, FENNEL, AND FARRO
Prep Time: 10 mins. | Cook Time: 10 mins. | Serve: 4

- ✓ ½ cup quick-cooking farro, cooked
- ✓ ½ lb. green beans, trimmed
- ✓ ½ lb. wax beans, trimmed
- ✓ 2 tbsp. olive oil, divided
- ✓ Kosher salt, to taste
- ✓ 1 tbsp. fennel seeds
- ✓ Pinch red pepper flakes
- ✓ 2 tbsp. white wine vinegar
- ✓ 1 tsp. honey
- ✓ ¼ cup toasted pistachios, chopped
- ✓ 1 small bulb fennel, very shaved
- ✓ Fennel fronds, for serving

1. Season green beans, and wax beans with salt.
2. Grease the griddle top with olive oil.
3. Preheat your outdoor Griddle by turning all its burner's knob to medium-heat setting.
4. Place the green and wax beans on the griddle top and cook for 5 minutes per side.
5. Toss farro, fennel seeds, honey and rest of the ingredients in a suitable bowl.
6. Toss in green and wax beans then mix well.
7. Serve.

Per Serving:
Calories: 114 | Fat: 10.3g | Carbohydrates: 23g | Fiber: 3g | Sugar: 2.6g | Protein: 2.5g | Sodium: 165mg

CHARRED PEPPERS WITH QUESO BLANCO
Prep Time: 10 mins. | Cook Time: 10 mins. | Serve: 2

- ✓ 1 lb. poblano peppers
- ✓ ½ lb. mini sweet peppers
- ✓ 2 bell peppers (yellow and orange)
- ✓ 2 jalapeños
- ✓ 1 tbsp. olive oil
- ✓ Kosher salt, to taste
- ✓ ½ cup half-and-half
- ✓ 6 oz. Monterey jack cheese, coarsely grated
- ✓ 3 slices white American cheese
- ✓ 1 lime
- ✓ ½ cup tortilla chips, crushed
- ✓ 1 tbsp. cilantro, chopped

1. Grease the griddle top with olive oil.
2. Preheat your outdoor Griddle by turning all its burner's knob to medium-heat setting.
3. Place the sweet and poblano peppers on the griddle top and cook for 5 minutes per side.
4. Season the peppers with black pepper and salt.
5. Blend half and half, cheese, jalapenos, lime juice, black pepper, salt and cilantro.
6. Divide the peppers into tortilla and top with the sauce.
7. Serve.

Per Serving:
Calories: 270 | Fat: 4g | Carbohydrates: 8g | Fiber: 2.3g | Sugar: 5g | Protein: 1.4g | Sodium: 219mg

RAINBOW VEGGIE KABOBS

Prep Time: 10 mins. | Cook Time: 20 mins. |Serve: 4

- ✓ 1 tsp. ground cumin
- ✓ ½ tsp. ground coriander
- ✓ ½ tsp. smoked paprika
- ✓ 6 tbsp. olive oil
- ✓ 2 lb. summer squash, cut into 1" chunks
- ✓ 1 pt. grape tomatoes
- ✓ 12 oz. small broccoli florets
- ✓ 8 oz. cremini mushrooms, halved
- ✓ 1 lime

1. Toss veggies with seasonings and rest of the ingredients in a bowl.
2. Grease the griddle top with olive oil.
3. Preheat your outdoor Griddle by turning all its burner's knob to medium-heat setting.
4. Thread the veggies on the skewers alternately.
5. Place the skewers on the griddle top and cook for 5-10 minutes per side until veggies are soft.
6. Serve.

Per Serving:
Calories: 280| Fat: 7.3g | Carbohydrates: 21g | Fiber: 1.3g | Sugar: 1.4g | Protein: 1g | Sodium: 168mg

SEARED PEPPERS

Prep Time: 10 mins. | Cook Time: 10 mins. |Serve: 4

- ✓ 3 mixed colored bell peppers
- ✓ 3/4 lb. mini sweet peppers
- ✓ 1 ½ tbsp. olive oil
- ✓ ¼ tsp. Kosher salt, to taste and pepper

1. Grease the griddle top with olive oil.
2. Preheat your outdoor Griddle by turning all its burner's knob to medium-heat setting.
3. Place the pepper on the griddle top and cook for 5 minutes per side.
4. Season the peppers with black pepper and salt.
5. Serve.

Per Serving:
Calories: 315 | Fat: 7.5g | Carbohydrates: 13g | Fiber: 2.5g | Sugar: 3.3g | Protein: 3g | Sodium: 162mg

VEGETABLE SKEWERS

Prep Time: 10 mins. | Cook Time: 10 mins. |Serve: 2

- ✓ 1 red pepper, cubed
- ✓ 1 zucchini, sliced
- ✓ 1 yellow or summer squash, sliced
- ✓ 10 bella mushrooms
- ✓ 1 red onion diced
- ✓ Oil
- ✓ Seasonings

1. Thread the veggies on the skewers
2. Grease the griddle top with olive oil.
3. Preheat your outdoor Griddle by turning all its burner's knob to medium-heat setting.
4. Place the skewers on the griddle top and cook for 5 minutes per side.
5. Serve.

Per Serving:
Calories: 355 | Fat: 4.5g | Carbohydrates: 21g | Fiber: 1.4g | Sugar: 2.3g | Protein: 3g | Sodium: 215mg

EGGPLANT WITH CHICKPEA CROUTONS

Prep Time: 10 mins. | Cook Time: 16 mins. |Serve: 2

- ✓ 3 tbsp. 1 tsp. olive oil
- ✓ 1 small onion, chopped
- ✓ 2 garlic cloves, pressed
- ✓ Kosher salt, to taste
- ✓ 1 cup chickpea flour
- ✓ 1 tbsp. lemon zest
- ✓ 2 tsp. lemon juice
- ✓ 2 medium eggplants (12 oz.), sliced
- ✓ ¼ cup plain full-fat yogurt

- ✓ 1 cup mint leaves, torn
- ✓ 2 tbsp. chopped chives

1. Grease the griddle top with olive oil.
2. Preheat your outdoor Griddle by turning all its burner's knob to medium-heat setting.
3. Place the eggplant slices on the griddle top and cook for 5 minutes per side.
4. Season the eggplant with onion and salt then cook for 1 minute.
5. In a blender, add rest of the ingredients and pulse until smooth.
6. Make 1 inches balls out of this chickpea dough and cook for 2-3 minutes per side.
7. Serve eggplant with the croutons.

Per Serving:
Calories: 114 | Fat: 9.3g | Carbohydrates: 28.5g | Fiber: 2.8g | Sugar: 3g | Protein: 1.4g | Sodium: 165mg

SWEET POTATOES WITH LEMON-HERB SAUCE
Prep Time: 10 mins. | Cook Time: 10 mins. |Serve: 2

- ✓ ½ small red onion, chopped
- ✓ 2 tsp. grated lemon zest plus ¼ cup juice
- ✓ 2 lb. sweet potatoes, well-scrubbed and sliced into ¼-in.-thick rounds
- ✓ 3 tbsp. olive oil, divided, plus more for serving
- ✓ Kosher salt, to taste and pepper
- ✓ 1 small Fresno chile, seeded and chopped
- ✓ 2 tbsp. hemp seed (optional)
- ✓ ¼ cup fresh mint, chopped
- ✓ Plain Greek yogurt, for serving

1. Season the sweet potatoes with black pepper, salt,
2. Mix lemon juice, black pepper, salt, Fresno chile, hemp seed and mint in a bowl.
3. Grease the griddle top with olive oil.
4. Preheat your outdoor Griddle by turning all its burner's knob to medium-heat setting.
5. Place the sweet potato slices on the griddle top and cook for 5 minutes per side.
6. Serve with lemon sauce on top.

Per Serving:
Calories: 161| Fat: 13.5g | Carbohydrates: 15g | Fiber: 4.8g | Sugar: 0.4g | Protein: 3.4g | Sodium: 75mg

EGGPLANT STIR-FRY
Prep Time: 10 mins. | Cook Time: 20 mins. |Serve: 4

- ✓ 3 red peppers, seeded and halved
- ✓ 3 yellow squash, sliced
- ✓ 3 courgettes, sliced
- ✓ 3 Japanese eggplant, sliced
- ✓ 12 chestnut mushrooms
- ✓ 1 bunch asparagus, trimmed
- ✓ 12 spring onions, roots cut off
- ✓ 2 tbsp. olive oil
- ✓ Salt and black pepper
- ✓ 3 tbsp. balsamic vinegar
- ✓ 2 garlic cloves, minced
- ✓ 1 tsp. fresh Italian parsley leaves, chopped
- ✓ 1 tsp. fresh basil leaves, chopped
- ✓ ½ tsp. fresh rosemary leaves, chopped

1. Season all the veggies with black pepper, salt, vinegar, rosemary, basil and parsley in a large bowl.
2. Grease the griddle top with olive oil.
3. Preheat your outdoor Griddle by turning all its burner's knob to medium-heat setting.
4. Place the veggies on the griddle top and cook for 5-10 minutes per side until tender.
5. Serve.

Per Serving:
Calories: 287 | Fat: 7.3g | Carbohydrates: 33g | Fiber: 1.8g | Sugar: 3.3g | Protein: 1.3g | Sodium: 165mg

DESSERT RECIPES

PINEAPPLE WITH MAPLE WALNUT ICE CREAM
Prep Time: 10 mins. | Cook Time: 8 mins. | Serve: 4

- 1 (16-oz.) can pineapple rings
- ¼ cup maple syrup
- Juice of 1 lime
- ¼ tsp. ground cinnamon
- Butter, clarified butter, or coconut oil
- 1 pint maple walnut ice cream, to serve
- Chocolate sauce, to serve

1. Preheat your outdoor Griddle by turning all its burner's knob to medium-heat setting.
2. Grease the griddle top with cooking butter and oil.
3. Mix well the lime juice, maple syrup, and cinnamon in a small bowl and leave aside.
4. Cook the pineapple for 3 to 4 minutes in the oil, flipping regularly.
5. When the pineapple has turned a golden hue, brush both the two sides of the rings with maple-lime syrup.
6. Drizzle with chocolate sauce and a small scoop of maple walnut ice cream.
7. Serve and enjoy!

Per Serving:
Calories: 226 | Fat: 7.5g | Carbohydrates: 21g | Fiber: 4.4g | Sugar: 1.4g | Protein: 6g | Sodium: 282mg

SWEET PEACHES
Prep Time: 10 mins. | Cook Time: 10 mins. | Serve: 2

- 2 peaches
- 3 tbsp. Sugar, turbinate
- ¼ cup of Honey
- Gelato, as desired

1. Preheat your outdoor Griddle by turning all its burner's knob to medium-heat setting.
2. Grease the griddle top with cooking spray.
3. Halve each fruit and remove the pits. Add some sugar on the top.
4. Cook on the hot griddle top for 5 minutes per side.
5. Top each serving with a dollop of gelato.
6. Serve and enjoy

Per Serving:
Calories: 302 | Fat: 5g | Carbohydrates: 20g | Fiber: 1.5g | Sugar: 2.3g | Protein: 5.3g | Sodium: 265mg

PINEAPPLE SUNDAES
Prep Time: 10 mins. | Cook Time: 8 mins. | Serve: 4

- 4 pineapple slices
- 4 scoops vanilla ice cream
- Dulce de leche, for drizzling
- 2 tbsp. sweetened shredded coconut, toasted

1. Preheat your outdoor Griddle by turning all its burner's knob to medium-heat setting.
2. Grease the griddle top with cooking butter and oil.
3. Mix well the lime juice, maple syrup, and cinnamon in a small bowl and leave aside.
4. Cook the pineapple for 3 to 4 minutes in the oil, flipping regularly.
5. When the pineapple has turned a golden hue, brush both the two sides of the rings with maple-lime syrup.
6. Drizzle with chocolate sauce and a small scoop of maple walnut ice cream.
7. Serve and enjoy!

Per Serving:
Calories: 182 | Fat: 13g | Carbohydrates: 22.1g | Fiber: 4.4g | Sugar: 2.9g | Protein: 6g | Sodium: 110mg

CINNAMON SUGAR PEACHES
Prep Time: 10 mins. | Cook Time: 10 mins. | Serve: 4

- ¼ cup ½ stick salted butter
- 1 Tbsp. 1 tsp. granulated sugar
- ¼ tsp. cinnamon
- 4 ripe yellow-flesh peaches, halved and pitted
- vegetable oil

1. Preheat your outdoor Griddle by turning all its burner's knob to medium-heat setting.
2. Grease the griddle top with butter.
3. Halve each fruit and remove the pits. Add some sugar on the top.
4. Cook on the hot griddle top for 5 minutes per side.
5. Top each serving with cinnamon.
6. Serve and enjoy.

Per Serving:
Calories: 214 | Fat: 7.5g | Carbohydrates: 24g | Fiber: 2.4g | Sugar: 1.6g | Protein: 4.1g | Sodium: 235mg

RUM-SOAKED PINEAPPLE
Prep Time: 10 mins. | Cook Time: 10 mins. | Serve: 4

- ½ cup dark rum
- ½ cup packed brown sugar
- 1 tsp. ground cinnamon
- 1 pineapple, cored and sliced
- favorite vanilla ice cream

1. Mix dark rum with brown sugar and cinnamon in a saucepan.
2. Soak the pineapple in the rum overnight then drain.
3. Preheat your outdoor Griddle by turning all its burner's knob to medium-heat setting.
4. Sear the pineapple slices on the griddle top and cook for 5 minutes per side.
5. Serve with ice cream on top.

Per Serving:
Calories: 300 | Fat: 4.8g | Carbohydrates: 30.1g | Fiber: 4g | Sugar: 3.5g | Protein: 4.8g | Sodium: 165mg

- 2 small baking apples
- 4 tbsp. maple cream caramel sauce, divided
- 6 tsp. chopped pecans, divided
- 2 scoops vanilla ice cream

1. Cut the apples into thick slices.
2. Preheat your outdoor Griddle by turning all its burner's knob to medium-heat setting.
3. Grease the griddle top with cooking spray.
4. Brush the apple slices with caramel sauce.
5. Cook on the hot griddle top for 5 minutes per side.
6. Top the apples with ice-cram and pecans.
7. Serve and enjoy.

Per Serving:
Calories: 304 | Fat: 7.1g | Carbohydrates: 28g | Fiber: 3g | Sugar: 3.9g | Protein: 1.8g | Sodium: 233mg

MONKEY GRILLED CHEESE
Prep Time: 10 mins. | Cook Time: 10 mins. |Serve: 1

- 2 slices white or brioche bread
- 1 tbsp. cream cheese, softened
- 2 tsp. creamy peanut butter
- ½ tsp. honey
- 1 tbsp. chocolate hazelnut spread
- ½ banana, sliced
- 2 tbsp. mini marshmallows
- 1 tbsp. butter

1. Spread cream cheese, peanut butter, hazelnut spread on top of both the bread slices.
2. Top one bread slice with banana and marshmallows.
3. Drizzle the honey on top and set a bread slice on top.
4. Preheat your outdoor Griddle by turning all its burner's knob to medium-heat setting.
5. Grease the griddle top with cooking spray.
6. Press the bread gently and sear on the griddle top for 5 minutes per side.
7. Serve.

Per Serving:
Calories: 330 | Fat: 7.3g | Carbohydrates: 33g | Fiber: 2.4g | Sugar: 3.4g | Protein: 4.4g | Sodium:265mg

GRILLED APPLES
Prep Time: 10 mins. | Cook Time: 10 mins. |Serve: 2

PEACH MELBA
Prep Time: 10 mins. | Cook Time: 16 mins. |Serve: 2

- 2 large ripe peaches
- ½ pt. raspberries
- 1 tbsp. sugar
- 1 ½ cup vanilla ice cream

1. Preheat your outdoor Griddle by turning all its burner's knob to medium-heat setting.
2. Sear the peaches on the griddle for 2- 3 minutes per side.
3. Mix raspberries with sugar in a saucepan and cook for 10 minutes on medium-low heat while mashing the slightly.
4. Drizzle the prepared raspberry sauce on top of the peaches and garnish with ice cream.
5. Serve.

Per Serving:
Calories: 234 | Fat: 8.3g | Carbohydrates: 31g | Fiber: 33.5g | Sugar: 3.2g | Protein: 4.3g | Sodium:265mg

CHOCOLATE AND BANANA PIZZA
Prep Time: 10 mins. | Cook Time: 8 mins. |Serve: 4

- 1 lb. fresh pizza dough
- ½ cup chocolate hazelnut spread
- 2 bananas

1. Spread pizza dough into a 9 inches round.

2. Preheat your outdoor Griddle by turning all its burner's knob to medium-heat setting.
3. Grease the griddle top with cooking spray.
4. Place the dough on the griddle top and cook for 3 minutes per side.
5. Spread the hazelnut spread on top and add bananas on top.
6. Cook for 2 minutes then slice and serve.

Per Serving:
Calories: 264 | Fat: 5.3g | Carbohydrates: 23g | Fiber: 1.3g | Sugar: 2.2g | Protein: 1.4g | Sodium: 165mg

FOOD CAKE WITH STRAWBERRIES
Prep Time: 10 mins. | Cook Time: 10 mins. |Serve: 4

- 1 ½ lb. strawberries
- 2 tbsp. balsamic vinegar
- 1 tbsp. sugar
- 1 store-bought angel food cake
- Whipped cream (optional)

1. Toss strawberries with vinegar and sugar in a bowl.
2. Preheat your outdoor Griddle by turning all its burner's knob to medium-heat setting.
3. Grease the griddle top with cooking spray.
4. Slice the angel food cake.
5. Cook on the hot griddle top for 5 minutes per side.
6. Top the cake with cream and berries.
7. Serve and enjoy.

Per Serving:
Calories: 245 | Fat: 10.3g | Carbohydrates: 28g | Fiber: 1.8g | Sugar: 1.7g | Protein: 2.8g | Sodium: 168mg

CARAMELIZED PINEAPPLE
Prep Time: 10 mins. | Cook Time: 10 mins. |Serve: 4

- 1 pineapple, sliced
- 2 tsp. vegetable oil
- ½ cup sweetened shredded coconut
- 2 ½ pt. fat-free vanilla frozen yogurt
- mint sprigs

1. Preheat your outdoor Griddle by turning all its burner's knob to medium-heat setting.
2. Grease the griddle top with cooking oil.
3. Cook pineapple slices on the hot griddle top for 5 minutes per side.
4. Top each serving with a yogurt, mint, and coconut.

5. Serve and enjoy.

Per Serving:
Calories: 234 | Fat: 7.5g | Carbohydrates: 20g | Fiber: 3.4g | Sugar: 2.5g | Protein: 4g | Sodium: 176mg

APRICOTS WITH BRIOCHE
Prep Time: 5 mins. | Cook Time: 6 mins. |Serve: 8

- 8 ripe apricots
- 2 tbsp. unsalted butter
- 2 tbsp. sugar
- 4 slice brioche (1 inch thick)
- 2 tbsp. Warm honey
- 2 cup vanilla ice cream

1. Preheat your outdoor Griddle by turning all its burner's knob to medium-heat setting.
2. Grease the griddle top with butter.
3. Cook apricots on the hot griddle top for 3 minutes per side and drizzle sugar on top.
4. Cook the brioche slices on the griddle top for 2-3 minutes per side.
5. Top the brioche slices with apricots, honey and ice cream.
6. Serve and enjoy.

Per Serving:
Calories: 293 | Fat: 3.4g | Carbohydrates: 24g | Fiber: 2.4g | Sugar: 2.1g | Protein: 2.5g | Sodium: 157mg

BANANA SPLITS
Prep Time: 10 mins. | Cook Time: 5 mins. |Serve: 4

- 4 bananas, cut the slit on top, vertically
- 4 tbsp. butter
- 1 pt. vanilla ice cream
- ½ cup chocolate syrup
- 1 Butterfinger candy bar, chopped
- whipped cream

1. Place the banana on a foil sheet and top each with equal amount of butter, chocolate syrup and candy.
2. Wrap the aluminum foil.
3. Preheat your outdoor Griddle by turning all its burner's knob to medium-heat setting.
4. Grease the griddle top with cooking spray.
5. Cook on the hot griddle top for 5 minutes.
6. Unwrap and top the bananas with cream and ice-cream.

7. Serve and enjoy.

Per Serving:
Calories: 260 | Fat: 3.8g | Carbohydrates: 21g | Fiber: 2.4g | Sugar: 2.2g | Protein: 2.5g | Sodium: 159mg

CHOCOLATE MARSHMALLOW BANANA
Prep Time: 10 mins. | Cook Time: 4 mins. |Serve: 1

- 1 banana, slit cut on top vertically
- 1 handful chocolate chips
- 1 handful mini marshmallows

1. Place the banana on a foil sheet and stuff the slit with chocolate chips and marshmallows
2. Wrap the aluminum foil.
3. Preheat your outdoor Griddle by turning all its burner's knob to medium-heat setting.
4. Grease the griddle top with cooking spray.
5. Cook on the hot griddle top for 2 minutes per side.
6. Unwrap and serve.

Per Serving:
Calories: 285 | Fat: 7.3g | Carbohydrates: 25g | Fiber: 2.4g | Sugar: 2.2g | Protein: 2.4g | Sodium: 155mg

DONUT ICE CREAM SANDWICH
Prep Time: 10 mins. | Cook Time: 10 mins. |Serve: 4

- 4 glazed donuts, cut in half
- 8 scoops vanilla ice cream
- Chocolate syrup, for drizzling
- whipped cream
- 4 maraschino cherries

1. Preheat your outdoor Griddle by turning all its burner's knob to medium-heat setting.
2. Grease the griddle top with cooking spray.
3. Cook donuts on the hot griddle top for 5 minutes per side.
4. Top the bottom half of the donut with equal amount of ice-cram chocolate syrup, cream and cherries.
5. Place the top half of the donut.
6. Serve and enjoy.

Per Serving:
Calories: 245 | Fat: 7.4g | Carbohydrates: 21g | Fiber: 2.1g | Sugar: 3.2g | Protein: 4.1g | Sodium:161mg

S'MORES ROLL-UP
Prep Time: 10 mins. | Cook Time: 10 mins. |Serve: 1

- 1 flour tortilla
- 1 handful mini marshmallows
- 1 handful chocolate chips
- 2 graham crackers

1. Spread chocolate chips, marshmallows, graham crackers on top of the tortilla.
2. Fold the tortilla into a roll and wrap it in a foil sheet.
3. Preheat your outdoor Griddle by turning all its burner's knob to medium-heat setting.
4. Grease the griddle top with cooking spray.
5. Place the tortilla roll on the hot griddle top for 5 minutes per side.
6. Serve and enjoy.

Per Serving:
Calories: 286 | Fat: 7.4g | Carbohydrates: 28g | Fiber: 1.4g | Sugar: 2.4g | Protein: 3.8g | Sodium: 163mg

CINNAMON APPLES
Prep Time: 10 mins. | Cook Time: 10 mins. |Serve: 4

- 4 cups chopped apples
- ¼ cup packed brown sugar
- ¼ cup white sugar
- 2 tbsp. butter
- 1 tbsp. cinnamon

1. Toss apples with brown sugar, sugar, butter and cinnamon in a bowl.
2. Preheat your outdoor Griddle by turning all its burner's knob to medium-heat setting.
3. Grease the griddle top with cooking spray.
4. Cook the apples on the hot griddle top for 10 minutes.
5. Serve and enjoy.

Per Serving:
Calories: 295 | Fat: 5.4g | Carbohydrates: 29g | Fiber: 3.4g | Sugar: 3g | Protein: 5.4g | Sodium: 230mg

RASPBERRY CREAM CHEESE PANINIS
Prep Time: 10 mins. | Cook Time: 10 mins. |Serve: 2

- 4 slices Panera Bread, cut in 4-inch circle
- 4 oz. cream cheese softened

- ✓ 4 tbsp. raspberry jam
- ✓ ½ cup chocolate ganache

1. Spread equal amount of cream cheese, raspberry jam and chocolate ganache on two bread slices.
2. Set the other two bread slices on top and press them gently.
3. Preheat your outdoor Griddle by turning all its burner's knob to medium-heat setting.
4. Grease the griddle top with cooking spray.
5. Cook the sandwiches on the hot griddle top for 5 minutes per side.
6. Serve and enjoy.

Per Serving:
Calories: 245 | Fat: 3.8g | Carbohydrates: 21g | Fiber: 3.8g | Sugar: 11.1g | Protein: 3g | Sodium: 43mg

BLUEBERRY CREAM CHEESE SANDWICHES
Prep Time: 10 mins. | Cook Time: 10 mins. | Serve: 2

- ✓ 4 slices Panera Bread, cut in 4-inch circle
- ✓ 4 oz. cream cheese softened
- ✓ 4 tbsp. blueberry jam
- ✓ ½ cup chocolate ganache

1. Spread equal amount of cream cheese, raspberry jam and chocolate ganache on two bread slices.
2. Set the other two bread slices on top and press them gently.
3. Preheat your outdoor Griddle by turning all its burner's knob to medium-heat setting.
4. Grease the griddle top with cooking spray.
5. Cook the sandwiches on the hot griddle top for 5 minutes per side.
6. Serve and enjoy.

Per Serving:
Calories: 258 | Fat: 13.8g | Carbohydrates: 15.1g | Fiber: 3.8g | Sugar: 1.1g | Protein: 6.3g | Sodium: 213mg

RAISINS COOKIES
Prep Time: 10 mins. | Cook Time: 4 mins. | Serve: 8

- ✓ 3½ cups all-purpose flour
- ✓ 1 cup granulated sugar
- ✓ 1½ tsp. baking powder
- ✓ 1 tsp. salt
- ✓ ½ tsp. baking soda
- ✓ 1 cup vegetable shortening
- ✓ 1 egg, beaten
- ✓ ¾ cup milk
- ✓ 1¼ cup raisins

1. Beat egg with milk, sugar in a mixing bowl until sugar is dissolved.
2. Stir in flour, baking powder, salt, baking soda then mix to make a dough.
3. Fold in raisins and mix evenly.
4. Spread the dough into ¼ inches thickness and cut out cookies using a cookie cutter.
5. Preheat your outdoor Griddle by turning all its burner's knob to medium-heat setting.
6. Grease the griddle top with cooking spray.
7. Cook the cookies on the hot griddle top for 2 minutes per side.
8. Serve and enjoy.

Per Serving:
Calories: 246 | Fat: 13.8g | Carbohydrates: 24g | Fiber: 3.8g | Sugar: 13g | Protein: 6.3g | Sodium: 213mg

ORANGE MARMALADE SANDWICH
Prep Time: 10 mins. | Cook Time: 10 mins. | Serve: 2

- ✓ 4 slices Panera Bread, cut in 4-inch circle
- ✓ 4 tbsp. orange marmalade
- ✓ ½ cup chocolate ganache

1. Spread equal amount of orange marmalade and chocolate ganache on two bread slices.
2. Set the other two bread slices on top and press them gently.
3. Preheat your outdoor Griddle by turning all its burner's knob to medium-heat setting.
4. Grease the griddle top with cooking spray.
5. Cook the sandwiches on the hot griddle top for 5 minutes per side.
6. Serve and enjoy.

Per Serving:
Calories: 244 | Fat: 18g | Carbohydrates: 29g | Fiber: 3.8g | Sugar: 1.1g | Protein: 6.3g | Sodium: 13mg

CHOCOLATE CHIPS COOKIES
Prep Time: 10 mins. | Cook Time: 4 mins. | Serve: 8

- ✓ 3½ cups all-purpose flour
- ✓ 1 cup granulated sugar

- ✓ 1½ tsp. baking powder
- ✓ 1 tsp. salt
- ✓ ½ tsp. baking soda
- ✓ 1 cup vegetable shortening
- ✓ 1 egg, beaten
- ✓ ¾ cup milk
- ✓ 1¼ cup mini chocolate chips

1. Beat egg with milk, sugar in a mixing bowl until sugar is dissolved.
2. Stir in flour, baking powder, salt, baking soda then mix to make a dough.
3. Fold in chocolate chips and mix evenly.
4. Spread the dough into ¼ inches thickness and cut out cookies using a cookie cutter.
5. Preheat your outdoor Griddle by turning all its burner's knob to medium-heat setting.
6. Grease the griddle top with cooking spray.
7. Cook the cookies on the hot griddle top for 2 minutes per side.
8. Serve and enjoy.

Per Serving:
Calories: 241 | Fat: 13.8g | Carbohydrates: 25g | Fiber: 3.8g | Sugar: 1.1g | Protein: 6.3g | Sodium: 213mg

CRANBERRY COOKIES

Prep Time: 10 mins. | Cook Time: 4 mins. | Serve: 8

- ✓ 3½ cups all-purpose flour
- ✓ 1 cup granulated sugar
- ✓ 1½ tsp. baking powder
- ✓ 1 tsp. salt
- ✓ ½ tsp. baking soda
- ✓ 1 cup vegetable shortening
- ✓ 1 egg, beaten
- ✓ ¾ cup milk
- ✓ 1¼ cup dried cranberries

1. Beat egg with milk, sugar in a mixing bowl until sugar is dissolved.
2. Stir in flour, baking powder, salt, baking soda then mix to make a dough.
3. Fold in cranberries and mix evenly.
4. Spread the dough into ¼ inches thickness and cut out cookies using a cookie cutter.
5. Preheat your outdoor Griddle by turning all its burner's knob to medium-heat setting.
6. Grease the griddle top with cooking spray.
7. Cook the cookies on the hot griddle top for 2 minutes per side.
8. Serve and enjoy.

Per Serving:
Calories: 233 | Fat: 13.8g | Carbohydrates: 23g | Fiber: 3.8g | Sugar: 1.1g | Protein: 6.3g | Sodium: 213mg

GINGERSNAP COOKIES

Prep Time: 10 mins. | Cook Time: 4 mins. | Serve: 8

- ✓ 1 tbsp. cinnamon powder
- ✓ 3½ cups all-purpose flour
- ✓ 1 cup granulated sugar
- ✓ 1½ tsp. baking powder
- ✓ 1 tsp. salt
- ✓ ½ tsp. baking soda
- ✓ 1 cup vegetable shortening
- ✓ 1 egg, beaten
- ✓ ¾ cup milk

1. Beat egg with milk, sugar in a mixing bowl until sugar is dissolved.
2. Stir in flour, cinnamon powder, baking powder, salt, baking soda then mix to make a dough.
3. Spread the dough into ¼ inches thickness and cut out cookies using a cookie cutter.
4. Preheat your outdoor Griddle by turning all its burner's knob to medium-heat setting.
5. Grease the griddle top with cooking spray.
6. Cook the cookies on the hot griddle top for 2 minutes per side.
7. Serve and enjoy.

Per Serving:
Calories: 257 | Fat: 13.8g | Carbohydrates: 24g | Fiber: 3.8g | Sugar: 1.1g | Protein: 6.3g | Sodium: 213mg

DOUBLE CHOCOLATE COOKIES

Prep Time: 10 mins. | Cook Time: 4 mins. | Serve: 8

- ✓ ½ cup cocoa powder
- ✓ ¼ cup mini chocolate chips

- 3½ cups all-purpose flour
- 1 cup granulated sugar
- 1½ tsp. baking powder
- 1 tsp. salt
- ½ tsp. baking soda
- 1 cup vegetable shortening
- 1 egg, beaten
- ¾ cup milk

1. Beat egg with milk, sugar in a mixing bowl until sugar is dissolved.
2. Stir in flour, cocoa powder, baking powder, salt, baking soda then mix to make a dough.
3. Fold in chocolate chips and mix evenly.
4. Spread the dough into ¼ inches thickness and cut out cookies using a cookie cutter.
5. Preheat your outdoor Griddle by turning all its burner's knob to medium-heat setting.
6. Grease the griddle top with cooking spray.
7. Cook the cookies on the hot griddle top for 2 minutes per side.
8. Serve and enjoy.

Per Serving:
Calories: 294 | Fat: 13.8g | Carbohydrates: 24g | Fiber: 3.8g | Sugar: 1.1g | Protein: 6.3g | Sodium: 213mg

DULCE COOKIES SANDWICH

Prep Time: 10 mins. | Cook Time: 4 mins. | Serve: 8

- 3½ cups all-purpose flour
- 1 cup granulated sugar
- 1½ tsp. baking powder
- 1 tsp. salt
- ½ tsp. baking soda
- 1 cup vegetable shortening
- 1 egg, beaten
- ¾ cup milk
- 1¼ cup dulce de leche

1. Beat egg with milk, sugar in a mixing bowl until sugar is dissolved.
2. Stir in flour, baking powder, salt, baking soda then mix to make a dough.
3. Spread the dough into ¼ inches thickness and cut out cookies using a cookie cutter.
4. Preheat your outdoor Griddle by turning all its burner's knob to medium-heat setting.
5. Grease the griddle top with cooking spray.
6. Cook the cookies on the hot griddle top for 2 minutes per side.
7. Allow the cookies to cool and top of the dulce de lech with dulce de leche.
8. Set the other half of the cookies on top.
9. Serve and enjoy.

Per Serving:
Calories: 236 | Fat: 13.8g | Carbohydrates: 21g | Fiber: 3.8g | Sugar: 1.1g | Protein: 6.3g | Sodium: 213mg

OREO COOKIES SANDWICH

Prep Time: 10 mins. | Cook Time: 4 mins. | Serve: 8

- ½ cup cocoa powder
- 3 cups all-purpose flour
- 1 cup granulated sugar
- 1½ tsp. baking powder
- 1 tsp. salt
- ½ tsp. baking soda
- 1 cup vegetable shortening
- 1 egg, beaten
- ¾ cup milk
- 1¼ cup vanilla ice-cream, frozen

1. Beat egg with milk, sugar in a mixing bowl until sugar is dissolved.
2. Stir in flour, cocoa powder, baking powder, salt, baking soda then mix to make a dough.
3. Spread the dough into ¼ inches thickness and cut out cookies using a cookie cutter.
4. Preheat your outdoor Griddle by turning all its burner's knob to medium-heat setting.
5. Grease the griddle top with cooking spray.
6. Cook the cookies on the hot griddle top for 2 minutes per side.
7. Allow the cookies to cool and top half of the cookies with a scoop of ice-cream.
8. Top the remaining half of the cookies on top.

9. Serve and enjoy.

Per Serving:
Calories: 256 | Fat: 13.8g | Carbohydrates: 32g | Fiber: 3.8g | Sugar: 1.1g | Protein: 6.3g | Sodium: 213mg

VANILLA COOKIES

Prep Time: 10 mins. | Cook Time: 4 mins. | Serve: 8

- 3½ cups all-purpose flour
- 1 cup granulated sugar
- 1½ tsp. baking powder
- 1 tsp. salt
- ½ tsp. baking soda
- 1 cup vegetable shortening
- 1 egg, beaten
- ¾ cup milk
- 2 tsp. vanilla extract

1. Beat egg with vanilla, milk, sugar in a mixing bowl until sugar is dissolved.
2. Stir in flour, baking powder, salt, baking soda then mix to make a dough.
3. Spread the dough into ¼ inches thickness and cut out cookies using a cookie cutter.
4. Preheat your outdoor Griddle by turning all its burner's knob to medium-heat setting.
5. Grease the griddle top with cooking spray.
6. Cook the cookies on the hot griddle top for 2 minutes per side.
7. Serve and enjoy.

Per Serving:
Calories: 237 | Fat: 12.8g | Carbohydrates: 15g | Fiber: 3.8g | Sugar: 1.1g | Protein: 6.3g | Sodium: 213mg

S'MORES PANINI

Prep Time: 10 mins. | Cook Time: 10 mins. | Serve: 1

- 2 white bread slices, cut in 4-inch circle
- 2 tbsp. chocolate
- 1 jumbo marshmallow toasted

1. Spread chocolate and marshmallow on the bread slice.
2. Set the other bread slice on top and press them gently.
3. Preheat your outdoor Griddle by turning all its burner's knob to medium-heat setting.
4. Grease the griddle top with cooking spray.
5. Cook the sandwich on the hot griddle top for 5 minutes per side.
6. Serve and enjoy.

Per Serving:
Calories: 295 | Fat: 7.3g | Carbohydrates: 28g | Fiber: 2.3g | Sugar: 3g | Protein: 1.8g | Sodium: 160mg

DULCE DE LECHE PANINI

Prep Time: 10 mins. | Cook Time: 15 mins. | Serve: 4

- 4 tbsp. dulce de leche
- 4 large croissants, cut in half
- 8 strawberries, sliced
- 8 large marshmallows, cut into 4 slices
- Cooking spray

1. Spread equal amount of dulce de leche, strawberries, and marshmallow on two croissant halves.
2. Set the other two croissant pieces on top and press them gently.
3. Preheat your outdoor Griddle by turning all its burner's knob to medium-heat setting.
4. Grease the griddle top with cooking spray.
5. Cook the sandwiches on the hot griddle top for 5 minutes per side.
6. Serve and enjoy.

Per Serving:
Calories: 124 | Fat: 7.4g | Carbohydrates: 23g | Fiber: 3.1g | Sugar: 3.3g | Protein: 2.4g | Sodium: 205mg

CHOCOLATE AND BRIE PANINI

Prep Time: 10 mins. | Cook Time: 10 mins. | Serve: 2

- 4 slices crunchy sourdough bread, cut in 4-inch circle
- 4 oz. Brie cheese, cut into slices
- 2 oz. milk chocolate, chopped
- 2 Tbsp. unsalted butter, melted

1. Spread equal amount brie cheese, milk chocolate and butter on two bread slices.
2. Set the other two bread slices on top and press them gently.
3. Preheat your outdoor Griddle by turning all its burner's knob to medium-heat setting.
4. Grease the griddle top with cooking spray.

5. Cook the sandwiches on the hot griddle top for 5 minutes per side.
6. Serve and enjoy.

Per Serving:
Calories: 240 | Fat: 2.5g | Carbohydrates: 33g | Fiber: 0.8g | Sugar: 1.5g | Protein: 2.5g | Sodium: 245mg

BRIE CHEESE SANDWICH

Prep Time: 10 mins. | Cook Time: 25 mins. |Serve: 1

- 1 oz. brie, rind removed, and sliced
- 1 English muffin, cut in half
- 1 fresh basil leaves, sliced
- 2 tbsp. sliced strawberries
- ½ tbsp. pepper jelly
- ½ tbsp. butter, melted

1. Spread brie, basil, strawberries, pepper jelly and butter on lower half of the muffin.
2. Set the other muffin half on top and press them gently.
3. Preheat your outdoor Griddle by turning all its burner's knob to medium-heat setting.
4. Grease the griddle top with cooking spray.
5. Cook the sandwich on the hot griddle top for 5 minutes per side.
6. Serve and enjoy.

Per Serving:
Calories: 247 | Fat: 3g | Carbohydrates: 23g | Fiber: 2.3g | Sugar: 2g | Protein: 2.8g | Sodium: 91mg

PEANUT BUTTER BANANA PANINI

Prep Time: 10 mins. | Cook Time: 10 mins. |Serve: 1

- 2 slices wholegrain bread
- 2 tbsp. natural peanut
- 10 bittersweet chocolate chips
- 1 avocado, peeled and mashed

1. Spread peanut butter, chocolate chips, avocado mash on a bread slice.
2. Set the other bread slice on top and press them gently.
3. Preheat your outdoor Griddle by turning all its burner's knob to medium-heat setting.
4. Grease the griddle top with cooking spray.
5. Cook the sandwich on the hot griddle top for 5 minutes per side.

6. Serve and enjoy.

Per Serving:
Calories: 90 | Fat: 7.1g | Carbohydrates: 27g | Fiber: 2.3g | Sugar: 3.3g | Protein: 1.3g | Sodium: 161mg

APPLE PIE PANINI

Prep Time: 10 mins. | Cook Time: 16 mins. |Serve: 4

- ½ cup mascarpone cheese
- 2 tsp. honey
- 4 tbsp. (½ stick) butter
- 8 slices cinnamon raisin bread, cut in 4-inch circle
- 1 Granny Smith apple, cored and sliced
- 2 tbsp. light brown sugar

1. Drizzle brown sugar over the apple.
2. Preheat your outdoor Griddle by turning all its burner's knob to medium-heat setting.
3. Grease the griddle top with butter.
4. Sear the apples on the griddle top and cook for 2-3 minutes per side.
5. Spread equal amount of mascarpone cheese, butter honey, and apple on four bread slices.
6. Set the other four bread slices on top and press them gently.
7. Cook the sandwiches on the hot griddle top for 5 minutes per side.
8. Serve and enjoy.

Per Serving:
Calories: 205 | Fat: 12.5g | Carbohydrates: 15g | Fiber: 6.4g | Sugar: 5.3g | Protein: 3.8g | Sodium: 235mg

NUTELLA DESSERT PANINI

Prep Time: 10 mins. | Cook Time: 10 mins. |Serves: 2

- 4 slices French bread, cut in 4-inch circle
- 6 tbsp. Nutella spread
- 6 tbsp. Marshmallow cream
- 1 large bananas sliced
- 2-3 tbsp. butter

1. Spread equal amount of Nutella, marshmallow cream and bananas on two bread slices.
2. Set the other two bread slices on top and press them gently.
3. Preheat your outdoor Griddle by turning all its burner's knob to medium-heat setting.
4. Grease the griddle top with butter.

5. Cook the sandwiches on the hot griddle top for 5 minutes per side.
6. Serve and enjoy.

Per Serving:
Calories: 234 | Fat: 3.8g | Carbohydrates: 25g | Fiber: 3.1g | Sugar: 4.3g | Protein: 2.3g | Sodium: 168mg

Measurement Charts

VOLUME EQUIVALENT (DRY)

US standards	Metric (Approximate)
1/8 tsp.	0.5 ml
¼ tsp.	1 ml
½ tsp.	2 ml
1 tsp.	4 ml
1 tbsp.	5 ml
¼ cup	15 ml
½ cup	59 ml
¾ cup	118 ml
1 cup	177 ml
2 cups	235 ml
3 cups	700 ml
4 cups	1 L

VOLUME EQUIVALENT (LIQUID)

US standards	US standards (ounces)	Metric (Approximate)
2 tbsp.	1 fl oz.	30 ml
¼ cup	2 fl. Oz.	60 ml
½ cup	4 fl oz.	120 ml
1 cup	8 fl. Oz.	240 ml
1 ½ cup	12 fl oz.	355 ml
1 pint or 2 cups	16 fl. Oz.	475
1 quart or 4 cups	32 fl. Oz.	1 L
1 gallon	128 fl. Oz.	4 L

WEIGHT EQUIVALENTS

US standards	Metric (Approximate)
1 ounce	28g
2 ounces	57g
5 ounces	142g
10 ounces	284g
15 ounces	425g
16 ounces (1 lb.)	455g
1 ½ pounds	680g
2 pounds	907g

TEMPERATURE EQUIVALENTS

Fahrenheit	Celsius (Approximate)

225 °F	107 °C
250 °F	120l °C
275 °F	135 °C
300 °F	150 °C
325 °F	160 °C
350 °F	180 °C
375 °F	190 °C
400 °F	205 °C
425 °F	220 °C
450 °F	215 °C
475 °F	245 °C
500 °F	260 °C

CONCLUSION:

Blackstone outdoor cooking station provides ample space for cooking. It also makes it easy to cook breakfast like pancakes, brown hash, bacon, and French bread. It comes with complete cookware for preparation and sausages. We highly recommend that you try a flat place to set up the appliance. The Blackstone griddle is one of the most reliable and robust griddles out there on the market. You can move this station around, set it up anywhere in your backyard and become the pitmaster you all wanted to be! So, chose your favorite recipes from this cookbook, set up your griddle outside and let's do some backyard cooking!

INDEX

A

adobo sauce, 40
aioli, 57
all-purpose flour, 59, 69, 93, 124, 125, 126, 127
allspice, 57, 61, 96, 115
almond flour, 11, 12, 13, 15
almonds, 87, 88, 89, 91, 114
amberjack, 94
ancho chilli, 82
anchovies, 85
anchovy, 44, 86
anchovy paste, 44
angel food cake, 122
apple, 6, 20, 43, 57, 62, 71, 75, 80, 95, 96, 108, 109, 121, 128
apricots, 80, 122
arugula, 19, 27, 29, 59, 107
asparagus, 20, 23, 61, 107, 115, 118
avocado, 11, 17, 30, 31, 33, 37, 41, 61, 62, 128

B

bacon, 5, 11, 15, 23, 25, 28, 29, 30, 33, 34, 37, 47, 48, 80, 81, 112, 116
baking powder, 10, 12, 13, 15, 16, 17, 18, 25, 124, 125, 126, 127
baking soda, 10, 16, 17, 18, 93, 124, 125, 126, 127
balsamic vinegar, 23, 27, 30, 31, 32, 37, 38, 50, 55, 58, 59, 63, 65, 66, 67, 73, 75, 104, 107, 113, 118, 122
banana, 16, 80, 121, 122, 123
barbecue rub, 24
barbecue sauce, 5, 6, 24, 33, 36, 57, 77
basil, 12, 29, 30, 31, 37, 42, 45, 55, 63, 64, 65, 66, 90, 95, 96, 97, 99, 101, 108, 111, 118, 128
bay leaf, 58, 85, 87, 99
BBQ sauce, 28, 47, 55
beef filets, 66
beef stock, 59
beef tenderloin, 58
beer, 4, 40, 93
bell pepper, 11, 14, 19, 20, 36, 37, 41, 42, 45, 48, 60, 77, 110, 111, 114, 115
biscuit baking mix, 114
black beans, 16, 50
black pepper, 10, 11, 13, 14, 15, 16, 18, 19, 20, 21, 23, 24, 25, 26, 27, 28, 29, 30, 31, 32, 36, 37, 38, 39, 41, 42, 43, 44, 45, 46, 47, 49, 51, 52, 53, 55, 56, 57, 58, 59, 60, 61, 62, 63, 64, 65, 66, 67, 68, 69, 71, 72, 73, 74, 75, 76, 80, 84, 85, 89, 90, 91, 93, 94, 96, 98, 99, 100, 101, 102, 103, 104, 107, 108, 109, 110, 111, 112, 113, 114, 116, 117, 118
black peppercorns, 68, 76, 81, 96
blue cheese, 31, 45, 59
blue cheese dressing, 45
blueberries, 10
blueberry jam, 124
Boston butt pork, 73
bourbon, 56, 116
bread, 6, 7, 12, 14, 15, 24, 30, 31, 36, 45, 47, 48, 59, 67, 86, 96, 99, 121, 124, 127, 128
breadcrumbs, 24, 30, 31, 47, 49, 59, 80, 87, 99
brie, 127, 128
Brie cheese, 127
brioche, 121, 122
brisket, 5, 55, 68
broccoli, 10, 11, 15, 46, 56, 65, 108, 117
broccolini, 97
brown rice, 44
brown sugar, 5, 24, 25, 28, 32, 38, 42, 46, 47, 49, 51, 55, 56, 59, 65, 66, 68, 73, 74, 75, 82, 116, 121, 123, 128
brussels sprouts, 113
buffalo mozzarella, 66
buffalo sauce, 43, 45
burger buns, 91
butter, 10, 11, 12, 13, 14, 15, 16, 17, 18, 19, 20, 21, 25, 28, 32, 33, 42, 43, 45, 46, 47, 48, 49, 50, 55, 56, 57, 58, 59, 60, 63, 65, 67, 68, 69, 72, 77, 80, 84, 88, 89, 97, 99, 100, 107, 114, 116, 120, 121, 122, 123, 127, 128
butternut squash, 107

C

cabbage, 63, 82, 85, 87, 88, 89, 108
Cajun seasoning, 56
candy bar, 122
canola oil, 3, 30, 32, 62, 64
caper berries, 88
capers, 86, 101
caramel sauce, 121
cardamom, 89
carrot, 32, 45, 57, 81
cauliflower, 11, 13, 15, 78, 112, 114, 115
cayenne pepper, 14, 19, 24, 25, 27, 31, 32, 37, 40, 48, 50, 61, 66, 85, 86, 95, 96, 99, 102, 103, 115
celeriac, 88
celery, 87, 95, 97
cheddar cheese, 14, 15, 19, 20, 21, 24, 28, 30, 33, 47
cherries, 123
chicken breasts, 36, 37, 38, 39, 40, 44, 45, 46, 47, 48, 50, 51
chicken drumsticks, 47
chicken stock, 77, 81
chicken tenders, 51, 52
chicken thighs, 28, 38, 39, 40, 42, 48, 49, 51
chicken wing sections, 43
chicken wings, 25, 43, 44, 49
chiles de árbol, 94
chili powder, 24, 27, 28, 32, 39, 40, 43, 47, 48, 49, 60, 68, 71, 77, 93, 99
chili-garlic sauce, 111
chipotle peppers, 40
chives, 11, 21, 23, 26, 33, 37, 55, 60, 62, 110, 112, 118
chocolate, 17, 18, 108, 120, 121, 122, 123, 124, 125, 126, 127, 128
chocolate chips, 17, 18, 123, 125, 126, 128
chocolate ganache, 124
chocolate hazelnut spread, 121
chocolate syrup, 122, 123
Chocolate syrup, 123
Chorizo, 4, 5, 16, 27, 79
cider vinegar, 6, 36, 43, 57, 62, 71, 75, 87, 109, 116
cilantro, 10, 24, 25, 30, 32, 39, 40, 41, 43, 50, 51, 60, 61, 62, 63, 65, 66, 74, 90, 93, 94, 95, 96, 97, 98, 100, 108, 111, 116, 117
clams, 96
cocoa powder, 17, 125, 126
coconut oil, 12, 120
coffee beans, 66
cooked chicken, 32, 45, 47
cooking oil, 14, 23, 27, 28, 38, 40, 44, 45, 56, 58, 59, 60, 61, 62, 68, 69, 77, 80, 82, 86, 87, 89, 90, 93, 94, 95, 96, 97, 98, 99, 107, 108, 111, 122
cooking spray, 11, 12, 13, 14, 15, 16, 21, 23, 24, 25, 26, 27, 28, 29, 30, 31, 32, 33, 34, 36, 37, 38, 39, 40, 41, 42, 43, 44, 45, 46, 47, 48, 49, 50, 51, 52, 53, 55, 56, 57, 58, 59,

61, 62, 63, 64, 65, 66, 67, 68, 69, 71, 72, 73, 74, 75, 76, 77, 78, 79, 80, 81, 82, 84, 85, 86, 87, 88, 89, 90, 91, 93, 94, 97, 98, 99, 100, 107, 109, 110, 112, 120, 121, 122, 123, 124, 125, 126, 127, 128
Cooking spray, 127
coriander, 23, 49, 57, 61, 62, 75, 78, 79, 80, 82, 86, 87, 88, 89, 90, 91, 96, 108, 114, 117
corn, 3, 27, 32, 41, 45, 46, 62, 63, 80, 81, 82, 97, 98, 114
corn syrup, 27
cornstarch, 64, 111
cotija cheese, 62
cottage cheese, 85
courgettes, 87, 118
crab, 99
cranberries, 125
cream cheese, 24, 29, 121, 123, 124
crème fraiche, 79
Creole seasoning, 39
croissant, 127
cucumber, 57, 67, 73, 91, 95
cumin, 20, 23, 24, 28, 30, 39, 40, 41, 49, 52, 60, 61, 62, 64, 74, 75, 78, 79, 82, 88, 89, 90, 91, 94, 96, 104, 109, 114, 115, 117

D

deggi mirch, 88
dehydrated onion flakes, 64
dill, 18, 36, 48, 57, 67, 73, 97, 98, 100, 101, 102, 103, 114
donuts, 123
dried Italian blend seasoning, 61
dry rub, 28, 91
dulce de leche, 126, 127
Dulce de Leche, 127

E

egg, 10, 11, 12, 13, 14, 15, 16, 17, 18, 19, 24, 30, 31, 49, 59, 66, 71, 93, 97, 98, 99, 100, 109, 124, 125, 126, 127
eggplant, 86, 88, 109, 111, 115, 118
English muffin, 128
eye fillet steak, 57

F

farro, 116
fennel bulb, 95, 96
fennel seeds, 75, 87, 88, 102, 116
fenugreek seeds, 86
ferment, 27

figs, 23, 31
filet mignon, 55, 57, 68
fish sauce, 49, 50, 57, 73, 76
fish stock, 96
five-spice powder, 81, 115
flank steak, 27, 58, 59, 62, 67, 73
flatbreads, 3, 76, 85
flour, 10, 11, 13, 16, 17, 18, 20, 41, 59, 61, 62, 69, 77, 80, 81, 93, 117, 123, 124, 125, 126, 127
French beans, 80
French fries, 59
Fresno chile, 118
Fresno peppers, 27

G

garam masala, 88
garlic, 6, 15, 19, 20, 24, 26, 27, 28, 29, 30, 31, 32, 36, 37, 38, 39, 40, 41, 42, 43, 44, 45, 46, 47, 48, 49, 50, 51, 52, 53, 55, 56, 57, 58, 59, 60, 61, 62, 63, 64, 66, 67, 68, 69, 71, 72, 73, 74, 75, 76, 77, 78, 79, 80, 81, 84, 85, 86, 87, 88, 89, 90, 91, 93,94, 95, 96, 97, 98, 99, 100, 101, 102, 103, 104, 105, 107, 108, 109, 110, 111, 113, 114, 115, 117, 118
garlic chili oil, 26
garlic leaves, 87
garlic powder, 6, 15, 24, 27, 28, 31, 32, 37, 39, 40, 41, 43, 44, 46, 48, 52, 53, 55, 61, 64, 67, 68, 69, 72, 73, 74, 75, 76, 99, 100, 101, 115
gem hearts, 82
ginger, 32, 42, 43, 45, 46, 49, 50, 51, 56, 63, 64, 67, 73, 74, 77, 80, 88, 89, 90, 95, 96, 105, 111, 115
goat cheese, 23, 26, 27, 31, 33, 107
graham crackers, 123
granulated sugar, 87, 120, 124, 125, 126, 127
grapefruit, 95
Greek seasoning, 101
Greek Seasoning, 29
green beans, 64, 78, 80, 116
green chilies, 16, 57
ground beef, 24, 59, 63, 64, 65, 67
ground buffalo meat, 28
ground chicken, 48
ground chuck, 23, 24
ground lamb, 85, 90
ground pork, 23, 24, 75
ground turkey, 21, 41, 47, 50, 52, 53
groundnut oil, 81
grouper, 93

gruyere, 11
guajillo chiles, 94, 108

H

habanero chili, 75
half-and-half, 116
halibut, 98, 101
Halloumi cheese, 29
ham, 14, 77
harissa, 74, 75, 85, 88, 91
harissa sauce, 74, 75
heavy cream, 10, 68
hemp seed, 118
herb de Provence, 12
Herb de province, 52
hoisin sauce, 73, 76
honey, 25, 29, 31, 36, 37, 38, 43, 48, 49, 51, 52, 55, 57, 58, 71, 72, 73, 77, 79, 80, 82, 87, 94, 95, 96, 97, 98, 108, 109, 113, 115, 116, 121, 122, 128
horseradish, 6, 58
hot dogs, 1, 28, 77
hot pepper paste, 44
hot sauce, 11, 45, 46
houmous, 88

I

ice-cream, 122, 126
Italian seasoning, 37, 51, 56

J

jack cheese, 16, 39, 40, 116
jalapeño, 29, 39, 51, 62, 93, 95
juniper berries, 87

K

kale, 13, 19, 44, 63
Kecap manis, 57
kefalotyri cheese, 86
ketchup, 59, 71, 77, 81
kiwi, 51

L

lamb chops, 84, 85, 86, 88, 90
lamb cutlets, 88, 89, 91
lamb loin chops, 84
lamb neck fillet, 87
lamb shoulder, 91
lean lamb, 87, 88
leeks, 116
leg of lamb, 86, 89, 90
lemon, 13, 19, 29, 30, 31, 32, 33, 37,

44, 48, 49, 51, 52, 55, 58, 59, 61, 63, 64, 65, 67, 73, 74, 76, 77, 78, 80, 82, 84, 85, 86, 87, 88, 89, 91, 93, 97, 98, 100, 101, 102, 103, 104, 108, 109, 112, 114, 115, 116, 117, 118
lemon grass, 89
lemon pepper, 13, 76
lemon-pepper seasoning, 51
lettuce, 46, 57, 86
lime, 25, 30, 32, 38, 40, 41, 43, 44, 45, 48, 49, 50, 56, 57, 60, 61, 62, 63, 66, 74, 76, 78, 79, 88, 89, 93, 94, 95, 96, 97, 98, 99, 100, 114, 116, 117, 120
lobster, 97, 99
London broil top-round steak, 55
long grain rice, 45, 78

M

mackerel, 103
mandarins, 95
mango, 51, 97, 98
manouri cheese, 29
maple syrup, 10, 16, 17, 18, 25, 57, 76, 120
Marinara sauce, 24
marshmallow, 127, 128
Marshmallow cream, 128
mascarpone cheese, 128
mayonnaise, 32, 44, 45, 93, 99
Mexican cheese, 39
milk, 10, 13, 14, 16, 17, 18, 21, 49, 100, 109, 115, 124, 125, 126, 127
mint, 27, 78, 86, 87, 88, 89, 90, 91, 97, 109, 114, 115, 118, 122
mirin, 27, 38, 42, 72, 77, 111
mixed salad leaves, 78
molasses, 71, 73, 85
Montreal marinade, 72
mozzarella cheese, 12, 37
muscovado sugar, 81
mushrooms, 7, 13, 19, 21, 23, 28, 29, 33, 45, 56, 64, 74, 78, 109, 113, 115, 117, 118
mustard, 6, 24, 28, 31, 36, 44, 49, 51, 52, 56, 58, 59, 62, 74, 75, 82, 86, 87, 99, 103, 104, 108, 110, 111, 113, 116

N

nectarines, 31
Nutella spread, 128
Nutrition yeast, 11
NY strip steak, 66

O

oats, 15, 16
olive oil, 3, 10, 12, 18, 19, 20, 21, 23, 25, 26, 29, 30, 31, 32, 36, 37, 38, 39, 40, 41, 42, 43, 44, 46, 48, 49, 50, 51, 52, 55, 56, 57, 58, 59, 60, 61, 62, 63, 64, 65, 66, 67, 69, 71, 72, 73, 74, 75, 76, 77, 78, 79, 80, 81, 82, 84, 85, 86, 87, 88, 89, 90, 91, 97,98, 99, 100, 101, 102, 103, 104, 105, 107, 108, 109, 110, 111, 112, 113, 114, 115, 116, 117, 118
olive tapenade, 76
olives, 12, 51, 64, 88, 98, 101
onion, 11, 13, 14, 15, 16, 19, 21, 24, 29, 30, 31, 32, 36, 38, 39, 41, 42, 44, 45, 46, 47, 48, 49, 50, 51, 52, 56, 59, 60, 61, 62, 63, 64, 65, 67, 68, 69, 71, 73, 74, 75, 76, 77, 78, 79, 81, 88, 89, 90, 91, 93, 94, 95, 96, 97, 98, 101, 107, 108, 110, 111, 113, 114, 115, 117, 118
onion powder, 14, 15, 31, 38, 39, 41, 48, 61, 68, 75, 101, 115
onion soup mix, 69
orange, 38, 65, 71, 75, 81, 82, 100, 104, 105, 115, 116, 124
orange marmalade, 38, 124
oregano, 29, 36, 37, 40, 46, 48, 50, 52, 55, 60, 64, 66, 67, 69, 73, 76, 84, 87, 88, 94, 101, 102, 103, 104, 108, 113

P

paprika, 5, 20, 23, 24, 27, 28, 31, 38, 40, 42, 43, 62, 68, 74, 75, 78, 79, 82, 88, 91, 95, 96, 99, 100, 101, 102, 104, 117
parmesan cheese, 13, 26, 48, 76, 113
parsley, 20, 23, 24, 29, 49, 52, 55, 56, 60, 63, 64, 65, 79, 80, 81, 84, 88, 98, 99, 100, 102, 103, 104, 108, 111, 114, 118
Passilla chiles, 108
peach, 43
peach preserves, 43
peanut, 32, 46, 57, 121, 128
pecans, 116, 121
Pecorino Romano, 24
Peppadews, 3, 23
pepper jelly, 128
Pico de Gallo, 60
pineapple, 42, 44, 47, 51, 62, 67, 76, 77, 79, 94, 100, 108, 109, 120, 121, 122
pistachios, 91, 116
pita, 36, 67, 73
pizza dough, 121
plantains, 108, 109, 112
plum, 30, 33, 85, 86, 95
plums, 29, 33, 85
poblano peppers, 116, 117
polenta, 65
pork chops, 1, 71, 72, 73, 74, 75
pork fillet, 77, 78, 79, 80, 82
pork fillet medallions, 77
pork loin, 74, 78
pork rashers, 76
pork ribs, 5, 71
pork shoulder, 5, 27, 73
pork spareribs, 81
pork tenderloin, 31, 76, 81
pork tenderloins, 74, 75
potato, 3, 6, 11, 14, 25, 26, 27, 29, 32, 33, 34, 78, 95, 96, 110, 118
potato flakes, 27
prosciutto, 80
Prosecco, 86
provolone, 56
prunes, 79
pumpkin puree, 15
pumpkin seeds, 108

Q

queso fresco, 41

R

rack of lamb, 86
raisins, 18, 116, 124
ranch dressing, 37, 112, 113
Ranch dressing, 112
ranch seasoning, 112
Ras El Hanout, 91
raspberries, 18, 121
raspberry jam, 124
red chard, 85
red chili flakes, 44, 49
red pepper flakes, 21, 24, 47, 55, 58, 60, 61, 64, 65, 69, 98, 99, 102, 103, 104, 109, 113, 116
red sauce, 100
ribeye steak, 60
rib-eye steaks, 63
rice vinegar, 25, 81
ricotta cheese, 12
rock sugar, 81
rocket, 89
rosemary, 23, 25, 26, 32, 33, 50, 52, 57, 58, 59, 68, 69, 71, 75, 85, 86, 87, 89, 90, 103, 110, 113, 118

round steak, 69
rum, 121
rump steaks, 57
rye, 45

S

sage, 13, 71, 75, 77, 80
sake, 27
salami, 113
salmon, 19, 21, 97, 98, 100, 101
salt, 6, 10, 11, 12, 13, 14, 15, 16, 17, 18, 19, 20, 21, 23, 24, 25, 26, 27, 28, 29, 30, 31, 32, 33, 36, 37, 38, 39, 40, 41, 42, 43, 44, 46, 48, 49, 50, 51, 52, 55, 56, 57, 58, 59, 60, 61, 62, 63, 64, 65, 66, 67, 68, 69, 71, 72, 74, 75, 80, 84, 85, 89, 90, 93, 94, 95, 96, 97, 98, 99, 100, 101, 102, 103, 104, 107, 108, 109, 110, 111, 112, 113, 114, 115, 116, 117, 118, 124, 125, 126, 127
sambal Oelek, 51
sausage, 24, 27, 30, 79
scallion, 20, 44
scallop, 104
sea bass, 103
seafood seasoning, 32
Serrano, 10
sesame oil, 3, 42, 44, 46, 63, 73, 77, 81
Sesame seeds, 38
shallot, 30, 40, 52, 65, 68, 80, 94, 108
sherry vinegar, 29, 109, 111
shredded coconut, 120, 122
shrimp, 1, 32, 94, 96, 99, 100, 101, 103, 104, 105
sirloin steak, 56, 61, 62, 65
skirt steak, 59, 60, 61, 62, 64, 65, 66
snap peas, 67, 77
snapper, 95
sour cream, 33, 39, 41, 58, 60
soy sauce, 25, 27, 32, 38, 42, 44, 45, 46, 47, 49, 50, 51, 56, 58, 63, 64, 67, 71, 72, 77, 80, 81, 100, 104, 105, 111
Spike Seasoning, 29
spinach, 13, 16, 20, 52, 58, 64, 98

Sriracha, 3, 4, 25, 42, 43, 50, 57, 114
Steak sauce, 59
stevia, 15, 104, 105
strawberries, 13, 122, 127, 128
sultanas, 80
Sumac, 115
summer squash, 45, 117
sun-dried tomatoes, 12
sunflower oil, 76, 80, 88
sunflower seeds, 108
Sunkist Minneola tangelo, 36
sweet chili sauce, 38, 114
sweet potatoes, 26, 29, 32, 79, 96, 118
sweet red chili sauce, 43
swerve, 12
Swiss cheese, 45
swordfish, 98

T

taco seasoning, 39, 50, 53
tahini paste, 85
tandoori spice, 97
tarragon, 96
tater tots, 112
teriyaki sauce, 81
thyme, 28, 40, 48, 49, 55, 56, 58, 59, 68, 75, 80, 82, 84, 85, 88, 89, 100, 102, 103, 104, 107, 108, 110, 111, 113, 115
tilapia, 98
tofu, 6, 19, 111
Tomatillos, 39
tomato, 10, 19, 20, 37, 38, 42, 47, 51, 59, 63, 66, 67, 73, 81, 82, 90, 96, 101, 107, 114
tomato paste, 38, 42, 47, 59
tortellini, 113
tortilla, 116, 117, 123
tri-tip steak, 56
trout, 94, 103
tuna, 1, 95, 102, 103
turkey breast, 50
turmeric, 11, 19, 20, 86, 89, 90, 91, 114

V

vanilla, 12, 13, 14, 15, 20, 114, 120, 121, 122, 123, 126, 127
vanilla extract, 20, 127
vegetable oil, 8, 14, 15, 16, 24, 27, 41, 45, 56, 59, 62, 67, 68, 69, 86, 99, 111, 112, 114, 120, 122
vegetable shortening, 124, 125, 126, 127
vinaigrette, 74, 94, 97, 108, 110

W

walnuts, 51
water, 2, 7, 8, 11, 12, 13, 16, 19, 20, 25, 27, 32, 33, 47, 49, 59, 61, 67, 69, 71, 73, 74, 84, 85, 104, 107, 108, 111, 112
wax beans, 116
whipped cream, 122, 123
white pepper, 31, 40, 95
white rice, 108
white sugar, 123
white vinegar, 10, 16, 17, 18, 47, 72, 82
whitefish, 93, 95, 96
whole chicken, 36
whole fish, 93
wine, 29, 36, 64, 65, 66, 69, 76, 77, 79, 80, 81, 82, 85, 86, 89, 110, 113, 116
wine vinegar, 29, 36, 64, 65, 66, 69, 76, 77, 82, 85, 86, 110, 113, 116
Worcestershire sauce, 28, 36, 44, 55, 59, 65, 71, 72, 86, 99

Y

yoghurt, 67, 73, 87, 88, 89, 91, 109
yogurt, 15, 43, 53, 58, 67, 73, 74, 78, 87, 89, 90, 109, 114, 115, 117, 118, 122

Z

zucchini, 16, 17, 26, 27, 31, 32, 36, 45, 47, 48, 66, 67, 90, 101, 110, 111, 112, 113, 115, 117

Thank you for reading this book. If you enjoyed it reading Please leave us a review on the website you bought it from. It would be so kindof you to help other readers buying this book and make a wise decision.

Thank You!

Made in United States
Orlando, FL
22 July 2022